Greene's Dictionary of Bible Names

*Every proper name in Scripture exhaustively
defined to help uncover hidden truths found
in God's Holy Word.*

Dr. Samuel Greene

Narrow Way Ministries International
About the Author & Ministry, visit:
www.nwmin.org

All proper names are spelled as translated in the
King James Version unless otherwise noted.

Printed in the United States of America
ISBN: 978-1-937199-88-3

PREFACE

In contemporary Western culture, personal names are little more than labels that distinguish one person from another, but in Biblical times, a person's name had a much deeper significance. A name in Scripture is often significant of the nature or character of a person, whether it be a person, angel or God Himself. This would apply to cities or places as well, where the name would give the revelation of the combined total nature or character of the people that lived there. God uses names to give us hidden revelation concerning His marvelous truth in the Word. Forever it will be this, "*It is the glory of God to conceal a thing: but the honour of kings is to search out a matter*," (Proverbs 25:2). Knowing the definition of the name of something can unlock great hidden truths and revelation that God intends for us to find.

This book is not a study on the principle of names in Scripture but is simply a supplemental resource giving the definitions of every proper name in Scripture as well as the covenantal names of God. For a deeper study on names, I have written a study manual on "The Principle of Names in Scripture" and encourage you to study for yourself the glorious truths of names in Scripture, further making this book an even more invaluable tool as you study God's precious Word!

So, my earnest desire and hope is that this resource placed in your hands will revolutionize the way you read, teach, preach, and receive from GOD when it comes to names in Scripture.

Jesus is Precious,

Brother Sam

DEDICATION

I dedicate this book to all the disciples at NWM churches and Bible schools and to the whole body of Christ.

ACKNOWLEDGEMENTS

Thanks to our editors, their diligence was much appreciated: Katie Greene, Emily Greene, Andrew Jensen, Aaron Jensen, & Norma Dunn.

Thanks to Terry Blake for her endless hours of typing.

Thanks to my faithful assistant, Andrew Jensen, whose motivation to seeing this project completed was invaluable.

Thanks to Elizabeth Roubos for her faithful donations that allowed this book to be produced.

Thanks to NWM Asheville for their time, support, and prayers in this long endeavor.

Thanks to my dear wife for all that she does and all that she allows in my life.

A special thanks to Jesus for giving the strength and inspiration for writing this book.

TABLE OF CONTENTS

THE ACTUAL NAMES OF GOD IN SCRIPTURE 7
EVERY PROPER NAME & DEFINITION IN SCRIPTURE 9
    A 11
    B 32
    C 44
    D 50
    E 54
    F 64
    G 64
    H 71
    I 84
    J 89
    K 108
    L 112
    M 116
    N 130
    O 137
    P 139
    Q 147
    R 147
    S 153
    T 173
    U 181
    V 183
    W 183
    X 183
    Y 183
    Z 184
BIBLIOGRAPHY 193
ABOUT THE AUTHOR 194

The Actual Names of God in Scripture

The names of God are expressions of His person, His presence, and His character, none of which can be fully comprehended by the human mind. It is only as we look at each of these names of God, can we begin to understand Him. There is no greater way to have a true image of God and His person than by receiving the revelation of the names He chose to reveal Himself by in the Scriptures.

The revelation of the name of God stands as the center of what we call revelation. God Himself is known where His name is made known. Since God's revelation of His name is an act of grace and enables us to have a greater personal understanding and communion with Him, we need to be ever so thankful for the "Word of God." What a treasure house it really is! Without it we would have no hope of knowing Him intimately. But now we can know Him, and even greater, we can know His wonderful character because of the revelation of His names are freely given to us if we would just search them out.

We find that these names come under several classifications. The first classification is called Elohistic, those names which have to do with the relationship of God with His creation. The name El signifies "to be strong, powerful." Elohim is the plural of El and speaks to us of the plurality of divine persons in the Godhead. El signifies the object of worship rather than a divine name. When the name El is used as a compound name it is usually associated with some power or attribute of God in respect to His creation. The second classification would be the redemptive names of God, or Jehovahistic name. All the others would be just what we would classify as the self-revealing names of God. Here we will give them in alphabetical order, all of them both Elohistic and redemptive, the self-revealing names of our great God:

Adon – To rule; sovereign, controller
Adonai (Genesis 15:2) – Master, Lord, owner – This name usually refers to Jesus.
Adon-Adonai – Jehovah our ruler – This name expresses God as the absolute Owner and Lord.
Adoni-Jah – Jehovah is Lord
El (Genesis 14:18) – To be strong, powerful, or mighty – singular; it is used of Father, Son & Holy Spirit
    a.   Father is El – Genesis 14:18-22
    b.   Son is El – Isaiah 7:14, Isaiah 9:6-9 (Emmanu-El)
    c.   Holy Spirit is El – Job 33:4, 37:10

Elah (Ezra 4:24) – Oak, an oak tree – This name symbolizes the durability of or the everlasting God. It can also indicate the God who identifies with His people in captivity (43 x's in Ezra and 46 x's in Daniel)
Eloah (Deuteronomy 32:15) – To fear, to worship, to adore. He is the adorable

one or worshipful one. He is the object of all worship. It is the singular of Elohim. It speaks of the totality of His being and the finality of His decisions.

Elohim (Genesis 1:1) – The plurality of divine persons – It describes God's greatness and glory, and it displays God's power and sovereignty.

El Elohe-Israel (Genesis 33:18-20) – The God of Israel

El Elyon – Most High God – This name combines the idea of God's highness with His might (Psalms 7:17, Psalms 47:2, Psalms 97:9)

El Olam (Genesis 21:33) – God of eternity, the everlasting God

El Roi (Genesis 16:13-14) – The well of Him that lives and sees.

El Shaddai – Almighty (All powerful one), all sufficient God (Genesis 17:1), His exhaustive bounty, the the breasty one, the resource of sufficiency, He who satisfies.

El Beth-El (Genesis 31:3, 35:7) – God of the house of God

Jah (Exodus 15:2, Psalms 68:4) – This is a shortened form of Jehovah. It means – the independent one, the Lord most vehement; it comes from a root that means – to be, to breathe. This says to us, "God is"

Jehovah (Genesis 2:4) – Self existent, eternal, ever loving one; it comes from a root – to be, to exist

Jehovah-Elohay – The Lord my God, my Lord (Judges 6:15, Judges 13:8), "He's my God"

Jehovah-Eloheenu – The Lord our God

Jehovah-Eloheka – The Lord your God (Exodus 20:2). This title speaks of God's relationship to His people, and their responsibility to Him.

Jehovah-Elohim – The Lord our Creator (Genesis 2:4, 9)

Jehovah-Gmolah – The God of recompenses (Jeremiah 51:6-8)

Jehovah-Elyon – The Lord, the blesser (Psalms 7:17)

Jehovah-Hasenu – The Lord, the maker (Psalms 95:6)

Jehovah-Jireh – The Lord, the provider, the Lord will see, the Lord is provision (Genesis 22:14)

Jehovah-Makkeh – The Lord shall smite you (Ezekiel 7:9)

Jehovah-M'Kaddesh – The Lord our sanctification (Exodus 31:13, Leviticus 20:8), the one who sets us apart unto Himself, the one who sanctifies us, empowers us to be holy (Exodus 19:5-6)

Jehovah-Nissi – The Lord, the banner (Exodus 17:15), the Lord my banner. The root word for Nissi means an ensign, a standard.

Jehovah-Raah or **Rohi** – The Lord our shepherd (Psalms 23:1)

Jehovah-Rapha – The Lord, our healer, the Lord is healing.

Jehovah-Sabaoth – The Lord, of hosts (I Samuel 1:3)

Jehovah-Shalom – The Lord is peace, the Lord our peace (Judges 6:24). Root word Shalom means – peace, good health, favor, whole, perfect, prosperity.

Jehovah-Shaphat – The Lord, the judge (Judges 11:27)

Jehovah-Shammah – The Lord, the ever present (Ezekiel 48:35). The Lord is there, the Lord is present.

Jehovah-Gibbor – The Lord, the mighty (Isaiah 42:13)

Jehovah-Tsidkenu – The Lord, our righteousness (Jeremiah 23:6, 33:16), the Lord, my righteousness

Jehovah Jehoshua Messiah – The Lord Jesus Christ (Matthew 1:21, Acts 2:36)

EVERY PROPER NAME & DEFINITION IN SCRIPTURE

A

Aaron (a'-ur-un) - Light. A shining light. Enlightened. Very high. To be high. A mountain of strength. Mountaineer. Lofty. A teacher. Rich. To shine.

Aaronites (a'-ur-un-ites) - Descendants of Aaron. Same as Aaron.

Ab (ab) - Fifth Jewish month. Grapes ripened. Figs ripened. Olives ripened.

Abaddon (ab-ad'-dun) - Destruction. The destroyer. Complete destruction. A destroying angel.

Abagtha (ab-ag'-thah) - Fortune. Happy. Great. Prosperous. Given by fortune. Father of the winepress.

Abana (ab-ay'nah) - Made of stones. Rocky. Her stones. A building. Permanent. Constancy; A sure ordinance. Steadfastness. Perennial.

Abarim (ab'-ar-im) - Regions beyond. Mountain beyond. Passengers. The passages.

Abba (ab'-bah) - Father. Daddy (It denotes a childlike intimacy and trust. It is a title of great respect.)

Abda (ab'-dah) - Servant or worshipper of God. Work. Something done. Service rendered. Bring to pass. Bondage.

Abdeel (ab'-de'-el) - Servant of God. Serving God. A vapor. A cloud of God.

Abdi (ab'-di) - Servant of Jehovah. Serviceable. My servant.

Abdiel (ab'-de'-el) - Servant of God.

Abdon (ab'-dun) - Hard bondage. Servitude. Servant. Cloud of judgment. A faithful servant. Service.

Abed-nego (ab-ed'-nego) - Servant or worshiper of Nebo. Servant of light. Servant of splendor. Servant of the sun. Shining.

Abel (Person) (a'-bel) - A breath. Vanity. Vapor. Something Transitory.

Abel (Place) (a'-bel) - A plain. Mourning. Weeping. Fading away.

Abel-beth-maachah (a'bel'-beth-ma'-kah) - Meadow of the house of Maachah. Mourning for the house of oppression. Depression. Grassy.

Abel Keramim (Cheramim) (a'-bel-ker-a'-mim) (NIV) - Mourning of the vineyards.

Abel-maim (a-bel-ma'-im) - Place of waters. Irrigating waters. Meadow of waters. Mourning of waters.

Abel-meholah (a'-bel-me-ho'-lah) - Meadow of dancing. Place of mirth. Mourning for sickness. Mourning of dancing. Root: A dance. To turn round. To twist oneself (In pain as of a woman in labor.) To dance in a circle.

Abel-mizraim (a'-bel-miz'-ra-im) - Mourning of Egypt. Meadow of Egypt. Mourning. Place of the weeping Egypt. Threshing floor of Atad.

Abel-shittim (a'-bel-shit-tim) - Plains or meadows of acacias. Mourning of thorns. Place of thorns.

Abez (a'-bez) - Whiteness. To be white. To glean. Conspicuous. An egg. Muddy. Dirty. Color of tin.

Abi (a'-bi) - My Father is Jehovah. The will of God. Fatherly. Motherly. My father. Ancestor. Founder.

Abia (ab-i'-ah) - Jehovah is Father. God my father. The Lord a father. Worshipper of Jah.

Abiah (ab-i'-ah) God my father. The Lord is my father. My father is Jah. A divinely, devout man.

Abi-albon (ab-i-al'-bun) - Father of strength. Most intelligent father. His father's strength. Valiant. My father is above understanding. Father of understanding.

Abiasaph (ab-i'-as-af) - Consuming father. Father of gathering. Remover of reproach. He took away His father. Gathering.

Abiathar (ab-i'-uth-ur) - Plenty. Father of Plenty. Father of abundance. Liberal. Excellent father. Father of the remnant. Father of superfluity. Surviving father.

Abib (a'-bib) - An ear of corn. Green ear. Green fruit. Ears of corn. First month of Jewish Calendar.

Abida (ab'-id-ah) - Father of knowledge. My father knows. Prayer of a father. Knowing. To know.

Abidah (ab'-id-ah) - Prayer of a father. My father knows. Knowing.

Abidan (ab'-id-an) - My father is judge. Father of judgment.

Abiel (a'-be-el) - Father of strength. My father is God. Strong. God my father.

Abiezer (ab-e-e'-zur) - My father will help. A father's help. A father's strength. Helpful. Is help. Father of helps. My father is my help.

Abiezite (ab-i-ez'-rite) - Descendants of Abiezer. My father will help. Father of helps. Is help.

Abigail #1 (ab'-e-gul) - The father's joy. Father of delight. Father of joy. Father of exultation. Source of joy. Cause of joy. Exultation. Joy. Gladness. My father is joy.

Abigail #2 (ab'-e-gul) (II Samuel 17:25) - Father of a heap. Father of a billow. Father of strength.

Abigibeon (ab-i-gib'-e-on) - Father of Gibeon.

Abihail (ab-e-ha'-il) - His father's strength. Father of might. Mighty. Father of light. Father of Splendor. The father of strength. Cause of Strength.

Abihu (a-bi'-hew) - He is my father. God is my father. Whose father is he. Worshipper of him. He to whom God is father.

Abihud (a-bi-hud) - Father of honor. Father of majesty. Father of praise. My father is majestic. Father of renown. Confession.

Abijah (a-bi'-jah) - God my father. Jehovah is my father. My father is Jah. The desire of the Lord. Worshipper of Jah. Whose father is God. The Lord is my father.

Abijam (a-bi'-jum) - Father of the sea. Father of light. Great desire. Seaman. Father of the west.

Abilene (ab-i-le'-ne) - A grassy place. Desolation. The father of mourning. Meadow. Brook.

Abimael (a-bim'-ah-el) - My father is God. My God is father. A corpulent father. Father sent from God. Whose Father is God.

Abimelech (a-bim'-e-lek) - Father of the king. My father is king. The king is my father.

Abinadab (a-bin'-ah-dab) - Father of nobility. My father is noble. Father of liberality. Source of liberality. My father a prince. Father of a vow. Father of willingness. Father of generosity.

Abiner (ab'-i-ner) - My father is a lamp.
Abinoam (a-bin'-o-am) - Father of beauty. Father of pleasantness. Father of grace. Graciousness. The comeliness of father. Gracious. Father of grace.
Abiram (a-bi'-rum) - Father of loftiness. Father is the exalted one. The renowned father. Father of Altitude. Father that is high. Proud. High father. Father of deceit. Lofty.
Abishag (ab'-e-shag) - Father of error. My father wanders. My father errs. Ignorance of the father. My father was a wanderer. Father's delight. My father seizes. My father causes wandering.
Abishai (ab'-e-sha-hee) - Father of a gift. My father's gift. Possessor of all that is desirable. Source of wealth. Source of giving. Father's sacrifice. Generous. The present of my father.
Abishaloam (a-bish'-ah-lum) - Father of peace. Father of peacefulness. Friendly.
Abishua (a-bish'-u -ah) - Father of welfare. Father of safety. Father of salvation. My father is salvation. Father of riches. Prosperous. Father of deliverance.
Abishur (ab'-e-shur) - The wall of my father. My father a wall. Uprightness. My father is a wall. Strong. Father of oxen. Father of beholding. Father of the singer. Stronghold. Father of uprightness.
Abital (ab'-e-tal) - Father of the dew. Father of the shadow. My father is dew. Good. Fresh. Gentleness. Refreshing.

Abitub (ab'-e-tub) - Father of goodness. Source of goodness. Good.
Abiud (a-bi'-ud) - Father of honor. Father of trustworthiness. The honor of the father. My Father is majesty. Father of praise.
Abnaim (ab-nah'-um) - A stone.
Abner (ab'-nur) - Father of light. The father's candle. Enlightening. Enlightener. My father is a lamp.
Abraham (a'-bra-ham) - Father of a multitude. Father of a great multitude. Father of mercy. Father of many nations. Loyalty. Faithfulness. Father of a great nation.
Abram (a'brum) - A high father. The exalted Father. Father of heights. High. Lofty. Thinker. High father. Honored father. Ambition. Father of elevation. Father of the lofty.
Abrech (Ab'-rech) - I will cause blessings. Tender father.
Absalom (ab'-sal-um) - Father of peace. My father is peace. Friendly. A father's peace. Peaceful.
Accad (ak'-kad) - A chain. Bond. Fortress. A vessel. Pitcher. Spark.
Accho (ak'-ko) - Sand heated. Sand made warm by the sun. To hem in. Hot sand. Close. Pressed together.
Aceldama (as-el'-dam-ah) - Field of blood.
Achab (a'-chab) - Brother of the father.
Achaia (ak-ah'yah) - Trouble. Wailing. Grief. A brother.
Achaicus (ak-ah'yah-cus) - Belonging to Achai. Trouble. Wailing. Sorrowing. Sad.
Achan (a'-kan) - Serpent. Vexation. Trouble. One that takes. He that troubleth.

Achar (a'-kar) - Tribulation. Trouble. To disturb. To trouble. Vexation. Disorder. Tumult. Troublesome. One that takes.

Achaz (a'-kaz) - Possessor. He took. One that takes. One that possesses.

Achbor (ak'-bor) - A mouse. A rat. Agility. Gnawing. Bruising.

Achim (a'-kim) - Jehovah will establish. Without winter. Wise. Sensible. Prudent. Preparing. Revenging. Confirming.

Achish (a'-kish) - Serpent. Charmer. Angry. A hard place. I will blacken. I will terrify. Of awe. Of reverence. Thus, it is. How it is.

Achmetha (ak'-meth-ah) - Fortress. A citadel. Brother of death. Summer house. Place of assemblage. Station.

Achor (a'kor) - Trouble. Tribulation. Troubled.

Achsa (ak'sah) - Distinquished ornament. Anklet. Garter. An ornament for the feet. Bursting the veil.

Achsah (ak'-sah) - Adorned. Ornament. Anklet. An ornament for the feet. Bursting the veil.

Achshaph (ak'-shaf) - Enchantment. I will be bewitched. Delusion. Obscure. Sorcery. Fascination. Poison. Tricks.

Achzib (ak'-zib) - A deceiver. Deceit. Lying. Liar. Of firmness. Falsehood. One that runs.

Acrabbim (ac-rab'-bim) - Steep of scorpions.

Adadah (ad'-ah-ah) - Festival. Forever adorned. Testimony of the assembly.

Adah (a'-dah) - Ornament. To adorn. Adornment. Beauty. Pleasure. Evidence. An assembly. Comeliness.

Adaiah (ad-a-i'-yah) - Jehovah has adorned. Pleasing to Jehovah. Whom Jehovah adores. Ornament of the Lord. Adorned of Jah. Witness of Jehovah. The witness of the Lord.

Adalia (ad-al-i-'yah) - Upright. The honor of Ized. Brave. Strong in mind. Enmity. One that draws water. Poverty. Cloud. Death.

Adam (ad'-um) - Earthy. Red earth. Of the ground. Taken out of the red earth. Ruddy. Red sandstone. A covenant breaker. Guilt. Earth born. A coverer of his transgressions. Red.

Adamah (ad'-am-ah) - Red earth. The ground. Bloody. Soil. Country. Husband. Land. Of blood.

Adami (ad'-am-i) - Human. My man. Red. Earthly.

Adar #1 (a'-dar) - Wide. Height. Glorious. Fire god. Fire. Adorned. High power. Eminent. Threshing floor. Greatness. The name of the twelfth Jewish month.

Adar #2 (a'-dar) - (Joshua 3:15) - Exceedingly glorious. Very excellent. Greatness. Ample.

Adar Sheni (a'-dar-she-ni) - Thirteenth Jewish Month.

Adbeel (ad'-be-el) - Sorrow of God. Languishing for God. Miracle of God. Chastened of God. Disciplined of God. Cloud of God. God has disciplined. Vapor.

Addan (ad'-dan) - Humble. Calamity. Sorrow. Firm. Strong.

Addar (ad'-dar) - Greatness. Height. Honorable. Very excellent. Exalted. Mighty one. Threshing floor.

Addi (ad'-di) - My witness. Adorned. Ornament. Held up by God. Prey.

Addin (ad'-din) - Adorned. Delicious. Voluptuous.

Addon (ad'-don) - Humble. Calamity. Misfortune. Basis. Foundation. The Lord. Powerful.

Ader (a'-dur) - A flock. Caretaker. An arrangement. A drove.

Adiel (a'-de-el) - Ornament of God. Praise or witness of God. The witness of the Lord.

Adin (a'-din) - Delicate. Ornament. Slender. Soft. Given to pleasure. Tender. Voluptuous. Dainty.

Adina (ad'-in'-ah) - Pleasant. Ornament. Voluptuous. Effeminate. Slender. Pliant. Delight. Pleasure.

Adino (ad'-in-o) - Whose pleasure is the spear. His bending of the spear. Delicate ornament. Luxuriousness. He wielded his spear.

Adithaim (ad-ith-a'-im) - Two-fold ornament. Double ornament. Assemblies. Double prey. God the ornament. Two ways.

Adlai (ad'-la-i) - Justice of Jehovah. Just. Weary. The prey is mine. My witness. My ornament.

Admah (ad'-mah) - Earthy. Red earth. Redness. Bloody.

Admatha (ad'-math-ah) - God given. Her earthiness. Cloud of death. Colored with brown. Color. Appraising. A mortal vapor. Appraising. A mortal vapor.

Adna (ad'-nah) - Pleasure. Eternal rest. Delight of his brother.

Adnah #1 (ad'-nah) - Pleasure. Favorite. Brother.

Adnah #2 (ad'-nah) - (II Chronicles 12:20) - Resting. Forever. Eternal rest.

Adonai - Lord. Master. To be lower. To judge. To domineer. Lord of the

dispersion. Lord. Master. The lightning of the Lord.

Adonijah (ad-on-i'-jah) - Jehovah is my Lord. My Lord God. My Lord is Jah. The Lord of the Lord. The Lord is my master.

Adonikam (ad-on-i'-kam) - My Lord has risen. The Lord of might. Lord of height. The Lord was exalted. My Lord is risen. The Lord is assisting. Whom the Lord sets up.

Adoniram (ad-on-i'-ram) - My Lord is high. My Lord has raised me. The Lord of might. Lord of height. The Lord was exalted. My Lord is risen. Lord of might and elevation.

Adonizedek (ad-on-i-ze'-dek) - Lord of justice. Lord of righteousness. Justice of the Lord.

Adoraim (ad-o-ra'-im) - Two Chiefs. Two -fold habitation. Double mound. A firm foundation. Strength of the sea.

Adoram (ad-o'-ram) - My Lord is high. The Lord of might. Lord of height. Adorned. High. Honor. Strength. Their glory. The Lord exalted Himself. Their beauty. Their power.

Adrammelech (a-dram'-mel-ek) - Magnificence of the King. King of fire. The adorned king. Honor of the king. Adar is king. The majesty of the king. Splendor of Molech. An idol. The cloak. Grandeur of the king. Power of the king.

Adramyttium (a-dram-mit'-te-um) - I shall abide in death. Not in the race. Court of death.

Adria (a'-dre-ah) - Without wood.

Adriel (a'-dre-el) - Flock of God. Honor of flock of God. My shepherder - the one who is very personally and intensely involved, in my life is my God. The honor of God.

Adullam (a-dul'-lam) - Justice of the people. Their testimony. Struck with terror. Their ornament. Resting place. Refuge. Their prey.

Adullamite (a-dul'-lam-ite) - Same as Adullam.

Adummim (a-dum'-min) - The red earth. The going up to Adummim. The going up of the red earths. Red spots. Bloody things. Earthy. Red. Bloody

Aeneas (e'-ne-as) - Praiseworthy. Praise. Of heavy birth. Laudable. Praised.

Aenon (e'-non) - Springs. Fountain. To praise. Great fountain. Fountains. Clouds of darkness. A cloud. His eye.

Agabus (ag'-ab-us) - A locust. A grasshopper. The father's joy. The father's feast.

Agag (a'-gag) - Flaming. To burn. To blaze as fire. Warlike. Lofty. I will over top. Very high. Roof. Flame. High. Upper floor.

Agagite (ag'-ag-ite) - Same as Agag.

Agar (a'-gar) - Same as Hagar. Flight. To flee. Fugitive. Immigrant. The sojourner. Mid-day. Stranger. Wandering. A valley. Deepness. A stranger. One that fears.

Agee (ag'-ee) - Fugitive. Deepness. A valley.

Agrippa (ag-rip'-pah) - One who at his birth causes pain. Horse hunter. Wild horse tamer. Born with difficulty.

Agur (a'-gur) - An assembler. A gatherer. A collection or reward. Gathered. Stranger. Gathered together. He who gathers.

Ahab (a'-hab) - Uncle. My father's brother. Friend of his father. Weakness of character.

Aharah (a-har'-ah) - After a brother. Brother of rach. Brother of breathing. Remaining brother. Great delay. After the brother. Brother of height. Brother's follower. A meadow of a sweet savor. A smiling brother.

Aharhel (a-har'-hel) - Behind the breastwork. What is behind. Hope is delayed. Behind the entrenchment. A fortress. Another host. The last sorrow. A brother's sheep

Ahasai (a-ha'-sa'i) - My holder or protector. Clear sighted. Possessor of God. My possessions. Protector. Whom Jehovah protects.

Ahasbai (a-has'-ba-i) - I flee to the Lord. To flee. Take refuge. Shining. I will trust in the Lord. I have taken refuge in Jehovah. Blooming. Trusting in me. A grown-up brother.

Ahasuerus (a-has-u-e'-rus) - King or mighty man. Prince of the people. Lion king. Prince. Clothed with majesty. Prince. Head. Chief. Also called Xerxes.

Ahava (a-ha'-vah) - Brotherhood. I shall subsist. Constant. Flowing river. Generating water. A stream. Essence. Being.

Ahaz (a'-haz) - Possessor. Helper. Jehovah has seized. Jehovah sustains. He holds. He has grasped. One that takes. One that passes.

Ahaziah (a-haz-i'-ah) - When Jehovah upholds. Jehovah holds. Jehovah possesses. Taken by God. The Lord took. The Lord sustains. Whom

Jehovah sustains. Seizure. Vision of the Lord.

Ahban (ah'-ban) - Brotherly. Brother of the prudent. Brother of intelligence. Intelligent brother. Vise. Possessor of understanding.

Aher (a'-hur) - Coming slowly. Following another. One that is behind. After. Defer. Delay.

Ahi (a'-hi) - Brother. My brother. Brother of Jehovah. Joining. My brethren.

Ahiah (a'-hi'-ah) - Brother of the Lord. Jehovah is my brother. Jehovah is my friend. Fellowship. Friend of God.

Ahiam (a-hi'-am) - A brother's mother. A mother's brother. Most firm union. Brother of a nation. Of the father.

Ahian (a-hi'-an) - Brotherly. Fraternal. Brother of a day. Brother of them. A firm union. Brother of wine.

Ahiezer (a-hi-e'-zer) - Brother of help (from the idea of surrounding). Girding. Defending. A brother's help. Helpful. Helping brother. Brother of assistance.

Ahihud #1 (a-hi'-hud) - Brother. Friend of the Jews (to make oneself a Jew.) Brother of majesty. Brother of excellence. Brother of praise. Brother of renown. Brother of honor. Brother of vanity. Witty brother. Brother of darkness. Brother of joy.

Ahihud #2 (a-hi'-hud) - (I Chronicles 8:7) - Joining of the union. Brother of a riddle. The mysterious.

Ahijah (a-hi'-jah) - Same as Ahiah. Brother of the Lord. Jehovah is my brother. Jehovah

is my friend. Fellowship with the Lord. Worshipper of Jehovah. Brother of grandeur.

Ahikam (a-hi'-kam) - Brother of rising up. Brother of the enemy (in the sense of rising up). My brother has risen. My brother has appeared. A brother has risen up. That is high. A brother who avenges.

Ahilud (a-hi'-lud) - Brother of one born. A birth of a brother. Pedigree. A brother begotten.

Ahimaaz (a-him'-a-az) - Brother of anger. A rascal. Powerful brother. My brother is counselor. Brother of strength. Brother of help. Brother of the council.

Ahiman (a-hi'-man) - Brother of gift. Who is my brother? My brother is gifted. A brother prepared. Likeness of a brother. Brother of a portion. Liberal. Brother of a man of fortune. Brother of the right hand.

Ahimelech (a-him'-el-ek) - Brother of the king. My brother is king. My brother is a king. My King's brother.

Ahimoth (a-hi'-moth) - Brother of death. Brother's death.

Ahinadab (a-him'-el-ek) - Brother of nobility. Brother of liberality. A noble. Willing brother. Brother of a vow.

Ahinoam (a-hin'-o-am) - Brother of grace. The brother pleasant. Brother of pleasantries. A brother's delight. My brother is joy. Beauty of the brother. Brother of motion.

Ahio (a-hi'-o) - Brotherly. His brother. Union of him. Brethren. His brother.

Ahira (a-hi'-rah) - Brother of evil. Joining of the fellowship. Unlucky. Brother of iniquity. Brother of the shepherd.

Ahiram (a-hi'-rum) - Brother of height. To lift up oneself. Exalted brother. Great slowness. High. Exalted. My brother is exalted. Brother of craft. Brother of protection.

Ahiramites (a-hi'-rum-ites) - Descendants of Ahiram. Same as Ahiram.

Ahisamach (a-his'-am-ak) - Brother of support. Brother of help. A brother supports. A brother aiding. Supporting brother. Brother of strength.

Ahishahar (a-hish'-a-har) - Brother of the dawn. Brother of the morning. Brother of the dew. Early. Brother of blackness.

Ahishar (a-hi'-shar) - Brother of firmness. The brother's stay. Brother of uprightness. Brother of song. Brother of a prince.

Ahithophel (a-hith'-o-fel) - Brother of folly. Impiety. Brother of ruin. Most sure union. Foolishness. Brother of foolishness.

Ahitub (a-hi'-tub) - Brother of goodness. Brother of benevolence. Benign. My brother is goodness.

Ahlab (ah'-lab) - Fatness. Fertility. A fertile place. Brother of the heart. Made of milk.

Ahlai (ah'-lahee) - Oh that! O would that. Would to God. Brother to me. Prayer of God. Wishful. Ornamental. Beseeching. Sorrowing. Expecting.

Ahoah (a-ho'-ah) - Same as Ahijah and Abiah. Brother of the Lord. Jehovah is my brother. Friend. A brother's need. Brother of rest. Joining of the Lord. A live brother. My thorn. My thistle.

Ahohite (a-ho'-hite) - Same as Ahoah.

Aholah (a-ho'-lah) - She has her own tent. A tent. An idolatrous sanctuary. A father's tent. His tabernacle. His tent. A symbolic name for Samaria.

Aholiab (a-ho'-lee-ab) - Tabernacle of my father. Her father's tent. Tent of the father. The tent of my father. Home. Tabernacle. Tent.

Aholibah (a-hol'-ib-ah) - My tabernacle in her. My tent is in her. A symbolic name for Judah. Aholah and Aholiboh represent Jerusalem and Samaria in their adulteries. (Ezekiel 23:4)

Aholibamah (a-hol'-ib-a'-mah) - Tent of the high place. My tent on high. Tent of high elevation. Tent of the height. My tabernacle is exalted.

Ahumai (a-hoo'-mahee) - Brother of waters. Dwelling near water. Brother of divine compassion. A meadow of waters.

Ahuzam (a-hoo'-zam) - Their possessions. Possession. Holding fast. Most full possession. Seizure. Possess. Hold. Seize. Their taking. Their possessing. Vision.

Ahuzzath (a-huz'-zath) - A possession. Holding fast. A thing possessed. A possession. Especially land. Seizing. Collecting.

Ai (a'-i) - A heap of ruins. Crooked. As it overturned. A ruin. A heap. Vulture.

Aiah (a-i'-ah) - A little hawk. A vulture. A bird of prey. Cry. Clamor. A falcon. A raven. A hawk. A cry. Alas. Woe.

Aiath (a-i'-ath) - Same as Ai. A heap of ruins. A heap. Eye. An hour. Fountain.

Aija (a-i'-jah) - Same as Ai and Aiath.

Aijalon (a-ij'-el-on) - A large stag. Place of gazelles. A swift hind. A deer-field. Much elevated. A chain. Strength. The place of deer.

Aijeleth Shahar (a-ij'-el-eth-sha'-har) - Title of Psalm 22. Morning. Hind. The hind of the morning dawn. The rising sun. A doe. The land of the morning. It is also a musical instrument.

Ain (a'-in) - Fountain. An eye. A fountain. A spring. Same as Aiath.

Ajah (a'-jah) - Same as Aiah. A little hawk. A vulture. A bird of prey. Hawk. The screamer.

Ajalon (aj'-a-lon) - Same as Aijalon. A large stag. Place of gazelle. A swift hind. Very elevated. A chain. A deer-field. A hind. Strength.

Akan (a'-kan) - Torques. Acute. Twisted. Oppression. A chain that binds. A chain that tortures. Twist.

Akel-Dama (a-kel'-da-ma) (Hebrew for Aceldoma) - Field of blood.

Akkub (ak'-kub) - Insidious. Cunning. Artful. Laid in wait. Subtle. Literally to take by the heel. Lewdness. Much delayed. Foot-print. Supplanting. Crookedness.

Akrabbim (ac-rah'-bim) - Assert if scorpions. Scorpions. Serpents. A scourge.

Al - Nothing. Nay. Neither. Not. Nor. Never.

Alameth (al'-am-eth) - Covering. Youthful vigor. Concealment. Hiding. A covering.

Alammelech (a-lam'-mel-ek) - Oak of the king. King's oak. The binding of kings. God is king.

Alamoth (al'-am-oth) - Virgins. Hiding places. Girls. After the manner of virgins. The soprano or female voice. Title of Psalm 46.

Albon (al'-bon) - Derivation. Uncertain. Probably. Father of strength.

Alemeth (al-e'-meth) - A hiding place. A covering. Cave. Hiding. Rest. Self. Sustain. Youth. Worlds. Upon the dead.

Alexander (al-ex-an'-dur) - Defending men. Man defender. Helper of men. One who turns away evil. One who assist men

Alexandria(ns) (al-ex-an'-dree-ah) - Same as Alexander.

Algum (al'-gum) - Not drunken ones. Not added ones.

Aliah (a-li'-ah) -   Same as Alvah. Evil. Iniquity. Sublimity. Much elevated. Moral perverseness.

Alian (a-li'-un) - Same as Alvan. Tall. Unrighteous. Sublime. Much exalted. Lift up. Restore. High.

Alleluia (al-le-loo'-yah) - Praise ye the Lord.

Allon (al'lon) - An oak. Other strong tree. Strong.

Allonbachuth (al'-lon-bak'-ooth) - Oak of weeping.

Almighty (ol-mit'-e) - Shaddai. The almighty.

Almodad (al-mo'-dad) - Immeasurable. Increasing with measure. Extension. The agitator. Measure of God. God is a friend.

Almon (al'-mon) - Hidden. Covering. Concealment. Hiding place.

Almon-diblathaim (al'-mon-dib-lath-a'-im) - Hiding of the two cakes. Hiding of troubles. Hidden in a cluster of figs.

Aloth (a'-loth) - Yielding milk. The heights. Mistresses. Possessed. Ascents.

Alpha (al'-fah) - The beginning. The first letter of the Greek alphabet.

Alphaeus (al-fe'-us) - Successor. Transient. Chief. Produce. Gain. Exchange. Compensation of God. Leader. A thousand. Learned.

Altaschith (al-tas'-kith) - Do not destroy. You may not destroy. Thou must not destroy. Thou must not corrupt. (The title of Psalms 57, 58, 59, 75.)

Alush (a'-lush) - A crowd of men. I will knead (bread). Mingling together. Desert. Desolation. Wild place.

Alvah (al'-vah) - Iniquity. Elevated. Evil. Perverseness. His rising up. His highness.

Alvan (al'van) - Unrighteous. Sublime. Their ascent. Iniquitous ones. Very exalted. Tall. Thick.

Amad (a'-mad) - Eternal people. Perpetual position. People of duration. Station. People of witness. A prey.

Amal (a-mal) - Troublesome. Labor. Sorrow. Worry. Iniquity.

Amalek (am'-al-ek) - A people that lick up or exhaust. People of lapping. A strangler of the of the people. Warlike. A dweller in the vale. Labor. Labor that is irksome.

Amalekites (am'al-ek-ites) - Descendants of Amalek. Same as Amalek.

Amam (a'-mam) - People. A gathering place. Mother. Gathering together. Fear of them.

Amana (am-a'-nah) - A confirmation. Truth. Integrity. Continuance. Faith. Something fixed. A covenant. Constant. A nurse. Constantly. A settled provision.

Amariah (am-a-ri'-ah) - Jehovah has said. Jehovah has promised. Whom Jehovah spoke of. The speech of the Lord. Word of God. God has promised. The Lord says. The integrity of the Lord.

Amasa (am'-a-sah) - Burden. Burden bearer. An exalter of the people. A forgiving people. Burdening. Sparing the people.

Amasai (am'-as-ahee) - Burden of the Lord. Burdensome. My burdens. He burdened. Jehovah has borne. Strong.

Amashai (am'-ash-ahee) - Carrying spoil. Burden bearer. People of my spoilers. He laid a burden. Gift of the people. Burdensome. The peoples' gift.

Amashi-ali (am-a-shi-a-li) - Same as Amaziah.

Amasiah (am-a-si'-ah) - Carried of the Lord. Burden of Jehovah. Jehovah is strong. Laden of Jah. Jah bears in his arms. He burdened. He loaded. Firm. Strength. Courageous.

Amaziah (am-a-zi'-ah) - Strength of the Lord. Made strong for the Lord. Jehovah strengthens. Jehovah has strength. Strength of Jah. He was brave. Firm. Strength. Courageous. Jehovah is mighty.

Amen (a'-men) - So be it. Very truly. Verily.

Amethyst (am'-e-thyst) - Dream stone. Literally. I shall be brought back, as from a dream.

Ami (a'-mi) - The beginning. Bond servant. Extended. Increased.

Faithful. Skilled. Mother. Fear. People.

Aminadab (a-min'-a-dab) - The kinsman is generous. Noble nation. My people are noble. My people are liberal. Same as Amminadab.

Amittai (a-mit'-tahee) - Truth of the Lord. True. Truthful. Truth of God. Faithful. Fearing.

Ammah (am'-mah) - Beginning. A cubit. Two ways. A mother. Head. Unit. Measure. My.

Ammi (am'-mi) - My people. A people. Tribe. Troops. Flock.

Ammiel (am'-me-el) - People of God. A devoted ally. A devoted kinsman of God. Servants of God. Worshippers of God.

Ammihud (am-mi'-hud) - People of praise. Men of praise worthiness. People of majesty. A nation of excellence. A nation of praise. People of splendor.

Ammihur (am-mi'-hur) - My people are noble.

Amminadab (am-min'-a-dab) - People of liberality. My liberal people. My people are willing. My kinsman is generous. He gave a people. Generosity. Kindred of a prince. My people is noble. My people is liberal.

Amminadib (am-min'-a-dib) - Same as Amminadab.

Ammishaddai (am-mi'-shad'-dahee) - People of the Almighty. Most powerful. To be strong. To act violently. To lay waste. An ally is the Almighty. Servant of the Almighty. The Almighty is my my kinsman. The Almighty is with me.

Ammizabad (am-miz'-a-bad) - People of the bountiful giver. The kinsman has endowed. People of the endower. He gave a people. Kindred of the giver. People of endowment. Dowry of the people.

Ammon (am'-mon) - Great people. Son of my people. Pertaining to the nation. People of strength. Tribal. People of Lot. Kinsmen. People.

Ammonites (am'-mon-ites) - Descendants of Ammon. Same as Ammon.

Amnon (am'-non) - Faithful. Intelligent. A faithful son. Made faithful. Fixed. Permanent. True. Tutor.

Amok (a'-mok) - Deep. Deepened down. A valley. Depth. Unsearchable.

Amon (a'-mon) - A nourisher. A nurse. A multitude. Faithful. Security. A workman. Very extended. True. Skilled. Trustworthy. Builder.

Amorite(s) (am'-o-rite(s)) - Mountaineer. A talker. A slayer. A bitter people. Dwellers on the summits. Prominence. Publicity. A rebel. Babbler.

Amos (a'-mos) - Burden. Burden bearer. Vigorous. Who is being born. Carried. Loading. Weighty. One with a burden. Strong.

Amoz (a'-moz) - Strong. Strength. Brass. Courageous. Vigorous. Robust. Burdensome. To impose. To inflict.

Amphipolis (am-fip'-o-lis) - A city surrounded by the sea. Around the city. Surrounded city.

Amplias - Enlarged. Large. Extended. Extensive.

Amram #1 (am'-ram) - Intensely red. A nation exalted. High people. People exalted. Their sheaves. Handfuls of corn.

Amram #2 (am'-ram) - People of exaltation.

Amramite(s) (am'-ram-ite(s)) - Descendants of Amram. Same as Amram

Amraphel (am'-raf-el) - One that speaks of dark things. An obscure speech. The circle of the few. Powerful people. Sayer of darkness. Fall of the sayer. Very gigantic. Speaker of hidden things. One that speaks of secrets.

Amzi (am'-zi) - Strong. Robust. My strength. Mighty.

Anab (a'-nab) - A place fertile in grapes. Place of cluster. To bear fruit. Grapetown. A grape. A knot.

Anah (a'-nah) - An answer. Answering. Respond. One who answers. One who sings. One who is poor. One who is afflicted. Speech.

Anaharath (an-a-ha'-rath) - Hollow way. Pass. The groaning of fear. Dryness. Gorge. Narrow path. Groaning. Wrath.

Anaiah (an-a-i'-ah) - Answered of the Lord. Jehovah has answered. Afflicted of Jah. Answered of Jah. He answered. Give account.

Anak (a'-nak) - Long necked. Giant. Neck chain. Length of neck. Collar. Ornament. Necklace.

Anakims (an'-ak-ims) - Descendants of Anak.

Anamim (an'-am-im) - Responding waters. Affliction of the waters. Answer of the waters. A fountain. Affliction. Sound of waters. Rock men. Men of rock. Answer.

Anammelech (a-nam'-mel-ek) - Idol of the king. Stature of the king. The king's answer. The affliction of the king. King of riches. Image of the king. King's rock. Poverty of the king.

Anan (a'-nan) - A cloud. He beclouds. He covers. Gracious hearing. Prophecy. Covering. Cloud.

Anani (a-na'-ni) - cloud of the Lord. Covered with God. My cloud. He heard me. Cloudy. Protect

Ananiah (an-an-i'-ah) - When Jehovah covers. Cloud of the Lord. Jehovah is protector. Jah has favored. Protected of God. Separated. Set apart.

Ananias (an-an-i'-as) Jehovah is gracious. The Lord has been gracious. Seperated. Set apart. The cloud of the Lord.

Anath (a'-nath) - An answer to prayer. Answer. Granting. Depression. Poverty. Affliction. A strong man. Song.

aAnathema (a-nath'-em-ah) - Something accursed.

Anathoth (an'-a-thoth) - Answers to prayers. Afflictions. Answers. A strong man.

Andrew (an'-drew) - Manliness. Manly. Strong. Conqueror. A strongman.

Andronicus (an-dron-ni'-cus) - Conqueror. Conquering men. Victory of man. A man excelling others.

Anem (a'-nem) - Two fountains. Double fountain. Their afflictions. Dual. Answer. Song. Affliction.

Aner (a'-nur) - Exile. To shake out. To drive out. Waterfall. Affliction. Affliction of light. Light. He shook off. Juvenility. Youth. Sprout. Answer. Song.

Anethothite (an'-e-thoth-ite) - Same as Anathoth.

Anetothite (an'-e-toth-ite) - Same as Anathoth.

Aniam (a'-ne-am) - Sorrow of the people. Sighing of the people. Groaning. Lamentation. The strength of the people. The sorrow of the people. A people.

Anim (a'-num) - Two fountains. Answerings. Singings. Afflicted.

Anna (an'-nah) - Grace. Free gift. Favored. Favor. Gracious. One who gives.

Annas (an'-nas) - Grace of Jehovah. Humble. Whom Jehovah graciously gave. One who answers.

Antichrist (an'-ti-krist) - Adversary to Christ. Against Christ. An opponent of the Messiah

Antioch (an'-te-ok) - Driven against. Who fights a chariot. Speedy as a chariot.

Antipas (an'-tip-as) - Likeness of his father. Against all. Against fatherland. For all.

Antipatris (an-tip'-at-ris) - Likeness of his father. Against (or instead of) one's country. For. Over against. For his father.

Antothijah (an-to-thi'-jah) - Prayers answered by Jehovah. Afflictions of Jehovah. Answers of Jah. Afflictions. Answers of the Lord. Songs of the Lord.

Antothite (an'-to-thite) - Belonging to Anathoth. Answers to prayer. A man of Anathoth.

Anub (a'-nub) - Bound together. To bind together. Strong. High. Clustered. A confederacy. Joined.

Apelles (a-pel'-leze) - Exclusion. Separation. Seclusion. Without receptacle.

Apharsachites (a-far'-sak-ites) - As causers of division. Dividing. Rend. Tear asunder.

Apharsattchites (a-far'-sath-kites) - I will divide the deceivers. Dividing. Tearing asunder. Rending.

Apharsites (a-far'-sites) - Dividing. Tearing asunder. Causers of division.

Aphek (a-'fek) - Strength. Restraint. Speaking. Soundness. Strong fortress. Restrained.

Aphekah (af-e'-kah) - Strength. Restraint. Fortress. Rapid stream. Vigor. Speaking.

Aphiah (af-i'-ah) - Rekindled. Refreshed. Revived. I will make to breathe. Breathing. Breeze. Groan speaking.

Aphik (a'-fik) - Channel. Strong. Restraint. Soundness. Strength. A stream.

Aphrah (af'-rah) - Dust. Dust heap. Female fawn.

Aphses (af'-seze) - Dispersion. The dispersed. The shattering. To disserve.

Apocalypse (ah-pok-uh-lips) - Uncovering.

Apocrypha (ah-pok-ruh-fuh) - Hidden.

Apollonia (ap-ol-lo'-ne-ah) - Belonging to Apollo. Utter destruction. Perdition. Destroyer. The sun. A city of Macedonia named for the pagan deity. Apollon.

Appolonius (a-poll-oh'-ne-us) - Destroying.

Apollos (ap-ol'-los) - A destroyer. Youthful god of music. One who destroys. Laying waste. The sun.

Apollyon (ap-ol'-le-on) - One that exterminates. Destroyer.

Appaim (ap'-pa-im) - Face. Presence. Two breathing places (i.e. The nostrils.) Two Persons. Double nosed. To send out. Double portion.

Apphia (af'-fee-ah) - That which is fruitful. A dear one. Productive. Endearment.

Appii Forum (ap'pe-i for'-em) - Persuasive mart. (Hebrew - I shall be nourished.) The forum or marketplace of Appius.

Aquila (ac'-quil-ah) - An eagle. Hebrew: I shall be nourished. Latin: Eagle. Greek: Immoveable.

Ar (ar) - City. Awakening. Uncovering.

Ara (a'-rah) - Congregation. A lion. Strong. I shall see. Cursing. Flock.

Arab (a'-rab) - Fugitive. Ambush. To lie in wait. To lie in ambush. Multiplying. Sowing. Sedition. A window. A locust. A court. A cave.

Arabah (ar'-ab-ah) - A plain. A Wilderness. A desert. The desert plain. Solitude. Serenity. Burnt up.

Arabia (a-ra'-be-ah) - Desert. Sterile. Of the mingled people. Mixed. Dusky. Evening. Ravens. Wilderness. Sense of sterility. Wild. Open place.

Arabian(s) (a-ra'-be-un) - Dweller in sterile region. Sense of sterility.

Arad (a'-rad) - Wild ass. Fugitive. Dragon.

Arah (a'-rah) - Wandering. Wayfarer. He wandered. The way. A traveler. Departure.

Aram (a'-ram) - High. Elevated. Lifted up. Exalted. Magnified. Highest. The Highland. Magnificence.

Aram Dammeseck (ar'-am dam'-me-sek) - An ancient name for Syria of Damascus.

Aramitess (a'-ram-i-tes) - Highlanderess. A female inhabitant of Aram. A woman of the highlands

Aram-naharaim (a'-ram-na-ha-ra'-im) - Psalm 60 title. Aram of the two rivers. Highland of the two rivers. Flowing. Stream. Exalted. Chosen of God.

Aram-zobah (a'-ram-zo'-bah) - Exalted station. Exalted conflict. Elevated. Height. Depression.

Aran (a'-ran) - Wild goat. Firmness. I shall shout for joy. An ark. Their curse. Goat of the rock. Stridulous.

Ararat (ar'-ar-at) - Mountain of descent. The curse reversed. The precipitation of a curse. The curse of trembling. Wilderness. Elevated. A bow. Holy land.

Araunah (a-raw'-nah) - Jehovah is firm. A large ash. A large pine. (Idea of a tremulous sound, as of a tall tree vibrating; idea of a tinkling sound as of a tall tree vibrating; idea of a creaking sound, as of a tall tree vibrating). An ark. A chest. I will shout for joy. Joyful shouting of Jehovah. Song. Joyful cry. A strong one. A herd. Jah is strong. Pine of God. Ash of God.

Arba (ar'-bah) - Four square. Perfect Stature. The croucher of Baal. The strength of Baal. Four. A giant. Square.

Arbah (ar'-bah) - Same as Arba.

Arbathite (ar'-bath-ite) - Same as Betharbel. House of the desert. An inhabitant of Arbah.

Arbel (ar'-bah) - Same as Betharbel. House of the ambush of God. Ambush.

Arbite (ar'-bite) - Ambush. To lie in wait. To lie in a bush. Inhabitants of Arabia.

Archelaus (ar-ke-la'-us) - Prince. People's chief. Ruling the people. Prince of the people. Ruling. A chief.

Archevite(s) (ar'-ke-vite(s)) - Inhabitants of Erech. Length. To make long. To prolong. From the beginning. Precedence.

Archi (ar'-kee) - Inhabitants of Erech. Length. To make long. To prolong. Ambush.

Archippus (ar-kip'-pus) - Master of the horse. Horse chief. Chief groom. Ruler of horses.

Archite (ar'-kite) - Length. To make long. To prolong. Ambush. Inhabitant of Erech.

Arcturus (ark-tu'-rus) - A moth. Consuming. A gathering together. Ambush. The bear's tail. Bearward. Great bear.

Ard (ard) - Fugitive. Descent. I shall subdue. One that commands. He that descends. To wander. Excellent. Ruling.

Ardites (ar'-dites) - Fugitive. Descent. I shall subdue. One that commands. He that descends. To wander. Excellent. Ruling.

Ardon (ar'-don) - Fugitive. Descendant. Ruling. A judgment of malediction. Very Magnificent. Roaming.

Areli (a-re'-li) - Lion of my God. Heroic. Valiant. A lion is my God. He cursed my God. The light of God. The vision of God. Son of a hero. A son of God.

Arelites (a-re'-lites) - Descendants of Areli. Same as Areli.

Areopagite (a-re-op'-a-jite) - Mortial peak. Hill of Mars. Employed. None given to members of the Court of Areopagus.

Areopagus (a-re-op'-a-gus) - Mortal Peak (the hill of Mars).

Aretas (ar'-e-tas) - Agreeable. A husbandman. Pleasing. Virtuous. Great.

Argob (ar'-gob) - Heap of stones. A rocky district. Strong. A lion's den. A lump of clay. Region of clods.

Aridai (a-rid'-a-i) - Gift of the plough. Gift of the bull. The lion is enough. Strong. Great. Shining. Distinguished. Delight of Hari.

Aridatha (a-rid'-a-thah) - Great or noble birth. The lion of the decree. Giving. What is worthy. Son of the great. Strong. Treacherous. Sixth son of Haman.

Arieh (a-ri'-eh) - Lion. Lion of Jehovah. A prince of Israel. Strong.

Ariel (a'-re-el) - Lion of God. Altar of God. God's altar hearth. Hero of God. Altar. Light of god.

Arim (ar'-im) - City of forests.

Arimathaea (ar-im-ath-e'-ah) - Lofty or high place. Placed on a height. Dead unto God. Lion. A lion dead to the Lord.

Arioch (a'-re-ok) - The mighty lion. Lionlike. Servant. The moon God. A lion. Venerable. Noble. Long. Great. Tall.

Arisai (a-ris'-a-i) - Like to a lion. Lionlike. The form of a lion. Arrow

Aristarchus (ar-is-tar'-cus) - Best ruling. The best ruler. Excellent ruler. The best prince.

Aristobulus (a-ris-to-bu'-lus) - Best counselor. Counseling in the best way. A good counselor.

Arkite (ar'-kite) - Fugitive. My gnawing. Length. Tusk.

Armageddon (ar-mag-ed'-don) - Height of Megiddo. Hill of Megiddo. Place of crowds. Hill of slaughter. Place of great crowd. Hill of fruits.

Armenia (ar-me'-ne-ah) - Mountain of descent. A bow. Mountains of Mini. The trembling light. The curse reversed. Precipitation of a curse.

Armoni (ar-mo'-ni) - Belonging to a palace. Pertaining to the palace. Belonging to a king's court. A chamberlain. Palatial. A fortress of the palace.

Arnan (ar'-nan) - Nimble. Active. Strong. Agile. Lion of perpetuity. Very swift. Noisy. Quick.

Arni (ar'-ni) - Rejoicing.

Arnon (ar'-non) - Murmuring. Roaring. A sounding torrent. A growling stream. Constant sounding. Rushing water. Rejoicing. Sunlight.

Arod (a'-rod) - Wild ass. Posterity. I will subdue. I will roam. Distinguished honor. Ruling fugitive. Hunchbacked.

Arodi (ar'-o-di) - A wild ass. Honor. Hunchbacked.

Arodites (a'-ro-dites) - Descendants of Arod. Wild ass. Posterity.

Aroer (ar'-o-ur) - A naked tree. Childless. Empty. Destitute. Nudity. Barren. Most sterile. Nudity of situation. Health. Tamarisk. Ruins.

Aroerite (ar'-o-ur-ite) - A naked tree. Childless. Empty. Patron. Descendants of Aroer.

Arpad (ar'-pad) - Support. To prop. Rest. Strength. The light of redemption. Spread out. Firm couch or bed. Resting place. I shall be spread out.

Arphad (ar'-fad) - Same as Arpad. Spread out. Sure bed or covering. Fortified city. Resting place. The light of redemption.

Arphaxad (ar-fax'-ad) - One that releases. A jar pouring forth. I shall fail at the breast. A healer. A releaser. Great diffusion. One that heals.

Artaxerxes (ar-tax-erx'-ees) - A great king. Honored king. Possessor of an exalted kingdom. The silence of light. Fervent to spoil. Warrior. The great one.

Artemas (ar'-te-mas) - Whole. Sound. Safe and sound. Gift of Diana.

Aruboth (ar'-u-both) - Flood gates. Lattice. Window. Openings.

Arumah (a-ru'-mah) - Elevated. I shall be exalted. High. Height. Lofty. A high place.

Arvad (ar'-vad) - Place of fugitives. Wandering. I shall break loose. Refuge. A refuge for the roving.

Arvadites (ar'-vad-ites) - A refuge. Wandering. A refuge for the roving. I shall break loose. Place of fugitives.

Arza (ar'-zah) - Earth. Firm. Delight. Earthiness.

Asa (a'-sah) - Physician. Healer. Cure. Healing. He healed. Curing.

Asahel (as'-a-hel) - Made of God. God has made. God is doer. Whom God made. The work of God. Creature of God. God made or constituted.

Asahiah (as-a-hi'-ah) - Made of Jehovah. Jehovah has made. The Lord hath wrought. The gracious answer of God. God created.

Asaiah (as-a'-yah) - Same as Asahiah. The Lord hath wrought. God created.

Asaph (a'-saf) - Collector. To collect together. To draw up. To gather up the rear. He that gathered or removed reproach. Jehovah has gathered together. Assembler. He hath taken away. One who completes. Who gathers together.

Asareel (a-sar'-e-el) - God is joined. Whom God has bound. Bound of God. I shall be a prince of God. God has collected. Right of God. The beatitude of God.

Asarelah (as-a-re'-lah) - Upright to God. Upright toward God. Right before God. Guided towards God. Joined to God. God has fulfilled with joy.

Asenath (as'-e-nath) - Who belongs to Neith. She who is of Neith (an Egyptian goddess). Dedicated. Beauty. Fairness. Peril. Misfortune.

Aser (a'-sur) - Fortunate. Happy. Greek form of the Hebrew name Asher.

Ashan (a'-shan) - Smoke. Vapor. Dust. Anger.

Ashbea (ash'-be-ah) - I conjure. I adjure. Man of Baal. Let me call as witness. I shall be made to swear. Adjuration.

Ashbel (ash'-bel) - Fire of Bel. Vain fire. Fire of old age. To waste away. Consume. Man of Baal. Flowing. Continually increasing. Determination of God. An old fire.

Ashbelites (ash'-bel-ites) - Descendants of Ashbel. Fire of Bel. Vain fire. Fire of old age. To consume. To waste away. Man of Baal.

Ashchenaz (ash'-ke-naz) - A fire is scattered. A fire that spreads.

Ashdod (ash'-dod) - A fortified place. A strong place. To be strong or powerful. Only in a bad sense to oppress. To spoil. To act violently. A friend to fire. Stronghold. Ravager. Effusion. Inclination. Theft. Expulsion. Exile. Castle.

Ashdodites (ash'-dod-ites) - Inhabitants of Ashdod. Divided rock. Fragment of hewn rock. To divide. To cut up.

Ashdoth (ash'-doth) - Divided rock. Fragment of hewn rock. To divide. To cut up. Streams.

Ashdothites - (ash'-doth-ites) - Same as Ashdodites. Inhabitants of Ashdod.

Ashdothpisgah (ash'-doth-piz'-gah) - Springs of Pisgah. To pour forth. Ravines of Pisgah. Spoilers of the survey. Divided rock. Fragment of hewn rock. To divide. To cut up.

Asher (ash'-ur) - Fortunate. Happy. Fortress. Proceeding right. Reciprocal activity. Blessedness. Happiness. Honesty. Prosperous.

Asherah (ashe'-rah) - She who enriches. An idol or image of Ashtoreth.

Asherites (ash'-ur-ites) - Descendants of Asher. Fortunate. Happy. Blessedness. Happiness. Honesty. Prosperous. Fortress. Proceeding right. Reciprocal activity.

Ashima (ash'-im-ah) - A goat without wool. A fault. An Offense. Guiltiness. I will make desolate. Crime. Fire of the sea. Lion. Straight. Heaven.

Ashkelon (ash'-ke-lon) - Migration. Taken. The fire of infamy. I shall be weighed. Weighing. Wandering. Weight. Balance.

Ashkenaz (ash'-ke-naz) - A fire is scattered. Spreading fire. Strong. Fortified. A fire that spreads. Same as Ashchenaz.

Ashnah (ash'nah) - Strong. Mighty. I will cause change. Fortification. Firmness. Hard. Firm. Change.

Ashpenaz (ash'-pe-naz) - Horse's nose. I will make prominent the sprinkled. Prompt assistance.

Ashriel (ash'-re-el) - Vow of God. I shall be prince of God. Right of God. The binding or blessedness of God.

Ashtaroth (ash'-ta-roth) - Star. Statues or groves of Astarte or Ashtoreth. Rich pastures. A wife. Flock. A pagan goddess.

Ashterathite (ash'-ter-a-thite) An inhabitant of Ashtaroth. Same as Ashtaroth.

Ashteroth (ash'-ta-roth) - Same as Ashtaroth.

Ashteroth Karnaim (ash'-te-roth-kar-na-im) - Ashteroth of the two horns or peaks. The crescent moons. Double horned mind readers.

Ashterothite (ash'-ter-o-thite) - Same as Ashteroth. Inhabitants of Ashteroth Karnaim. Ashteroth of the two horns or peaks. Two crescent moons.

Ashtoreth (ash'-to-reth) - Queen of heaven. She who enriches. Abundance of riches. Thought searching. (This idol that was represented as a woman with the head of an ox; she was worshipped as the moon.)

Ashur (ash'-ur) - Blackness. Black. A watcher. Freeman. I shall be early sought. Successful. Happy in nobility. Blessed.

Ashurbanipal (ash'-ur-ba'-nip-al) - Asher is creating an heir.

Ashurites (ash'-ur-ites) - Inhabitants of Ashur. Blackness. Black. A watcher. Freeman. I shall be early sought. Successful. Happy in nobility. Blessed.

Ashvath (ash'-vath) - Fabricated. Wrought. Sleek. Shiny. Bright. Shining. Delight. Firmer. Stronger.

Asia (a'-she-ah) - Orient. Slime. Mire. Full of mud. Boggy.

Asiel (a'-se'-el) - Created by God. God has made. The work of God. God is doer or maker.

Askelon (as'-ke-lon) - Migration. Taken. The fire of shame. Contempt. Weight. Balance. The fire of infamy.

Asnah (as'-nah) - A bramble. A dweller in the thorn bush. To be sharp. Thorn bush.

Asnapper (as-nap'-pur) - The swift. A dangerous bull. Asnap the great. Very quick. Leader of an army. Unhappiness. Increase of danger.

Aspatha (as'-pa-thah) - Given by the horse. Horse given. The enticed gathered. Foal of a horse.

Asriel (as'-re-el) - Vow of God. God is joined. God has bound together. Right of God. Help of God. God has filled with joy.

Asrielites (as'-re-el-ites) - Descendants of Asriel. The prohibition of God.

Asshur (ash'-ur) - A step. Going forward. Lifted up. Exalted. Level plain. Successful.

Asshurim (ash'-u-rim) - Steps. Going forward. Mighty ones. Successes. Liers in wait. Beholders. Honest.

Assir (as'-sur) - Captive. Prisoner. Firmly bound. Imprisoned. Fettered.

Assos (as'-sos) - Approaching. Nearer. Firm. Coming near.

Assur (as'-sur) - A step. Going forward. Lifted up. Exalted. Level plain. Successful.

Assyria (as-sir'-e-ah) -Successful. Country of Assur. Success. Step. Hero. Mighty.

Assyrians (as-sir'-e-uns) - A step. Lifted up. Exalted. Level plain. The land named for Asshur.

Astaroth (as'-ta-roth) - Queen of heaven. She who enriches. Increase of a flock. Abundance of riches. Accessions.

Asuppim (a-sup'-pim) - Collected. A collection of offerings. House of gatherings. Storehouse. Gatherings. To gather for any purpose.

Asyncritus (a-sin'-cri-tus) - Incomparable. Disciple. Unsocial.

Atad (a'-tad) - Bramble. Buckhorn. A thorn. A thistle. A black thorn. A thorn tree. To pierce. Thorn bush.

Atarah (at'-a-rah) - A crown. Crowning. Ornament.

Ataroth (at'-a-roth) - Crown. An ornament.

Ataroth-adar (at'-a-roth-a'-dar) - Crowns of greatness. Crowns of glory. Crowns of flocks.

Ataroth-addar (at'-a-roth-ad'-dar) - Crowns of greatness. Crowns of glory. Crowns of power. Crown of Addar.

Ater (a'-tur) - Bound. Shut-up. Shut. Dumb. Binder. Left-handed (i.e. shut as to the right-hand). Maimed. Oppression. Misfortune. Ruin. Lame.

Athach (a'-thak) - Lodging place. Your due season. Declination. Sojourn. Bending. Turning aside. To sojourn. Lodging. Thy time. Stopping place.

Athaiah (ath-a-i'-ah) - Whom Jehovah made. Made opportunity of the Lord. Jehovah is helper. Jah's due season. The hour of the Lord. God is helper. The Lord's time. God made it opportunely.

Athaliah (ath-a-li'-ah) -Taken away of the Lord. Whom Jehovah has afflicted. Jehovah is strong. Due season of Jah. Afflicted of God. The time of the Lord. The Lord took away. Jah has constrained.

Athenains (a-the'-ne-uns) - Uncertainty. Arriving. Inhabitants of Athens.

Athens (ath'-ens) - Uncertainty. The capital of Attica. Named after the goddess of wisdom, Athene. Without increase.

Athlai (ath'-lahee) - Afflicted of the Lord. Jehovah is strong. My due times. The removal by God. To compress. Constringent. Compress. My hour of time.

Atroth (a'-troth) - Crowns. Crown of their rapine.

Attai (at'-tahee) - Opportune. Opportunity. Seasonable. My due seasons. Removal by God. My hour. Timely.

Attalia (at-ta-li'-ah) - Jah's due season. Gentle father. Noble. Increasing. Sending. That increases or sends.

Attalus (at'-al'-uss) - Increased.

Augustus (aw-gus'-tus) - Venerable. Sacred. Kingly. Radiant. August. Eminent. Renowned. Consecrated. Majestic. Holy.

Ava (a'-vah) - Overturning. Perverted. Overthrow. Ruin. Iniquity.

Aven (a'-ven) - Nothingness. Perverseness. Vanity. Iniquity. Idolatry. Force. Riches. Sorrow. Wickedness.

Avim (a'-vim) - Inhabitants of desert places. Perverters. Villagers. Wicked or perverse men. Dwellers among the ruins. Peasants.

Avims (a'-vims) - Peasants. Dwellers among the ruins. Perverters. Villagers. Wicked or perverse men. Inhabitors of desert places.

Avites (a'-vites) - Perverters.

Avith (a'-vith) - Ruins of a city. Anything subverted. Wandering. Wickedness. Ruins. Hut. Village. Wicked.

Ayyah (ah'-ya) - Heap. Ruin.

Azal (a'-zal) - Noble. Root of a mountain. Deep rooted. He has reserved. Near. Separated.

Azaliah (az-a-li'-ah) - Whom Jehovah has reserved. Reserved of the Lord. Jehovah is noble. Jehovah has spared. He separated. God has reserved. Select. Jah has reserved. Near the Lord.

Azaniah (az-a-ni'-ah) - Whom Jehovah hears. Jehovah is hearer. Jehovah has given ear. Heard of the Lord. God heard. Help from Jah. Lord's weapons. Hearing the Lord. Jehovah is hearer.

Azarael (a-zar'-a-el) - Whom God helps. Helped of God. God is a helper. The strong one. God helped.

Azareel (a-zar-e-el) - Whom God helps. Helped of God. God is a helper. God assisted.

Azariah (az-a-ri'-ah) - Helped of the Lord. Whom Jehovah aids. Jehovah is keeper. Jehovah has helped. God assisted. God protects. He that hears the Lord.

Azaz (a'-zaz) - Strong. He was strong. Strong one. Jehovah is strong.

Azazel (a-za'-zel) - Goat of departure. The scape-goat.

Azaziah (az-a-zi'-ah) - Strengthened of the Lord. Whom Jehovah strengthened. Jehovah is strong. He was strong. Strength of the Lord.

Azbuk (az'-buk) - Strength emptied. Pardon. Exhaustion of strength. Stern depopulater. Devastation.

Azekah (a-ze'-kah) - Hedged or fenced round. Dug over. Strength of walls. Tilled. Broken-up. Tilled over. A place tilled.

Azel (a'-zel) - Separated. Distinguished noble. Noble. Reserved.

Azem (a'-zem) - Strength. Strenuous. Bone. Strong as a bone.

Azgad (az'-gad) - Worship. Supplication. Strong of fortune. A mighty troop. Strength of God. A troop has arrived. Strong army. Stern troop. Strong in worship or supplication. God is strong. A gang of robbers. A strong army.

Aziel (a'-ze-el) - Comforted of God. Whom God strengthens. God is might. God comforteth. Strengthened of God. God has nourished.

Aziza (a-zi'-zah) - Strong. Robust. Mightiness. Strength. Strengthfulness.

Azmaveth (az-ma'-veth) - Strong to death. Death is strong. Strong counsel. Death was near. Strong one of death. Strong as death. Strong death. A he-goat.

Azmon (az'-mon) - Strong. The mighty. Very secure. Bonelike strong. Fortress. Our strength. Bone of a bone. Bonelike.

Aznoth-tabor (az'-noth-ta'-bor) - Ears. Ears you will purge. The arms. Summits of Tabor. The ears of election. To listen. Hear. Perceive. The ears of purity or contrition. The ears of Tabor. Peaks.

Azor (a'-zor) - Helper. Strong help. One who helps. Helpful. A court.

Azotus (a-zo'-tus) - A stronghold. A strong place. Expulsion. Exile. Ravager. Greek name for Ashdod.

Azriel (az'-re-el) - Help of God. God is helper.

Azrikam(az'-ri-kam) - Help against an enemy. My help has risen. Reviving. Rising up. Help of an enemy. Help.

Azubah (a-zu'-bah) - Forsaken. Deserted. Desolation.

Azur (a'-zur) - Helper. Helpful. He that assists or is assisted. Strong help.

Azzah (az'-zah) - Strong. Fortified.

Azzan (az'-ran) - Very strong. Sharp. Strong one. A thorn. Their strength.

Azzur (az'-zur) - Helper. A strong one. Strong help. One who assists.

B

Baal (ba'-al) - Lord. Master. Possessor. Controller. Owner. Possessor of anything. Captain. Chief.

Baalah (ba'-al-ah) - Mistress. Lady. Possessing. My master. Her idol. She that is governed or subdued. A spouse. Rich.

Baalath (ba'-al-ath) - Mistress. Lady. Possessing. My master. A mistress of a ship. A rejoicing. Our proud lord. Rich. Her lord. Mistress-ship.

Baalath-beer (ba'-al-ath-be'-ur) - Having a well. Lady of the Well. Holy well. A mistress of a well. Subjected pit.

Baal-berith (ba'-al-be'-rith) - Lord of covenants. Master of a covenant. Idol of the covenant.

Baale (ba'-al-eh) - Plural of Baal. Lord. Master. Possessor. Controller. Possessor of anything. Owner. Masters of Judah.

Baal-gad (ba'-al-gad) - Lord of fortune. Master of a troop. Idol of fortune or felicity. The lord of Gad. Baal has a troop.

Baal-hamon (ba'-al-ha'-mon) - Lord of a multitude. Place of a multitude. Master of a multitude. Who rules a crowd. Baal having a great multitude.

Baal-hanan (ba'-al-ha'-nan) - Lord of compassion. The lord is gracious. Baal is gracious. Lord of grace. Baal gave graciously.

Baal-hazor (ba'-al'-ha'-zor) - Having a village; fence or castle. Lord of the court. Lord of trumpeting. Lord of Hazor. Baal has a trench.

Baal-hermon (ba'-al-her'-mon) - Place of the nose. A devoted master. Lord of Hermon. Having a fortress. Possessor of a thing cursed or possessor of destruction.

Baali (ba'-al-i) - My lord. My master. Owner. Lord over me. My idol.

Baalim (ba'-al-im) - Idols of Baal. Lords. Masters. False gods. Idols. Master.

Baalis (ba'-al-is) - Son of exultation. In rejoicing. The lord of joy or rules. Lord of the banner. In exultations. A proud lord. A rejoicing. With exultation. Son of joy.

Baal-meon (ba'-al-me'-on) - Place of habitation. The master of a dwelling. Master of the people. Idol or master of the house. The habitation of Baal. Lord of Meon.

Baal-peor (ba'-al-pe'-or) - Lord of the opening. A master of open space. An idol. The lord of opening, or gap.

Baal-perazim (ba'-al-per'-a-zim) - Place of breaches. Place of overwhelming. A master of breaches. God of divisions. Possessor of breaches.

Baal-shalisha (ba'-al-shal'-i-shah) - Having a third. The third in rank. The third idol. The god that presides over three. Place of triangle. Lord of Shalisha.

Baal-tamar (ba'-al-ta'mar) - Place of or having palm trees. The master of a palm tree. Lord of the palm. Place of the tree. Lord of palms.

Baal-zebub (ba'-al-ze'-bub) - Lord of the fly. Lord of flies. The master of a fly. The prince of evil spirits. God of the fly. God of wandering or flies.

Baal-zephon (ba'-al-ze'-fon) - Lord of the north. The master of the north. Master of winter. Hidden. Secret. The idol or possession of the north. Lord of the unknown. Lord of the secret. Lord of winter.

Baana (ba'-a-na) - Son of response. Son of grief. Son of affliction. Brutish. By hearing.

Baanah (ba'-a-na) - Son of response. Son of grief. Son of affliction. Brutish. In the answer. By afflicting. Answering.

Baara (ba'-ar-ah) - Kindling of the moon. New moon. The burning one. Brutish. A flame. Purging. Increase of the moon.

Baaseiah (ba-as-i'-ah) - Work of the Lord. Work of Jehovah. Jehovah is bold. Self master. In making. In pressing together. Work of God.

Baasha (ba'-ash-ah) - Wicked. Evil. Boldness. Offensive. He who lays waste. Confusion by mixing. To compress. To stink. He that seeks. With pleasure. He who seeks. Baal hears.

Babel (ba'-bel) - Confusion. To confound. Native etymology is Bab-il. The gate of God. Mixture. Mingling. Chaos.

Babylon (bab'-il-un) - Same as Babel. Confusion of tongues.

Babylonians (bab-il-o'-ne-ans) - Inhabitants of Babylon. Same as Babel. Confusion of tongues. Confusion.

Babylonish (bab-il-o'-nish) - Inhabitants of Babylon. Confusion. To confound. Mixture. Mingling. Choose. Wholly cast off.

Baca (ba'-cah) - Weeping. Valley of misery. A mulberry tree. Lamentation. Mulberry trees.

Bachrites (bak'-rites) - Descendants of Becher. First born. To come first. A youth.

Bachuth (bak'-uth) - Oak or other strong tree.

Bah (bah) - Young.

Baharumite (ba-hu'-rum-ite) - Inhabitant of Bahurim. Village or town of young men. Youth. Young men.

Bahurim (ba-hu'-rim) - Village or town of young men. Chosen ones. Young men. Youth. Choice. Warlike. Valiant. Loved.

Bajith (ba'-jith) - House. Place. Habitation. The house. Temple. Temple of Baal. Idol. A house. Temple of gods.

Bakbakkar (bak-bak'-kar) - Diligent searching. Searcher. Most diligent search. Wasting of the mountains.

Bakbuk (bak'-buk) - A bottle. Emptied of everything. A flagon or hollow cruse. Complete emptying of a bottle. Flask. The sound a bottle makes when emptied.

Bakbukiah (bak-buk-i'ah) - Emptying of wasting of Jehovah. Wasting by Jehovah. Effusion of Jehovah. The exhausting or emptying of God. Jehovah's pitcher.

Balaam (beh'-lam) - Destruction of the people. Swallowing up the people. The disturber of the people. A pilgrim. The devouring of the lord of the people. Foreigner. The ancient of the people. Absorption. Destruction. Age. Stranger. Lord of the people.

Balac (ba'-lak) - Same as Balak.
Wasting. Licking up. To make empty.
Who lays waste. Opening. Waster.
Baladan (bal'-adan) - Bel is his lord.
Having power. Not a lord. A son he
has given. Bel has power. One
without judgment. Having power and
riches.
Balah (ba'lah) - Decayed. Waxed old.
Failure. Withhold. Great fear. Terror.
Balak (ba'-lak) - Same as Balac.
Wasting. Licking up. To make empty.
Waster. Emptying. Destroying. Empty.
Who lays waste or destroys. Opening.
Vacant. Destroyer.
Bamah (ba'-mah) - High place. An
eminence or high place. Elevation. A
high place. A fortress. A sanctuary for
idols.
Bamoth (ba'-moth) - High places for
idols. Height. High places or heights.
Bamoth-baal (ba'-moth-ba'-al) - High
places of Baal.
Bani (ba'-ni) - Build. Built. Posterity.
My son. Built-up.
Baptist (bap'-tist) - To dip repeatedly.
To immerse. To submerge.
Bar (bar) - Son.
Barabbas (ba-rab'-bas) - Son of Abba.
Son of a father. Son of return. Son of
shame. Son of his father.
Barachel (bar'-ak-el) - Blessed of God.
Whom God blesses. God has blessed.
That bows before God.
Barachias (bar'-ak-i'-as) - Whom
Jehovah blesses. Blessing of the Lord.
Barak (ba'-rak) - Lightning. Thunder.
Thunderbolt. A gleam. Flashing.
Barhumite (bar'-hu-mite) -
Inhabitants of Bahurim. Village or
town of young men. Son of the

blackened. In the pitied. Young.
Youth. Choice. Warlike. Valiant.
Bariah (ba-ri'-ah) - Fugitive. Prince.
Turned to flight. A serpent. As fleeing.
Bar-jesus (bar-je'-sus)- Son of Jesus.
Son of Joshua.
Bar-jona (bar-jo'-nah) - Son of Jona.
Son of John or Johanan. Jehovah is
gracious. Son of a dove. Son of Jonas.
Barkos (bar'-cos) - Son after his
father. Partly-colored. The son cut off.
Painter. A son like his father.
Barnabas (bar'-na-bas) - Son of
exhortation. Son of prophecy. Son of
consolation. Son of the prophet. Son
of encouragement.
Barnea (bar'-ne-a) - Sanctuary.
Barsabas (bar'-sab-as) - The son of
return. Son of rest. Son of Saba. A son
that suspends the water. Man. Son of
the host. Son of the oath. Son of the
Sabbath.
Bartholomew (bar-thol'-o-mew) - Son
of Talmai. Abounding in furrows. A
son that suspends the water. A
furrow.
Bartimaeus (bar-ti-me'-us) - Son of
Timaeus. Honorable. Son of one
esteemed. Son of the honorable.
Unclean.
Baruch (ba'-rook) - Blessed. Who is
blessed. To be blessed.
Barzillai (bar-zil'-la-i)- Iron of the
Lord. Most firm and true. Strong.
Made of iron. Iron-hearted. Son of
contempt. Iron of God.
Bashan - (ba'-shan) Soft. Sandy soil. A
soft rich soil. The shame of them.
Fruitful. Soft earth. In the tooth. Level
ground.
Bashan-havoth-jair (ba'-shan-ha'-
voth-ja'-ur) - Fruitful. Village of Jair.

Bashemath (bash'-e-math) - Pleasant smelling. Fragrant. Perfumed. Spice. Fragrance. Confusion of death. In desolation. Delight. Sweet-smelling perfume.

Basmath (bas'-math) - Pleasant smelling. Fragrant. Perfumed spice. Spicy. Fragrance. Delight.

Bathrabbim (bath-rab'-bim) - Daughter of many. Daughter of mighty ones. Daughter of a city. Daughter of a multitude.

Bath-sheba (bath'-she-bah) - Daughter of an oath. Daughter of seven. Daughter of crying. Daughter of opulence. The daughter of satiety. The seventh daughter.

Bathshua (bath'-shu-ah) - Daughter of an oath. Daughter of seven. Daughter of crying. Daughter of opulence. Daughter of prosperity. Seventh daughter. Daughter of Shua.

Bavai (bav'-a-i) - With the desire of the Lord. By the mercy of the Lord. My goings. Wishes. Wisher. With the desire of God.

Baz (baz) - Peel.

Bazlith (baz'-lith) - A making naked. Asking. Stripping. To peel. With prayers. A peeling. Nakedness.

Bazluth (baz'-luth) - A making naked. Asking. Stripping. Nakedness. To bare. With supplications.

Bdellium (bdel'-li-um) - In turbidity.

Bealiah (be-a-li'-ah) - Possession of the Lord. Jehovah is Lord. Mastered of Jah. Jah is master. The god of an idol. In an assembly. The Lord exercised authority.

Bealoth (be'-a-loth) - City corporations. Rulers. Daughters of the city. Mistresses. Citizens. Cast under. Possessed. Possessors.

Bebai (beb'-a-i) - With the desires of the Lord. Fatherly. My cavities. Void. With the desire of God.

Becher (be'-ker) - First born. Young camel. Youth. The firstborn. First fruits. First begotten.

Bechorath (be-ko'-rath) - Offspring of the first born. First birth. First born. First fruits. Primogeniture.

Bedad (be'-dad) - Son of Adad. Separation. Solitary. Alone. In the bosom.

Bedan (be'-dan) - Fat. Robust. In judgment. Son of judgment. Servile. Strong. With judgment.

Bedeiah (be-de'-yah) - In the protection of the Lord. Servant of Jehovah. Isolated of Jah. According to judgment.

Bedejah (be-de'-yah) - By the power of God. Servant of Jehovah.

Beeliada (be-e-li'-ad-ah) - The Lord has known. For whom the Lord cares. The Lord knows. An open idol. The Lord knew. Known by Baal. Baal knows.

Beelzebub (be-el'-ze-bub) - Lord of the fly. Lord of the flies. The master of a fly. Lord of wandering or flies. Dung god. Same as Baalzebub.

Beer (be'-ur) - A well. A pit. Declaring.

Beera (be-e'-rah) - A well. Expounder. Declaring.

Beerah (be-e'-rah) - A well. Expounder. Wells.

Beer-elim (be'-ur-e'-lim) - Well of the mighty ones. Well of the heroes. Well of the gods. The well of Elim. The well of oaks.

Beeri (be-e'-ri) - Well of God. Expounder. Man of the well. My well. Fountain. Illustrious. Fountained. Man of the fountain.

Beer-lahai-roi (be'-ur-la'-hahe-ro'-e) - The well of the life of vision. The well of her that lives and of him that sees. Preserves me in life. The well of the living who sees me. The fountain of the vision of life. The well of him that liveth and seeth me. The well of the living God looking on me. Well of the living one.

Beeroth (be-e'-roth) - Wells. Explaining.

Beerothite (be-er'-o-thite) - Inhabitants of Beeroth. Wells. Explaining. One from Beerothite.

Beersheba (be-ur'-she-bah) - The well of the oath. The seventh well. Well of seven. Well of the Seven.

Beeshterah (be-esh'-te-rah) - House or temple of Astarte. In her flock. Increase. Flocks.

Behemoth (be'-he-moth) - The water ox. Beasts.

Bekah (be'-kah) - Part. Half. A cleft. Division. Half a shekel.

Bel (bel) - Lord. Confused. Confounded. Master. Chief. Lord or nothing.

Bela (be'-lah) - Devouring. Swallowing. Destruction. Consumption. Swallowing up. Destroying. Consuming.

Belah (be'-lah) - Same as Bela. Absorbing. Devouring. Swallowing. Destruction. Consumption. Swallowing up. Destroying. Consuming.

Belaites (be'-lah-ites) - Descendants of Bela. Absorbing. Devouring.

Swallowing. Destruction. Consumption. Swallowing up. Destroying. Consuming.

Belial (Be'-le-al) - Worthless. Without help. Wicked. Wickedness. Without profit. Vile. Perverse. A worthless, lawless fellow.

Belshazzar (bel-shaz'-ar) - Bel, protect the king. The lord's leader. Master of treasure. Lord of destruction straitened. The fire of Bel. Belus the splendor of brightness. Bel has formed a king. Bel has protected the king.

Belteshazzar (bel-te-shaz'-ar) - Bel protected his life. The lord's leader. Preserve his life. Lord of straitened's treasure. Prince of power. Who lays up treasures in secret. Belus hid his glory. Maintainer of the Lord. Protect his life,

Ben (ben) - Son. Edification of the family. To build. A son. A son, as a builder of the family name

Benaiah (ben-ay'-ah) - Whom Jehovah has built. Built up of the Lord. Jehovah is intelligent. God has built. Son of the Lord. God built. Son of my people.

Benabinadab (ben-a-bin'-ah-dab) - Son of Abinadab.

Ben-ammi (ben-am'-mi) - Son of my nation. Son of my people. Son of my own kindred. Son of my kindred. The son of the people. Kindred.

Ben-dekar (ben-de'kar) - Son of Dekar.

Bene-berak (be'-ne-be'-rak) - Son of lightning. Son of Barak. Sons of lightning.

Ben-geber (ben-ge'-ber) - Son of a strong man.

Bene-jaakan (be'-ne-ja'-a-kan) - Son of Jaakan. One who turns. Son of necessity. Sons of one who will oppress them. Sons of a family. Son whom the chain surrounds.

Ben-hadad (ben'-ha-dad) - Son of the most high or eminent. The beloved son. Son of the god Hadad. Son of the lot caster. Son of the shouter. Son of Hadad. The son of the honored. Sons of sorrow.

Ben-hail (ben-ha'-il) - Son of strength. Son of valor. Son of might. Sons of might. The son of activity. The son of the host. Warrior. Strong.

Ben-hanan (ben-ha'-nan) - Son of one who is gracious. Sons of grace. Son of kind one or very gracious. He hath given a son graciously.

Ben-hesed (ben-he'-sed) - Faithfulness.

Ben-Hur (ben-hur') - Son of Hur.

Benimi (be-ni'-mi) - Our sons.

Beninu (ben'-i-nu) - Our son or posterity. Our edification. Son of us. Our son.

Benjamin (ben'-ja-min) - Son of the right hand. Son of my days. Son of old age. The manifestation of divine power. Son of my right hand. Fortunate. Dexterous.

Benjamites (ben'-ja-mites) - Descendants of Benjamin. Same as Benjamin.

Beno (be'-no) - His son.

Ben-oni (ben-o'-ni) - Son of my sorrow. Son of my strength. The son of my last effort.

Ben-zoheth (ben-zo'-heth) - Son of most violent transportation. Corpulent. Strong. Son of releasing.

Family of sons. Son of separation. Son of Zoheth.

Beon (be'-on) - House of habitation. Indwelling. In affliction. By affliction. In answering. House of On.

Beor (be'-or) - Torch. Lamp. Burning. Shepherd. Foolish. Mad. A torch. Taking away.

Bera (be'-rah) - Son of evil. Gift. Excellence. In the evil. A well. Declaring. Distinguished for virtue and art.

Berachah (ber'-a-kah) - Blessing. Benediction. Prosperity. Liberal. Bending the knee.

Berachiah (ber'-a-ki'-ah) - Whom Jehovah has blessed. Blessed of the Lord. Jehovah is blessed. Bending the knee. Speaking well of the Lord. The blessing of the Lord.

Beraiah (ber-a-i'-ah) - Created of the Lord. Whom Jehovah has created. Jehovah has created. Jah is maker. The choosing of the Lord. The Lord has chosen or created.

Berea (be-re'-a) - To stabilize. Stable. Steadfast. Sure. The pierced. The beyond. Heavy. Weighty. Region beyond.

Berechiah (ber-e-ki'-ah) - Whom Jehovah has blessed. Blessed of the Lord. Jehovah is blessed. Bending the knee.

Bered (be'-red) - Place of hail. Hail. Seed.

Beri (be'-ri) - Expounder. Man of the well. Well of God. Fountain well. My son. My corn.

Beriah (be-ri'-ah) - In calamity. A calamity of his house. In evil. Unfortunate. Trouble. Evil. In fellowship. In envy. In calamity or trouble. Tragedy. Misfortune.

Beriites (be-ri'-ites) - Inhabitants of Beriah. In calamity. A calamity in his house. In evil. Unfortunate.

Berites (be'-rites) - Inhabitants of Beri. Expounder. Man of the well. Well of God. Wells.

Berith (be'-rith) - A covenant. Confederate. To eat together.

Bernice (bur-ni'-see) - Victorious. Carrying off victory. One that brings victory. Bringing victory.

Berodachbaladan (ber-o'-dak-bal'-ad-an) - Berodach has given a son. Baldan = Bel is his lord. The son of death. The mighty Lord. The son of Merodach. Bold. The causer of oppression is not a lord. An idol. The son of death.

Berothah (ber-o'-thah) - Wells of the Lord. The place of wells. A cypress tree. Wells. Wells of God. Cypress-like. Of a well.

Berothai (ber'o-thahee) - My wells. Wells of God. The diety worshipped in the cypress.

Berothite (be'-ro-thite) - Inhabitants of Beeroth. Wells.

Beryl (ber'-yl) - She will impoverish.

Besai (be'-sahee) - A sword. Victory. Treading down. Conqueror. Domineering. By the healing of God. A despising. Dirty.

Besodeiah (bes-o-di'-ah) - In the council of the Lord. Familiar with Jehovah. In Jah's secret. Intimate of Jehovah. Counsel of the Lord. By the covering of God. Counsel of Jehovah. Given to trust in Jehovah.

Besor (be'-sor) - Fresh. Cool. Cold. The bringer of good tidings. Glad news. Incarnation.

Betah (be'-tah) - Confidence. Security. Refuge. Safety.

Beten (be'-ten) - Belly. The womb. To be Hollow. Valley. Abdomen.

Beth (beth) - House.

Bethabara (beth'-ab'a-ra) - House of passage. A ferry-house. The house of confidence. Place of solitude. Place of passage.

Beth Acacia (beth-a-ka'-sha) - House of Acacia.

Beth-anath (beth'-a-nath) - House of response. A place of echo. House of affliction. The place of answering or replies.

Beth-anoth (beth'-o-noth) - Same as Bethanath. House of response. House of echo. House of affliction. Place of response or echo.

Bethany (beth'-a-ny) - House of affliction. House of response. House of dates or figs. Out of affliction comes fruit. The house of song. House of humility. Date-house. House of unripe figs.

Beth-arabah (beth'-ar'-ab-ah) - House of the desert. House of sweet smell. Place of Solitude.

Beth-aram (beth'-a-ram) - House of the lofty or of the exalted. The house of their hill. Mountain house. House of height. House of night. House of the height.

Beth-arbel (beth-ar'-bel) - House of the ambush of God. Those of courts. The place of the greatest brightness.

Beth-aven (beth-a'-ven) – House of vanity or idols. The house of iniquity.

Idolatry. House of trouble. House of naught or badness.

Beth-azmaveth (beth az'-ma-veth) - House strong with death. House of death's strength. The house of death's power. House of Azmaveth. House of a family.

Beth-baal-meon (beth-be'-al-me'-on) - House or place of habitation of Baal. House of the Lord of the dwelling. An idol of the dwelling place. Baal's dwelling place.

Beth-barah (beth-ba'-rah) - Place of the ford. A place of cutting through. House of eating or choice. House of the ford or crossing. The house of his son. The chosen house.

Beth-birei (beth-bir-e-i) - House of my creation. House of my creator. House of a creative one. The abode of the chosen one.

Beth-car (beth'-car) - House of battering rams. House of pasture. House of measure. The house of the lamb. The place of the house of pasture.

Beth-dagon (beth-da'-gon) - House of Dagon. House of a fish (an idol). House of the fish god. The house of corn. House of an idol. Place of the most distinguished fish.

Beth-diblathaim (beth-dib-lath-a'-im) - A house of two cakes of figs. The house of dried figs. House of the double fig-cake. House of dry figs. Place of troubles.

Beth-el (beth'-el) - House of God.

Beth-elite (beth'-el-ite) - Inhabitants of Bethel. House of God. One from Bethel.

Betheden (beth'-e-den) - House of delight.

Beth-eked (beth-e'-ked) - Of the shepherds. House of shearing.

Beth-emek (beth-e'-mek) - House or place of the valley. House of deepness.

Bether (be'-thur) - Dividing. Separation. A place cut off. Division. Craggy. Place of division. Cut up into sections. Split.

Bethesda (beth-ez'-dah) - House of mercy. Place of the flowing water. House of pity or mercy. House of kindness. House of grace.

Beth-ezel (beth-e'-zel) - House of firmness. The house close by. The next house. The neighbor's house. A neighbor's house. House of nearness. A fixed dwelling. Adjoining house.

Beth-gader (beth-ga'-der) - House of the wall. Walled place. The house for a mouse. House of the well. House of the hedge. House of walls.

Beth-gamul (bet-ga'-mul) - House of the recompensed. House of the weaned. Camel house. House of recompense. House of reward. Place of recompense.

Beth-haccerem (beth-hak'-se-rem) - House of the vineyard. House of the vine. The place of the vine.

Beth-hanan (beth-han'-an) House of the mountain.

Beth-haran (beth-ha'-ran) - House of the lofty. House of joyful shouter. House of grace. A house very high. House of the heights.

Beth-hogla (beth-hog'-lah) - House of the partridge. A place abounding in partridges. House of the languished feast. The place of the partridge.

Beth-hoglah (beth-hog'-lah) - House of the partridge. A place abounding in partridges. House of the languished feast. The place of the partridge.

Beth-horon (beth-ho'-ron) - House of place of the great cavern or holes. The house of wrath. Consumers house. Cavernous house. Hollow. The place of the great cave. Cave-house. The house of hollowness.

Beth-jesimoth (beth-jes'-im-oth) - House of the deserts. A place situated in barren waste. House of the wastes. House of desolation. Place of desolation.

Beth-jeshimoth (beth-jesh'-im-oth) - House of the deserts. A place situated in barren waste. House of the wastes. House of desolation. Place of desolation.

Beth-lebaoth (beth-leb'-a-oth) - House or place of lionesses. A place abounding in lions.

Beth-lehem (beth'-le-hem) - House of bread. House of flesh. Place of bread.

Bethlehemite (beth'-le-hem-ite) - Inhabitants of Bethlehem. House of bread or flesh. Place of bread.

Beth-lehem-judah (beth'-le-hem-ju'-dah) - House of bread and praise. House of flesh.

Beth-maachah (beth-ma'-a-kah) - House of oppression. House of country. House of attrition.

Beth-marcaboth (beth-mar'-cab-oth) - House of chariots. House of bitterness wiped out. The place of chariots.

Beth-meon (beth-me'-on) - House of habitation. House of Baal. House of the dwelling place. Dwelling place.

Beth-millo (beth-mil'-lo) - Place of the mound.

Beth-nimrah (beth-nim'-rah) - House of pure water. House of the leopardess. House of leopards. House of rebellion. A place abounding in waters.

Beth-palet (beth-pa'-let) - House or place of escape. Place of refuge or asylum. House of escape or flight. House of expulsion.

Beth-pazzez (beth-paz'-zez) - House of dispersion. House of dividing asunder. House of destruction.

Beth-peor (beth-pe'-or) - House or temple of the hiatus. A house wide open. A place for idol worship. House of worship of idols. House of gaping. House of the openings.

Beth-phage (beth'-fa-je) - House of unripe figs. Green fig house. House of my month. Place of figs.

Beth-phelet (beth'-fe-let) - House or place of escape. A place of refuge or asylum. Same as Bethpalet.

Beth-rapha (beth-'ra-fah) - House of Rapha. House of a giant. Place of fear. House of the healer. House of health. House of healing. House of the giant.

Beth-rehob (beth'-re-hob) - House of breadth. House of region or wilderness. House of the broad way. House of the street. Place of room. Place of a street.

Bethsaida (beth-sa'-dah) - House of fish. House of provision. House of hunting. House of fruits. Place of fishing. Fishing house. Place of fruit.

Beth-shan (beth'-shan) - House of quiet. House of rest. House of the sharpener. House of the sun. House of peace or ease. Place of security.

Beth-shean (beth-she'-an) - Same as Bethshan. House of quiet. House of rest. House of peace or ease. Place of security. House of the sun. House of the sharpener.

Beth-shemesh (beth'-she-mesh) - House of the sun. The house of the light of the sun.

Beth-shemite (beth'-shem-ite) - Inhabitants of Bethshemech. House of the sun. The house of the light of the sun.

Beth-shittah (beth-shit'-tah) - House of acacia. Abounding in acacias. House of the scourge. Place of acacia.

Beth-tappuah (beth-tap'-pu-ah) - House of apples. Abounding in apples. House of the breather. Place of the apple or citron tree. House of apricots.

Bethuel (beth-u'-el) - Virgin of God. Separated of God. A relation to God. Abode of God. Dweller in God. Filiation of God. House of God. A place consecrated to God.

Bethul (beth-ul) - Virgin. Separated. Abode of God.

Beth-zur (beth'-zur) - House of the rock. Place of the rock. House of rocks.

Betonim (bet'-o-nim) - Cavities. Pistachio nuts. Nuts. Bellies. Hollows. To purge.

Beulah (be-u'-lah) - Married. A married woman. Inhabited.

Bezai (be'-zahee) - In the labor of the Lord. Birth. Root. Shining. High. Eggs. By the speed of God. Conqueror. My fine linen. Garments. Victor.

Bezaleel (be-zal'-e-el) - In the shadow of God. Under God's shadow. Protection of God. Under his protection. Under the shade of God.

Bezek (be'-zek) - Flash of lightning. A spark. Lightning or brightness. Lightning in chains.

Bezer (be'-zer) - Gold ore. Defense. Strong. Gold one. Munition. Silver. Ore. Gold. Vine branches. Protection. Stronghold. An inaccessible spot. Fortress.

Bichri (bik'-ri) - Juvenile. First born. Youthful. First fruits.

Bidkar (bid'-kar) - Son of thrusting through. A piercer. Servant of Kar. In sharp pain. In stabbing. Stabbing. In compunction. Most diligent search. Stab or assassin.

Bigtha (big'-thah) - Given by fortune. In the winepress. Great. Gift of God.

Bigthan (big'-than) - Gift of fortune. Giving meat. A giver of pastry. In their winepress. In the press. Great. Garden. Gift of God.

Bigthana (big'-than-ah) - Given of fortune. In their winepress. Great. Gardener. Gift of God.

Bigvai (big'-vahee) - Happy. Of the people. In my bodies. With exultation. Husbandman. Fortunate.

Bildad (bil'-dad) - Son of contention. Contender. Lord Adad. Old friendship with love. Confusing (by mingling) love. A prince. Most separated.

Bileam (bil'-e-am) - Same as Balaam. Destruction of the people. Swallowing up the people. Conquest. The ancient of the people. The devourer. Absorption. Foreigner. Place of conquest.

Bilgah (bil'-gah) - Consolation. Reviving. Cheerful. Bursting forth. Ancient countenance. Recreation. Desistance. Cheerfulness. Brightness.

Bilgai (bil'-gahee) - Consolation of the Lord. Bursting forth. My comforts. First born. The first born. Cheerfulness. The delight of God. Desistent.

Bilhah (bil'-hah) - Timidity. In weakness. In languishing. Decrepitude. In the tongue. Bashfulness. Unconcerned. Terror. Alarm. Timid.

Bilhan (bil'-han) - Modest. Tender. Bashful. Their decrepitude. In the tongue. Timid. Foolish. Great trouble.

Bilshan (bil'-shan) - Son of tongue. Son of eloquence. Searcher. Inquirer. In slander. In the tongue. Their lord's earnest desire. Eloquent.

Bimhal (bim'-hal) - Son of circumcision. In circumcision. In weakness (by mixture). Circumcised. In peace.

Binea (bin'-e-ah) - Gushing forth. Wanderer. Son of the Lord. A fountain.

Binnui (bin'-nu-ee) - Building up. A building of family-ship. Built up. Building. A building up.

Birsha (bur'-shah) - Son of wickedness. In wickedness. Thick. Strong. An evil. A son who beholds. A man fat and taken with wickedness,

Birzavith (bur'-za-vith) - Selections of olives. Choice olives. Olive well. Wounds. To pierce with holes. Well of the olive tree. To separate.

Bishlam (bish'-lam) - In peace. Peaceful. Son of peace. Born in a time of tranquility. Peace.

Bithiah (bith-i'-ah) - Daughter (worshipper) of Jehovah. Daughter of Jah. Daughter of the Lord. Worshiper.

Bithron (bith'-ron) - Great division. A region divided by mountains and valleys. The broken or divided place. A broken place. Divisions. A craggy spot. Great separation. Valley.

Bithynia (bith-in'-e-ah) - A violent pushing. Violent precipitation. Belly.

Bizjothjah (biz-joth-jah) - Contempt of Jehovah. Despite. Contempt. Contempt of the Lord.

Biztha (biz'-thah) - Eunuch. Booty. Bound. Great. Despite.

Blastus (blas'-tus) - A shot. A sprout. A sucker. A bud. That buds or brings forth. To germinate. To spring.

Boanerges (bo-an-er'-jees) - Sons of thunder. Sons of rage. Commotion. Son of thunder.

Boaz (bo'-az) - In him is strength. Come in strength. Strength. Fleetness. The first born. Alacrity. Strength.

Bocheru (bok'-er-u) - His first born. Youth. First born. He is first born.

Bochim (bo'-kim) - Weepers. The place of weeping or mulberry trees. Of those weeping.

Bohan (bo'-han) - Thumb. Stumpy. In them. The thumb.

Booz (bo-oz) - In him is strength. Strength in him.

Boscath (bos'-cath) - Elevated ground. In poverty. To swell up. Swelling. Bombast. Loftiness.

Bosor (bo'-sor) - Burning. Torch. Lamp. Taking away. Shining.

Bozez (bo'-zez) - Shining. Glistening. Surpassing white. Blooming. Mud. Bog. Height. Glittering. White.

Bozkath (boz'-kath) - Elevated ground. A swelling (as of dough). Swelling up. To blister. Height. Swelling. A swell of ground.

Bozrah (boz'-rah) - Fortification. A vintage. A sheepfold. Besieged. In tribulation or distress. Wasteful. Shepherd. Stronghold.

Bukki (buk'-ki) - Emptying of the Lord. Wasting from Jehovah. Mouth of Jehovah. Devastation sent by Jehovah. Void. Proved of Jehovah. Exhaustion.

Bukkiah (buk-ki'-ah) - Emptying of the Lord. Wasting from Jehovah. Mouth of Jehovah. Devastation sent by Jehovah. Wasting. The dissipation of the Lord. Wasted. Proved of Jehovah.

Bul (bul) - Rain. Withering. Increase. Produce. Old age. Perishing. Changing. Change produced by rain.

Bunah (boo'-nah) - Prudence. Understanding. Building. Discretion.

Bunni (bun'-ni) - My understanding. I am built. Built. Building me. Building me up.

Buz (buz) - Contempt. To despise. Despised. Plundered.

Buzi (boo'-zi) - Contemned of Jehovah. My contempt. To disrespect.

Buzite (boo'-zite) - Descendants of Buz. Contempt. To despise. Despised. Plundered.

C

Cabbon (cab'-bon) - Cake. As the prudent. As the builder. As though understanding. Measure of grain. To heap up cake.

Cabul (ca'-bul) - Fetter. Bound. Displeasing. Dirty. Worthless. Sterile. Unproductive. Received as a pledge limit. Border.

Caesar (se'-zur) - One cut out. Severed. Hairy. Cutting.

Caesar Augustus (se'-zur-aw-gus'-tus) - Caesar - One cut out. Augustus - Venerable. Sacred. Kingly.

Caesarea (ses-a-re'-ah) - Severed. Pertaining to Caesar. Hairy. Cutting.

Caesarea Philippi (ses-a-re'-ah-fil-ip'-pi) - Caesarea - Severed. Philippi – lover of horses. Caesar's city of Philippi.

Caiaphas (cah'-ya-fus) - A searcher. He that seeks with diligence. As comely. One that vomiteth. Depression. Humiliation. Seeking diligently.

Cain (cain) - Possession. Acquisition. Fabrication. A purchase. Maker. Fixity. A lance.

Cainan (ca'-nun) - Possession. Acquisition. A purchase. Being purchased. Their smith. A possessor. Fixed. Ample possession. Purchaser.

Calah (ca'-lah) - Old age. Completion. Seasonable. Full age. Favorable. Opportunity. Holy gate. Maturity.

Calamus (cal'-a-mus) - Sweet stalk. Reed.

Calcol (cal'-col) - Sustenance. Sustaining. Who nourishes.

Comprehended. Nourishing. Nourishment. Consuming all things.

Caleb (ca'-leb) - Bold. Impetuous. A dog. Wholehearted. Hearty. A crow. A basket. Forcible. Firmly bound. Determination.

Caleb-ephratah (ca'-leb-ef'-ra-tah) - Caleb - Bold. Impetuous. A dog. Hearty. Firmly bound. Ephratah - Fruitful. Fruitfulness.

Calneh (cal'-neh) - Fortified dwellings. The wall is complete. Our consummation. Fortress. Defense of concealment.

Calno (cal'-no) - Fortified dwellings. His perfection. Our consummation. Altogether himself. Futility. Enclosure of a dwelling.

Calvary (cal'-va-ry) - Skull. Place of the skull. A bare skull.

Camon (ca'-mon) - Abounding in stalks. Standing corn. A riser up. Standing place. Fastness. Firm subsistence. An elevation.

Cana (ca'-nah) - Place of reeds. Zealous. Acquired. Zeal. Jealousy. Possession.

Canaan (ca'-na-an) - Merchants. Trader. Servant. Low region. Low. Lowland. Humbled. A trafficker. One that humbles or subdues. Humiliated. Flat. The greatest abasement. Subjection. To be low.

Canaanites (ca'-na-an-ites) - Inhabitants of Canaan. Same as Canaan. Of the people of zealots. Merchants. Trader. Servant. Low. Low region. Lowland. A trafficker. Zealous. Humbled. One that humbles or subdues. Humiliated. Flat. The greatest abasement. Subjection. To be low.

Canaanitish (ca'-na-an-i-tish) - Referring to Canaan. Merchants. Trader. Servant. Low region. Low. Lowland. Humbled. A trafficker. One that humbles or subdues. Humiliation. Flat. The greatest abasement. Subjection. To be low.

Candace (can'-da-see) - Queen of ruler of children. Who possesses contrition. Prince or ruler of servants.

Canneh (can'-neh) - Surname: Flattering title. Distinguished. Inclosure of a habitation.

Capernaum (ca-pur'-na-um) - City of consolation. Village of comfort. The field of repentance. City of comfort. Village of Nahum.

Caphthorim (caf'-tho-rim) - Pomegranate. Crowns. Place of rock towers. Hebrew plural of Caphtor.

Caphtor (caf'-tor) - Crown. Knop. Pomegranate. A button. As if to interpret. He bowed down to spy out. A sphere. A wreath. Seeking and inquiring. A wreath or crown. Hollow goblet.

Caphtorim (caf'-to-rim) - Pomegranate. Crowns. Place of rock towers. To encircle.

Cappadocia (cap-pa-do'-she-ah) - Province of good horses. Branded unreal. Cutting off. Distermination.

Carbuncle (car'-bun-cle) - Lighting stone. She shot forth. I will kindle.

Carcas (car'-cas) - Severe. An eagle. As the bound one. The covering of a lamb. Vulture.

Carchemish (car'-ke-mish) - Fortress of refuge. A fed lamb. To cut off. A lamb. As taken away. Fortress of Chemosh. The defense of concealment. Withdrawn.

Careah (ca-re'-ah) - Bald. Ice. Bald head. Bare.

Carmel (car'-mel) - Circumcised lamb. Harvest. Full of ears of corn. Fruitful field. Park. Fertile. A planted field. Garden. Orchard. Vineyard. A green field. Fruitful.

Carmelite (car'-mel-ite) - A native or inhabitant of Carmel. Same as Carmel.

Carmelitess (car'-mel-i-tess) - A woman of Carmel. Same as Carmel. Fruitful field. Park.

Carmi (car'-mi) - My vineyard. Lamb of the waters. Vinedresser. Noble. Fruitful. Sprung from his father. Gardener.

Carmites (car'-mites) - Descendants of Carmi. Vinedresser. My vineyard. Noble. Fruitful. Sprung from his father. Gardener. Lamb of the waters.

Carpus (car'-pus) - Fruit. The wrist. Fruitful.

Carshena (car-she'-nah) - Illustrious. Spoiler. Slender. A lamb. Sleeping. Plowman. Shining. A slender man. Distinguished.

Casiphia (cas-if'-e-ah) - Silver of the Lord. Desirable. Longing of Jah. Covetousness. Money. White. Shining. In silver.

Casluhim (cas'-loo-him) - Their boundary protected. As forgiven ones. Hopes of life. A shining people. People of Kasluh. Pardoned.

Castor (cas'-tor) - A girl. Damsel. Maiden. Separation. Beaver. Castor and Pollux – sons of Jupiter of heathen mythology.

Cedron (se'-drun) - Very black. Full of darkness. Intensely. Turbid. Great obscurity. A wall. Black. Sad. Very dark. Gloomy.

Cenchrea (sen'-kre-ah) - Millet. Small pulse. Granular.

Cephas (se'-fas) - A stone. A rock or stone.

Cesar (ce'-zar) - A name applied to those who are cut out of the womb.

Chalcedony (chal-ced'-o-ny) - Copper like. Flower like.

Chalcol (kal'-kol) - Sustenance. Sustaining. Who nourishes. Maintaining. Supplying. Sustained. I am made superior. Son of Mahol.

Chaldaeans (kal-de'-uns) - As clod breakers.

Chaldea (kal-de'-ah) - The land of the Chaldeans. Astrologer. Wanderers. As demons increasing. Occultism.

Chaldeans (kal-de'uns) - Astrologer. Wanderers. A magician or professional astrologer. As it were demons.

Chaldees (kal'-dees) - Astrologer. Wanderers.

Chanaan (Ka'-na-an) - Merchants. Servant. Low region. Humiliated.

Chapmen (chap'-men) - The search-men.

Charashim (car'-a-shim) - Craftsmen. A carpenter or mechanic. Of the magicians.

Charchemish (car'-ke-mish) - Fortress of refuge. The defense of concealment. Same as Carchemish.

Charran (car'-ran) - Same as Haran. Very dry. Grievous. A singing or a calling out. Very scorched or dry.

Chebar (ke'-bar) - Abundant. Vehement. Great. A river. Force or strength. Length. A great while. Joining. Strength. Power.

Chedorlaomer (ke'-dor-la'-o-mer) - Handful of sheaves. To bind sheaves.

Sheaf band. Servants of the god Lagamar. To make merchandise. Glory of Laomer. He that dwells in a sheaf. Roundness of a sheaf. A king. Handful.

Chelal (ke'-lah) - Completion. Completeness. Perfection. Completed. As night. Perfect. Ornament.

Chelluh (kel'-loo) - Consumed of the Lord. Union. Determine ye Him. Consume ye Him. All. Robust. Perfect. The expectation. Of hope. OF GOD. All completed.

Chelub (ke'-lub) - Binding together (like a basket). Wicker basket. Bird's cage. Boldness. A coop. A basket. Binding. Trap cage.

Chelubai (ke-loo-bahee) - Binding together of the Lord. My baskets. He altogether against me. Forcible. Bold. The bold. The valiant.

Chemarims (kem'-a-rims) - Persons dressed in black attire. To be warm. Affectionate. As changed ones. Black ones. Idolatrous priests. Blackness. Sadness. Mourning. An ascetic.

Chemosh (ke'-moth) - The swift. Subduer. Cut off. As if departing or fleeing. Handling. Stroking. Taking away. To subdue with quickness. Vanquisher.

Chenaanah (ke-na'-a-nah) - Merchant. One who bends the knee. Subduer. Flat. As if afflicted. Broken in pieces. Low. Humiliated. Son of Bilhan. Humiliation.

Chenani (ken'-a-ni) - Perfecter. Firm. Creator. As my perpetuator. My pillar. Jehovah has established. He has established. Planted.

Chenaniah (ken-a-ni'ah) - Established of the Lord. Whom Jehovah supports. Jehovah is firm. Preparation. As perpetuated of Jah. God has established or planted.

Chepharhaammonai (ke'-far-ha-am'-mo-nahee) - Village of the Ammonites. A village protected by walls.

Chephirah (ke-fi'-rah) - Village. A young lioness. Covert. A little lioness. The village. Town. A hamlet.

Cheran (ke'-eran) - Lamb. Union. Lute. As shouting for joy. Anger. Lyre. A great ram.

Cherethims (ker'-e-thims) - Executioners. Exiles. Those cut off. Cutting. Piercing. Slaying. Life guardsmen. Who tears or exterminates.

Cherethites (ker'-e-thites) - Same as Cherethims. Executioners. Exiles. He that is cut off. Cutting. Piercing. Slaying. Life guardsmen. Who cuts. Executioner.

Cherith (ke'-rith) - Separation. Gorge. Cut off. Cutting. Piercing. Slaying. Torrent of the gorge.

Cherub (ke'-rub) - Celestial. As if contending. Held fast. Like to majesty. A keeper. A warden. A guard.

Cherubim (cher'-u-bim) - Plural of cherub. Celestial. As if contending. Held fast. Like to majesty. A keeper. A warden. A guard.

Chesalon (kes'-a-lon) - Firm confidence. Hope. Foolish confidence. As extolled. Strength. Fortress. Slope. Sure confident. Fertile.

Chesed (ke'-sed) - Increase. Conqueror. A devil. As borrower. As a devil. Gain.

Chesil (ke'-sil) - Orion. Constellations. A fool. Foolishness. Stupid. Silly. Carnal. Ungodly. Hope. Fertile.

Chesulloth (ke-sul'-loth) - Confidences. Fearfulness. Fatness. The loins. Loins. Compassion. Fattened.

Chezib (ke'-zib) - Lying. Deceptive. False. Deceitful.

Chidon (ki'-don) - Great destruction. Javelin. Dart. Great misfortune.

Chileab (kil'-e-ab) - Accomplished of the father. Perfection of the father. Like to a father. Totality. Exaltation. Restraint of father. A father's hope.

Chilion (kil'-e-on) - Pining. Consuming. Wasting away. Complete. Consumption. Finished. Perfect. Anxious expectation.

Chilmad (kil'-mad) - As learned. As a disciple. Teaching or learning. Closed. Hedge. Fence. Inclosure. A defense.

Chimham (kim'-ham) - Great desire. Longing. Pining. As confusion. As they. Like to them. Of a pallid face.

Chinhan (kim'-han) - Their longing.

Chinnereth (kin'-ne-reth) - Harp. A lyre. Harp shaped. Harps.

Chinneroth (kin'-ne-roth) - Plural of Chinnereth. Harps. Harp shaped. Lyres.

Chios (ki'-os) -Snowy. An unlucky throw of the dice. Open. Opening. A serpent.

Chisleu (kis'-lew) - Like a quail. His confidence. Hope. Ninth month of the Hebrew calendar. Hunter. Rashness. Confidence.

Chislon (kis'-lon) - Firm confidence. Hope. Trust. Strong. Confidence. Strength. Sure.

Chisloth-tabor (kis'-ki-oth-ta'-bor) - Confidence of Tabor i.e., it's fortifications. Foolish confidences you will purge. Fears. Purity. Loins. Loins of Tabor. The defenses of Tabor. Loins or flanks of Tabor.

Chittim (kit'-tim) - Subduers. Smiters. Bruisers. Breakers in pieces. Gold. Those that bruise. An islander. Bruises. To afflict.

Chiun (ki'-un) - Statue. Image. Established. Pillar as set up. An idol.

Chloe (clo'-e) - Green herb. Covered with green vegetation. Tender sprout. Verdant.

Chorashan (cor-a'-shan) - Smoking furnace. Furnace of smoke. To be hot. Anger.

Chorazin (co-ra'-zin) - A furnace of smoke. The secret. Here is a mystery. Secret.   Place of the proclaiming. Woody places.

Chozeba (ko-ze'-bah) - Lying. Deceiver. Falsehood. Men liers in wait. Deceitful. Untruthful. Fallacious.

Christ (krist) - Anointed. Consecrated.

Christians (kris'-tyans) - Christ like. A follower of Christ. Anointed ones.

Chrysolyte (chry'-so-lyte) - Gold stone.

Chrysoprasus (chry'-so-pra'-sus) - Golden green. Golden achievement.

Chub (cub) - Christ's thorn. Clustered. A thorn. A sort of thorn.

Chun (kun) - Firm. To establish. Making ready. Founding. Stability. To stand upright

Chushan-rishathaim - Two-fold malicious. Ethiopian. The wickedness of Ethiopia. Blackness of iniquities. Great fear. Commotions. Troubles.

Chuza (cu'-zah) - Modest. A mound. A measure. The seer or prophet. Little jug. Possession.

Cilicia (sil-ish'-yah) - Hair cloth. The land of Celix. Which rolls or overturns. A stone.

Cinneroth (sin'-ne-roth) - Same as Chinneroth. Harp. A lyre. A harp. Harps. Lyres.

Cis (sis) - Same as Kish. Snaring. Bird catching. Greek form of Kish. Hunting of God. A bow.

Clauda (claw'-dah) - Lame. Surging. A lamentable voice. Breaking of water.

Claudia (claw'-de-ah) - Same as Clauda. Lame. Mild. Good. Merciful.

Claudius (claw'-de-us) - Lame. Whining. Mild. Good. Merciful. Celebrated.

Claudius Lysias (claw'-de-us-lis'-e-as) - Claudius - Lame. Lysias – He who has the power to set free. Releaser. Lame dissolution. Mild. Good. Merciful. Celebrated.

Clement (clem'-ent) - Kind. Merciful. Mild. Good. Gentle.

Cleopas (cle'-o-pas) - The whole glory. Renowned father. Famed of all. Glory of his father.

Cleophas (cle'-o-fas) - My exchanges. The whole glory. Glory of his father.

Cnidus (ni'-dus) - Nettle. Age. He bound.

Col-hozeh (col-ho'-zeh) - Wholly a seer. He sees all things. All-seeing. Every prophet.

Colosse (co-los'-see) - Monstrosities. Punishment. Correction. Violent taking away. Evasion.

Colossians (co-los'-yuns) - Monstrosities. Punishment. Correction. Violent taking away. Evasion.

Conaniah (co-na-ni'-ah) - Jehovah hath established. Stability of the Lord. Strength of the Lord. Jah hath sustained. Jehovah establishes. The Lord has set up.

Coniah (co-ni'-ah) - Established of the Lord. When Jehovah has set up. Strength of the Lord. Jah hath sustained. The Lord has established.

Cononiah (co-no-ni'-ah) - Jehovah has established. Stability of the Lord. The Lord has appointed. Treasurer of tithes.

Coos (co'-os) - Summit. A public prison. Top. Sheep. A form of Cos.

Coral (co'-ral) - Heights.

Corban (cor'-ban) - A gift offering. An offering to God in fulfillment of a vow.

Core (co'-re) - Baldness. Bald. Bare. Thin. Frozen. Greek form of Korah.

Corinth (cor'-inth) - Satiated. Which is satisfied. Ornament. Beauty. Horn. Top of a mountain.

Corinthians (co-rin'-the-uns) - Inhabitants of Corinth. Satiated. Which is satisfied. Beauty. Ornament. Horn. Top of a mountain.

Corinthus (co-rin'-thus) - Another spelling for Corinth. Satiated. Which is satisfied. Beauty. Ornament. Horn. Top of a mountain.

Cornelius (cor-ne-le-us) - The beam of the sun. Pitiless full. Of a horn. Hard as horn.

Cosam (co'-sam) - Most abundant. Divining. Abundant hunting.

Coz (coz) - Thorn. Nimble. The thorn of the nimble. A troublesome enemy. To vex. To loathe

Cozbi (coz-bi) - Lying. Deceiver. Deception. Deceitful. A liar. Sliding away. False.

Crescens (cres'-sens) - Growing. Increase. Fleshly Shadow. Increasing.

Crete (creet) - Fleshly. Carnal. Cut off. Given to the flesh.

Cretes or Cretians (cre'-shuns) - Fleshly. Carnal. Cut off. Given to the flesh. Inhabitants of Crete.

Crispus (cris'-pus) - Curled. Curly hair. Crisp.

Cumi (coo'-mi) - Arise.

Cush (cush) - A black countenance. Full of darkness. Black. Ethiopia. Fair. Fairness. Fright.

Cushan (cu'-shan) - A black countenance. Full of darkness. Black. Ethiopia. Fair. Fairness. Fright. Belonging to Cush. Great fear. Same as Cush.

Cushi (cu'-shi) - A black countenance. Full of darkness. Black. Ethiopia. Fair. Fairness. The fear of God.

Cuth (cuth) - Crushing. Fair. Fairness. Burning. Fear.

Cuthah (cu'-than) - Crushing. Place of crushing. Fair. Fairness. Burning. Fear. Treasure house. Same as Cuth.

Cyprus (si'-prys) - Love. A blossom. Sun. A Persian king. Fair. Fairness.

Cyrene (si-re'-ne) - Supremacy of the bridle. A wall. Coldness. The floor.

Cyrenian (si-re'ne-an) - Supremacy of the bridle. A wall. Coldness. The floor. A native of Cyrene. Belonging to Cyrene.

Cyrenius (si-re'-ne-us) One who governs. Who governs. Who reigns. Spearman. Warrior.

Cyrus (si'-rus) - The sun. Lovely. A blossom. A succeeder. Inheritor. An heir. Possess thou the furnace. As miserable. As heir. Persian king. Sun. Light. Spiritual sense.

D

Dabareh (dab'-a-reh) - A sheep walk. Manner of speaking. Pasture. The word. The thing. A bee. Obedient. The saying or word.

Dabbasheth (dab'-ba-sheth) - Flowing with honey. Camel hump. A hump. A sticky mass.

Daberath (dab'-e-rath) - A sheep walk. Manner of speaking. Pasture. A subject. The word. The thing. A bee. Obedient. The saying or word. Same as Dabareh. Led. Submissive.

Dabrasheth (dab'-re-sheth) - Hump of a camel. He whispered shame.

Dagon (da'-gon) - Honored fish. A national idol and god of the Philistines It had the head, arms and body of a man, but the body terminated in a fish. Corn. A fish. An idol. An excellent fish. Fish-god.

Dalaiah (dal-a-i'ah) - Whom Jehovah has delivered. Jehovah is deliverer. Drawn of Jah. The poor of the Lord: Jehovah delivers.

Dalmanutha (dal-ma-nu'-thah) - Slow firebrand. Hebrew - poor portion. A bucket. A branch. Widowhood. Exhausting. Leanness. Bereavement.

Dalmatia (dal-ma'-she-ah) - Deceitful. Deceitful lamps. Vain brightness. Vain splendor.

Dalphon (dal'-fon) - Proud. Strenuous. Dropping. The house of caves. Dripping.   Weeping. Earnest. Swift.

Damaris (dam'-a-ris) - Calf. A heifer. A yoke-bearing wife. A little woman. Little wife. Joined. Gentle.

Damascenes (dam-as-senes)- Inhabitants of Damascus. Activity. Moist with blood. Silent is the sackcloth weaver. Very red.

Damascus (da-mas'-cus) - Activity. Moist with blood. Sackcloth weaver is going about or dwelling. A sack full of blood. The similitude of burning. He was red. Alertness. Very red. Bloody sack. The oldest standing city in the world.

Dan (dan) - Judging. Judge. He that judges. Judgment. Mighty one. Domination. He judged. Human judgment.

Daniel (dan'-yel) - Judge of God. One who delivers judgment in the name of God. My judge is God. God is my judge. He that judges. Judgment of God. God my judge. God judged. Divine judgment.

Danites (dan'-ites) - Descendants of Dan. Judging. Judge. He that judges. Members of the tribe of Dan. Judgment. Mighty One. Domination. He judged. Human judgment.

Dan-jaan (dan-ja'-an) Judge of the woodland. The judge will afflict. The judge is greedy. Judge of purpose. Judgment. He heard.

Dannah (dan'-nah) - You have judged. Judgment. Low land. Murmurings. Stronghold: Sinking of the earth. Low ground.

Dara (da'-rah) - Bearer. The arm. Generation. House of the shepherd or companion. Holder. Pearl of wisdom. He knew. Race of shepherds.

Darda (dar'-dah) - Pearl of wisdom. He compassed knowledge. Dwelling of knowledge. Home of knowledge.

Pearl of knowledge. Bearer. Most wise.

Darius (da-ri'-us) - A restrainer. Governor. A possessor by succession. He that informs himself. A king. Investigation. The dwelling will be full of heaviness. He who enforces and inquires. Coercer. Conservator.

Darkon (dar'-kon) - Thrusting through. Bearer. Scattering. The dwelling of lamentation. Of generation. Of possession. Carrier. Great haste.

Dathan (da'-than) - Belonging to a fountain. Belonging to law or to a fount. Judgment. Law. Their law. Their decree. Law or rites. Fount. Strong. A goal. Pillar. Rites. Laws. Of a fountain.

David (da'-vid) - Beloved. Well-beloved. Loving. Dear.

Debar (de'-bar) - Sanctuary.

Debir (de'-bur) - An oracle. Speaker. A recess i.e., the inner part of the temple where the ark of the covenant was placed and where responses were given. An orator. A word. Sanctuary. Inner sanctuary.

Deborah (deb'-o-rah) - Eloquent. An orator. Bee. Her speaking. Word. Thing. A bee. Wasp. A bee in the sense of orderly motion.

Decapolis (de-cap'-o-lis) - Ten cities. Containing ten cities. Region of ten cities.

Dedan (de'-dan) - Leading forward. Low. Their friendship. In judgment. Their breasts. Friendship. A judge. Two persons. Progress. Increase. Low country.

Dedanim (ded'-a-nim) - Same as Dedan. Leading forward. Low. Their

friendship. In judgment. The descendants of Dedan. Meaning doubtful. Hebrew plural of Dedan. Their breasts. Friendships. A judge. Two persons. Progress. Increase. Low country.

Dehavites (de-ha'-vites) - Villagers. The sickly.

Dekar (de'-kar) - Thrusting through. Lance bearer. Piercing. Perforation. The piercer. Force. Stab. A branch. A force. A thrusting through.

Delaiah (del-a-i'-ah) - Drawn up of the Lord. Whom Jehovah has freed. Jehovah is deliverer. Delicate. Dainty one. The poor of the Lord. Freed by Jehovah. God raised up. Jah has delivered.

Delilah (de-li-lah) - Delicate. A drawer of water. Poor. Small. Head of hair. Languishing. Lustful. Dainty one. Thin. Gentle. Tender.

Demas (de'-mas) - Popular. Ruler of people. Ruler or governor of the people.

Demetrius (de-me'-tre-us) - Belonging to Demeter (Demeter was the goddess of agriculture and rural life). Mother earth. Belonging to corn. The mother of the people. The goddess of corn.

Derbe (der'-by) - Tanner. Tanner of skin. Covered with skin. A sting. Prickly. Juniper.

Deuel (de-oo'-el) - Invocation of God. God is knowing. Know ye God. The knowledge of God. Known of God.

Deuteronomy (doot'-er-an'-e-me) - Second law. Repetition of the law.

Devil (de-vil) - Slander. Traducer. Accuser. Adversary.

Diamond (dia'-mond) - He will smite down.

Diana (di-an'-ah) - Justice. One who judges. Flow restrained. Complete light. Luminous. A great mother. Perfect. Just now. Prompt. This day.

Diblaim (dib'-la-im) - Two cakes of figs. Double embrace. Twin balls. Cluster of figs. Cakes. Two cakes. Pressure. Straitness.

Diblath (dib'-lath) - Cake. Place of the fig cake. Paste of dry figs. Circle: Fruitful. Fertile.

Diblathaim (dib-lath-a'-im) - Two cakes of figs. Double embrace. Twin balls.

Dibon (di'-bon) - Weeping. Pining. Wasting. Full of understanding. Abundance of knowledge. A wasting away. Secure rest. River-place.

Dibon-gad (di'-bon-gad') - Wasting of Gad. Great understanding. Abundance of sons. Troop. Secure rest.

Dibri (dib'-ri) - Promise of the Lord. On the pasture born. My word. An orator. Eloquent. Talkative. A word. My saying. Jah distributes promise.

Didymus did'i-mus) - Double. Twin. A twin.

Diklah (did'-lah) - A palm tree. Palm grove. The beaten-small fainted. That is poor.   Place of palms. His diminishing.

Dilean (dil'e'-an) - A large gourd. Cucumber field. Brought low in affliction. That is poor. Species of the gourd.

Dimnah (dim-nah) - Dunghill. Dung. Dung heap.

Dimon (di'-mon) - Secure fast. Undisturbed silence. The quieter.

Abundance of blood. Where it is red. River bed. Rest. Bloody.

Dimonah (di-mon'-nah) - Sufficient numbering. Feminine of Dimon. Dung hill. Rest.

Dinah (di-na) - Judged. Vindicated. Justice. She that is judged. Judgment. Who judges. One who judges. Avenged.

Dinaites (di-na-ites) - Judgment. A cause.

Dinhabah (din'-ha-bah) - She gives judgment. Giving judgment. He gives judgment. Robbers den. Furnishing oily fatness. Concealment.

Dionysius (di-on-ish'-yus) - Divinely touched. The God of wine. From heaven. Divine inspiration.

Diotrephes (di-ot'-re-feez) - Loves preeminence. Nourished by Jupiter.

Dishan (di'-shan) - Gazelle. Wild goat. Antelope. Leaping. Their threshing. Their treading. A threshing. A genus of the great deer.

Dishon (di'-shon) - Same as Dishan. Gazelle. Wild goat. Antelope. Leaping. Their threshing. Their treading. Fatness. Ashes. The leaper.

Dizahab (diz'a-hab) - A place abounding with gold. Golden. Region of gold. Having gold. Rich in gold.

Dodai (do'-dahee) - Beloved of the Lord. Amatory. Love.

Dodanim (do'da-nim) - Leaders. A leader. Love. Progress. Increase.

Dodaveh (do'-da-vah) - Love of the Lord. Jehovah is loving. Love. Beloved of Jehovah. The love of God. Jah is friend.

Dodo (do'-do) - Beloved of the Lord. Jehovah is loving. His beloved. His uncle. Amatory. Beloved.

Doeg (do'-eg) - Fearful. Anxious. Timid. Sorrowful. Careful. Earnest.
Dophkah (dof'-kah) - Knocking. Beating. Literally - you have beaten. A knock. A knocking. Drover. Pressure of water. Cattle-driving.
Dor (dor) - Habitation. Circle. Circle of the years of life. Dwelling. Generation.
Dorcas (dor'-cas) - Gazelle. An emblem of beauty. A female roe - deer. A roe. Antelope.

Dothan (do'-than) - Two wells or cisterns. Judgment. Law. Their decree. Their sickness. Custom. Wells. Double cistern. Double fountain.
Drusilla (dru-sil'-lah) - Watered by the dew. Sprinkled with dew.
Dumah (doo'-mah) - Silence. Resemblance. Fig. Death.
Dura (doo'-rah) - Circle. Habitation. Same as Dor. Circle or circuits. In roundness. Dwelling.

E

Easter (east'-er) - Passover.

Ebal (e'-bal) - Stone. Stony. A heap of ruins. Heap of bareness. Bare. Heaps of confusion. Ancient heaps. Mount of stone. Desert dwellers. Very thick fat.

Ebed (e'bed) - Servant. Slave. Laborer. A servant.

Ebed-melech (e'-bed-me'-lek) - Servant of the king. Slave of the king. The king's servant. Servant of a king. Minister.

Eben-ezer (eb-en-e'-zur) - Stone of help. The Lord helped us.

Eber (e'-bur) - He who passed over. The region beyond. A passer over. A shout. Beyond the other side (as having crossed over). One that passes. Anger. Beyond. The other side. Across. Passage.

Ebiasaph (e-bi'-a-saf) - Father of increase. The father that gathers together. The father of gathering. The father that adds. Gatherer. He removed his father.

Ebronah (eb-ro'-nah) - Passage of the sea. Crossing over. Passage over. Being angry. Extremity. Gateway. Transitional.

Ecclesiastes (e-kle'-ze-as'-tez) - Preacher. A preacher.

Ed (ed) - Witness. A witness.

Edar (e'-dar) - Flock. Drove. An arrangement. To master. To keep flock in order or ranks.

Eden (e'-dun) - Paradise. A place of delight. Delight. Pleasantness. Pleasure. Plain.

Eder (e'-dur) - Same as Edar. Flock. Drove. An arrangement. To muster. To keep flock in order or ranks.

Edom (e'-dum) - Red. Red earth. Bloody.

Edomites (e'-dum-ites) - Inhabitants of Edom. Red. Red earth. Bloody.

Edrei (ed'-re-i)- Strong. A valley for a flock. Goodly pasture. A very great mass. Mighty. Plantation. Sufficient pasturage.

Eglah (eg'-lah) - A girl. A heifer. Chariot. Round. Calf. A calf to go round.

Eglaim (eg'-la-im) - Two pools. Drops of dew. Double reservoir. Drops of the sea. A double pond. Twin springs. On the limits. Two ponds.

Eglon (eg'-lon) - A fine bull calf. i.e., large and fat. A strong heifer. Circle. Chariot. Same as Eglah. Round. Calf-like. Young bull. Remarkable calf.

Egypt (e'-jipt) - Black. Oppressors. Double straits. That troubles or oppresses. Anguish. A hemming in. Limiting. Black land. Tribulation.

Egyptian (e-jip'-shun) - An oppressor. Double straits. Black land. Tribulation.

Egyptians (e-jip'-shuns) - Inhabitants of Egypt. An oppressor. Double straits. Black land. Tribulation.

Ehi (e'-hi) - My brother. Unity. Brotherly. Fellowship. Union. Connection.

Ehud (e'-hud) - Joined together. Strong union. He that praises. Union. Strong. Praise. Portion.

Eker (e'-ker) - Offspring. A shoot. One transplanted. Barren. Foreigner. Rooting up. A root.

Ekron (ec'-ron) - Uprooting. Emigration. A rooter out. Barrenness.

Torn away. Extermination. Barren place. Eradication. Uprooted. Great emigration.

Ekronites (ec'-ron) - inhabitants of Ekron. Uprooting. Emigration. A rooter out. Barrenness. Torn away. Extermination. Barren place. Eradicated. Uprooted. Great emigration.

El (el) - Might.

Eladah (el'-a-dah) - God adorns. Ornament of God. Whom God clothes. God has adorned. The eternity of God. God has decked. Whom God puts on or fills with Himself.

Elah (e'-lah) - Oak. An oak tree. Like a tree. The denunciation of a curse. A proper name for God -Elah. The Arab word for God is Allah. An oak. A curse. Perjury. Strength.

Elam (e'-lam) - Hidden time. Eternity. Youth. High. Their heaps. Suckling them. Eternal. A young man. A virgin. A secret. Hidden. High land. The longest duration.

Elamites (e'-lam-ites) - Inhabitants of Elam. Hidden time. Eternity. Youth. High. Their heaps. Suckling them. Eternal. A young man. A virgin. A secret. Hidden. Highland. The longest duration.

Elasah (el'-a-sah) - Whom God made. God is doer. The doings of God. God created. God has made. God is creator.

Elath (e'-lath) - Terebinths. A grove. An oak tree. An imprecation. Mightiness. A hind. Strength. An oak. A grove. Palm grove. Juniper. Trees.

El-beth-el (el-beth'-el) - Strong house of God. The God of the house of God. God of God's house. The God of Bethel.

Eldaah (el'-da-ah) - Whom God called. God has known. Knowledge of God. God of knowledge. Whom God calls. Asking God.

Eldad (el'-dad) - Whom God loves. The love of God. God has loved. God is a friend. Favored of God.

Elead (e'-le-ad) - Whom God praises. God is witness. God continues. Witness of God. God defender. God as testified. God applauds. God has strengthened.

Elealeh (el-e-a'-leh) - Whither God ascends. The ascension of God. Burnt offering of God. The exalted God. God is exalted.

Eleasah (el-e'-a-sah) - Whom God made. God is doer. God is helper. God made.

Eleazar (el-e-a-zar) - Whom God helps or aids. The help of God. God is helper. God has helped.

El-elohe (el-el-o'-he) - God of gods. God.

El-elohe-Israel (el-el-o'-he-iz'-rah-el) - God is the God of Israel. The mighty God.

Eleph (e'-lef) - A great multitude. The abode of a great multitude. A disciple learning. With the art. A thousand. Ox.

Elhanan (el-ha'-nan) - Whom God graciously gave. God was gracious. God has been generous. Mercy of God. Grace. God is gracious. God is kind. God gave graciously.

Eli (e'-li) - Jehovah is high. A foster son. Adopted of the Lord. My ascension. My God. My God. Elevated. The offering or lifting up. Ascent. Summit. Raised up. My foster child. Lofty.

Eliab (e'-le-ab) - My God is father. Whose father is God. God, my father. God is a father. God is the father. God is my father. God a father.

Eliada (e-li'-a-dah) - Whom God knows. Whom God acknowledges and cares for. God is knowing. God kindly regarded. Knowledge of God. Known of God. God knows and cares for.

Eliadah (e-li'-a-dah) - Same as Eliada. Whom God knows. Whom God acknowledges and cares for. God is knowing. God kindly regarded. Knowledge of God. Known of God. God knows and cares for.

Eliah (e-li'-ah) - Same name as Elijah. God-Lord. Strength of the Lord. God is Jehovah. My God is Jah. God the Lord. God Jehovah. The strength of God.

Eliahba (e-li'-ah-bah) - Whom God hides. God does hide. My God the father. God will hide.

Eliakim (el-li'-a-kim) - Whom God sets up i.e., establishes and causes to stand. God will raise up. God does establish. Resurrection of God. God is raising. God is setting up. My God arises.

Eliam (e'-le-am) - God's people. The people of my God. God is one of the family. God's founder of the people. The people of God. God is gatherer. People's God. God of the people.

Elias (e-li'-as) - Same as Elijah. God-Lord. Strength of the Lord. God is Jehovah. God Himself. Greek from of Elijah.

Eliasaph (e-li'-a-saf) - Whom God added. God has added. God is gathered. The Lord increaseth. Added of God. God is protector.

Eliashib (e-li'-a-shib) - Whom God restores. Whom God leads back again. God will restore. God is requiter. God has restored. The God of conversion. God recompensed or restored. God restores.

Eliathah (e-li'-a-thah) - God comes. To whom God comes. God has come. God of the coming one. Thou art my God. Most severe grief. God of consent. God is come.

Elidad (e-li'-dad) - Whom God loves. God has loved. God is a friend. My God is lover. Beloved of God. Loved of God. Love of God. God of his love.

Eliel (e'-le-el) - To whom God is God. To whom God is strength. God is God. God. God of gods. Strength of strength.

Elienai (e-li-e'-nahee) - God of my eyes. Unto Jehovah my eyes are raised. Unto God are my eyes. The God of my eyes. My eyes toward Jehovah. To God mine eyes.

Eliezer (e-li-e'-zur) - God of help. My God is help. God is my help. Help. The help of my God. God is helper.

Elihoenai (e-li-ho-e'nahee) - God the Lord of my eyes. To Jehovah are my eyes. My eyes toward Jehovah. Same as Elioenai.

Elihoreph (e-li-ho'-ref) - God of the reward. To whom God is the reward. The God of winter. God of harvest rain. God is a reward. God of autumn. God of harvest grain.

Elihu (e-li'-hew) - Whose God is he. He is my God. He is God. Himself. My

God is Jehovah. He is my God Himself. My God is He. God he is.

Elijah (e-li'-jah) - God-Lord. Strength of the Lord. My God is Jehovah. The Lord God. God the Lord. God-Jehovah. Spiritual vision. Jehovah is my God.

Elika (e-li'-kah) - God of the congregation. Strength of the congregation. God is rejector. God has spewed out. Pelican of God. God his rejector. God of rejection. The congregation of God. God has rejected.

Elim (e'-lim) - A grove of oaks. Palms. Mighty ones. The rams. The strong. Stags. Trees. Oaks. Large trees.

Elimelech (e-lim'-e-lek) - God of the King. My God the King. God is King. My God is King.

Elioenai (e-li-o-e'-nahee) - God the Lord of my eyes. To whom my eyes are directed. Toward him are my eyes. To him are my fountains. Toward Jehovah my eyes. Mine eyes are toward God. To Jehovah are my eyes.

Eliphal (el'-i-fal) - When God judges. God the judge. God is judge. God has judged. The God of deliverance. A miracle of God. God his judge. God hath judged.

Eliphalet (e-lif'-a-let) - God of salvation. God the Savior. To whom God is salvation. The God of deliverance. God delivers. The deliverance of God. God of escape. God is deliverance.

Eliphaz (el'-if-az) - My God is fine gold. God the strong. To whom God is strength. My precious God. God is dispenser. My God has refined. The endeavor of God. God is strong. The joy of God. God of gold. God is victorious.

Elipheleh (e-lef'-e-leh) - God distinguishes him and makes him eminent. Jehovah is distinction. Distinguished. My God set thou apart. God delivers. God distinguishes. Who exalts God. Whom God makes distinguished.

Eliphelet (e-lef'-e-leh) - God of salvation. God the Savior. To whom God is salvation. God of escape. God delivers. The deliverance of God.

Elisabeth (e-liz'-a-beth) - God of the oath. God is her oath. A worshipper of God. To whom God is the oath. God of the covenant. Oath of my God. My God has sworn. Salvation of God.

Eliseus (el-i-se'-us) - God his salvation. Greek form of Elisha = God the Savior. To whom God is salvation. God of salvation. God is savior. The look and face of salvation.

Elisha (e-li'-shah) - God the Savior. To whom God is salvation. God of salvation. God is Savior. The salvation of God. God the deliverer. Face or sight of God. God his salvation.

Elishah (e-li'-shah) - God the Savior. To whom God is salvation. God of salvation. God is Savior. My God has disregarded. It is God. The lamb of God. God that gives help. Firm-binding. God saves. God is salvation.

Elishama (e-lish'-a-mah) - God the hearer. My God will hear. God is hearer. God has heard. God hearing. Whom God hears.

Elishaphat (e-lish'-a-fat) - God the judge. God judges and defends him. Whom God judges. God is judge. God has judged. My God judgeth. God of judgment.

Elisheba (e-lish'-e-bah) - God of the oath. God is her oath. A worshipper of God. To whom God Is the oath. God of the covenant. Oath of my God. My God has sworn. God covenant. My God is fulness.

Elishua (e-lish'-oo-ah) - God the rich. God of affluence. God is rich. God is salvation. God of crying. God of supplication. Opulence. God is my salvation. God is salvation. The help of God. God of riches.

Eliud (e-li'-ud) - God of Judah. God is majesty. God is my praise. God of majesty. God is majestic.

Elizaphan (e-liz'-a-fan) - God hides i.e., defends him. Whom God protects. God is protector. God has concealed: God a protector. God has hid or protects.

Elizur (e-li'-zur) - God the rock. God is my rock. God is a rock. God is my strength. My Rock. Rock of God. God his rock.

Elkanah (el-ka'-nah) - God has redeemed. Possession of God. Whom God possessed. God hath created. God is jealous. God is possessing. God the zealous. The zeal of God. God creates. God has obtained.

Elkeshai (el'ka-shaw) - Hardness or rigor of God.

Elkoshite (el'-ko-shite) - God my bow and my defense. The gathered of God. A man of Elkeshai. God obtained. God's bow and power or might. Defense.

Ellasar (el'-la-sar) - Declension of God. God is chastener. Revolting from God. Oath of a prince. Oak of Assyria.

Elmadam (el-mo'-dam) - Immeasurable. Increasing. Without measure. Extension. The God of measure. Immense.

Elnaam (el-na'-am) - God of pleasantness. Whose pleasure God is. God is pleasant. God's fairness. God his delight. God has judged. God is his delight.

Elnathan (el-na'-than)- God gave. When God gave. God has given. God is giving. The gift of God. Conscience which God bestows.

Eloi (e-lo'-ee) - My God. Oak. Grove. Strong.

Elohim (e-lo'-hem) - God. Oak. Grove. Strong. Elohim is the abstract expression for absolute Deity.

Elon (e'-lon) - Magnificent oak. An oak tree. Strong. Might. Grove. A strongman. A remarkable oak.

Elon-beth-hanan (e'-lon-beth-ha'-nan) - Oak of the house of grace. Might of the house of the gracious giver. The house of grace or mercy. Oak house He gave. Oak of Hanan.

Elonites (e'-lon-ites) - Descendants of Elon. Magnificent oak. An oak tree strong and mighty. Grove. A strong man. A remarkable oak.

Eloth (e'-loth) - Same as Elath. Terebinths. A grove. Mightiness. Grove of strong trees.

Elpaal (el-pa'-al) - God the maker. To whom God is the reward. God is a reward. God is working. God's work. God his reward. The work of God. God has wages.

Elpalet (el-pa'-let) - God is deliverance. Same as Eliphalet - God of salvation. God the Savior. To whom

God is salvation. God is escape. God delivers. Deliverance of God.

El-paran (el-pa'-ran) - Strong. Oak of Paran. Oak of much digging. The power of their adoring. (Strong applied to a state, with the idea of robust: of a tree, like a terebinth or turpentine tree that abounds in foliage and lives for a thousand years.)

Eltekeh (el'-te-keh) - God fearing. Whose fear is God. Let God spue you out. Of grace or mercy. God is its fear. Fear of God. Care of God. Meeting place.

Elteketh (el'-te-keth) - The case of God.

Eltekon (el'-te-kon) - God the foundation. Whose foundation is God. A place established on God. Made straight of God. God is straight. The establishing of God. Founded by God.

Eltolad (el-to'-lad) - God of the generation. God's race. Whose posterity is from God. The generation of God. Allied to God. God its posterity.

Elul (e'-lul) - A vain thing. Nothingness. Cry or outcry. Name of the sixth Jewish month.

Eluzai (e-loo'-zahee) - God of my congregation. God is my praise. God is my strength. God is my gathering strength for flight. God is defensive. God my strength.

Elymas (el'-i-mas) - A wise man. A magician. A sorcerer. Corrupter.

Elzabad (el'-za-bad) - God gave. Whom God gave. God has endowed. God has bestowed. The dowry of God. Given of God. God has given or bestowed. God is endowing.

Elzaphan (el'-za-fan) - God hides. God defends him. Whom God protects. God has concealed. God has protected. God of the northeast wind. God a protector. God has hid. God of treasure. Same as Elizaphan.

Emerald (em'-er-ald) - Enameled.

Emims (e'-mims) - Terrors. Horrors. Terrible men. Giants. The fearful. Fears. Formidable people.

Emmanuel (em-man'-uel) - God with us.

Emmaus (em'-ma-us) - Hot springs. In earnest longing. People despised or obscured. Warm springs. Warm wells.

Emmor (em'-mor) - An ass. Greek form of Hamor.

En (en) - Fountain.

Enam (e'-nam) - Two fountains. The double. A congregation. Double fountain.

Enan (e'-nan) - Having eyes. A fountain. Cloud. A great fountain.

Endor (en'-dor) - Fountain of habitation. The eye of a generation. Fountain. Habitation. Fountain of dwelling.

Eneas (e'-ne-as) - I praise. Praise of Jehovah. Uttering praise. Laudable.

En-eglaim (en-eg'-la-im) - Fountain of two calves. The eye of a heifer. Eye. Spring of two heifers.

En-gannim (en-gan'-nim) - Fountain of the gardens. Eye. A garden. Fountain of gardens.

En-gedi (en-ghe'di) - Fountain of the kid. The eye of a kid. Eye. Kids' fountain. Fountain of the cutting down.

En-haddah (en-had'-dah) - Fountain of sharpeness. Fountain of swiftness. Fountain of joy. Swift spring. Quick sight. Well of gladness. Fountain of quick flowing. Flowing strongly.
En-hakkore (en-hak'-ko-re) - Fountain of the calling. Fountain of prayer. Fountain of him that called or prayed: Fountain of the crier. Fountain of him who calleth.
En-hazor (en-ha'-zor) - Fountain of Hazor. Fountain of the village. Fount of trumpeting. The grass of the well. Fountain of defense.
En-mishphet (en-mish'-pat) - Fountain of judgment. The eye of judgment.
Enoch (e'-noch) - Initiated. Initiating. Teacher. Dedicated. Consecrated. Experienced. Disciplined. Instructed. Taught.
Enon (e'-non) - Cloud. Mass of darkness. Fountain. Eye.
Enos (e'-nos) - Man. Man in his frailty. Feeble. Mortal. Sick. Despaired of. Mortal man. Forgetful. Decaying. A miserable of sick man. Mankind. Man as mortal.
Enosh (e'-nosh) - Same as Enos. Man. Man in his frailty. Mortal. Sick. Despaired of. Mortal man. Forgetful. Decaying. A miserable or sick man. Mankind. Man as mortal.
En-rimmon (en-rim'-mon) - Fountain of the pomegranate. Well of weight. Fountain of pomegranates. Fountain very high.
En-rogel (en-ro'-ghel) - Fountain of the fuller (washing). Fount of the spy. The fuller's fountain. The well of searching. Foot fountain. Fountain of a traveler.

En-shemesh (en-she'-mesh) - Fountain of the sun. Fountain.
En-tappuah (en-tap'-poo-ah) - Fountain of the apple tree. Fountain of the apple. Fountain.
Epaenetus (ep-en'-e-tus) - Laudable. Worthy of praise. Praised.
Epaphras (ep'-a-fras) - Commended. Charming. Foamy: Covered with foam.
Epaphroditus (e-paf-ro-di'-tus) - Lovely. Handsome. Charming: Agreeable. Comeliness. Fascinating.
Epenetus (ep-en'-e-tus) - Laudable. Worthy of praise: Same as Epaenctus.
Ephah (e'-fah) - Darkness. Obscurity. A measure. Weary. Tired. Weariness. Gloomy.
Ephai (e'-fahee) - Wearying of the Lord. Great languishing. Fatigued. Obscured. My shadows. My coverings. My fowls. Birdlike. Weariness of God. Languid.
Epher (e'-fur) - A young hart. Calf. Mule. Young calf. Dustiness. Dust. Lead. Gazelle. A young hind. A young animal.
Ephes-dammim (e'-fes-dam'-min) - Extremity of bloods. Boundary of blood. Nothing but blood. Effusion of blood. Loss of blood. End of blood.
Ephesians (e-fe'-zheuns) - Inhabitants of Ephesus. Desirable. Beloved. A giving away. To relax. Loosening. The end.
Ephesus (ef'-e-sus) - Desirable. Beloved. A giving away. To relax. Loosening. The end. Permitted.
Ephlal (ef'-lal) - Judgment. Judicious. Judging. Praying. Judge. The judgment of God.

Ephod (e'-fod) - Covering. Vestment of the High Priest. Image. A short cloak. Oracle giving. Oracular.

Ephphatha (ef'-fath-ah) - Be opened.

Ephraim (e'-fra-im) - Two-fold increase. Very fruitful. Doubly fruitful. Double ash-heap. Fruitful. Increasing. Double grainland. Posterity. Twin fruit.

Ephraimites (e'-fra-im-ites) - Inhabitants of Ephraim. Very fruitful. Doubly fruitful. Double ash-heaps. Fruitful. Increasing. Double grainland. Posterity. Twin fruit.

Ephrain (e'-fra-im) - A great and choice fawn. Double dust. Same as Ephron. Dust. Large young hind. Of two fawns.

Ephratah (ef'-rat-ah) - Fruitful. Ash heap. Dust. Fruitfulness. Very great fruitfulness. Fertility.

Ephrath (e'-frath) - Fruitful. Fruitful land. A shyness. Dust. Fruitfulness. Posterity.

Ephrathite(s) (ef'-rath-ites) - Inhabitants of Ephrath. Fruitful. Fruitful land. A shyness. Dust. Fruitfulness. Posterity.

Ephron (e'-fron) - A great and choice fawn: Of or belonging to a calf. Full of dust. Strong. Fawnlike. Large young fawn. Dust.

Epicureans (ep-i-cu-re'-ans) - A helper. Defender. Followers of Epicurus. Help. Assistance.

Er (er) - Watcher. Awake on the watch. Stirring up. Watchman. A troop. Watchful. Crouch.

Eran (e'-ran) - Watchful. Their awaking. Their stirring up. Intensive form of Er. Follower. A great troop. Watching.

Eranites (e'-ran-ites) - Descendants of Eran. Watchful. Their awaking. Their stirring up. A great troop. Watching. Followers.

Erastus (e-ras'-tus) - Beloved. Lovely. Amicable.

Erech (e'-rek) - Length. Health.

Eri (e'-ri) - Watcher of the Lord. Worshipper of Jehovah. My watcher My awakening. My stirring up. My city watching i.e., worshipping Jehovah.

Erites (e'-rites) - Descendants of Eri. Watcher of the Lord. Worshipper of Jehovah. My watcher. My awakening. My stirring up. My city. Watching i.e., Worshiping Jehovah.

Esaias (e-sah'-yas) Same as Isaiah. Salvation of the Lord. Jehovah is helper. Salvation is of the Lord. Jehovah has saved. The Lord has helped. The New Testament name for Isaiah.

Esarhaddon (e'-zar-had'-dun) - Gift of fire. A restrainer of joy. Victorious. Ashur has given brothers. Captivity of the fierce. I will chastise the fierce. That closes the point. Joy. Cheerfulness. Prince of great power.

Esau (e'-saw) - Covered with hair. Hairy. He that acts or finishes. Rough. He that acts or makes rough. All hairy. Doing. Finishing.

Esek (e'-sek) - Strife. Contention. Oppression. Quarrel. Dispute.

Esh-baal (esh'-ba-al) - Fire of Baal. A man of Baal. The fire of the idol. Baal's man.

Eshban (esh'-ban) - Very red. Intelligence. Man of understanding. Fire of discernment. Wise hero. Vigorous. Fire of the sun.

Eschol (esh'-col) - A cluster of grapes or flowers. Cluster of grapes. A bunch especially of grapes.
Eshean (esh'-e-an) - Support i.e., a place of confidence. Held up. Close binding.
Eshek (e'-shek) - Oppression. Strife. Violence. Oppressor.
Eshkalonites (esh'-ka-lon-ites) - (Same as Ashkelon). Migration. Inhabitants of Ashkelon.
Eshtaol (esh'-ta-ol) Woman requesting. I will be entreated. A strong woman. Entreaty. Asked of a woman. A receding. Hollowing out.
Eshtaulites (esh'-ta-u-lites) - Inhabitants of Eshtaol. Woman requesting. I will be entreated. A strong woman. Entreaty. Asked of a woman. A receding. Hollowing out.
Eshtemoa (esh-te-mo'-ah) - Women of fame. Obedience. I will make myself heard. The bosom of a woman. Fame of woman. Listening post.
Eshtemoh (esh'-te-moh) - Same as Eshtemoa. Obedience. Woman of fame. I will make myself heard. The bosom of a woman. Fame of woman. Listening post.
Eshton (esh'-ton) - Womanly. Rest. Restful. Fond of woman. Luxurious. Womanish.
Esli (es'-li) - Reserved of the Lord. Jehovah has reserved. God at my side. Near me. He who separates. Separated for God. Same as Azaliah.
Esmachiah (es'-mok-e-ah) - Joined to the Lord.
Esrom (es'-rom) - Same as Hezron. Enclosed. Enclosure. Surrounded by a

wall. Sure defense. Dart of joy. Division of a song.
Esther (es'-thur) - Star. She that is hidden. Secret. Hidden. A green myrtle. Happiness.
Etam (e'-tam) - A place of ravenous creatures. Wild beasts' lair. Their bird. Abundance of rapacious birds. Place of birds of prey.
Etham (e'-tham) - Boundary of the sea. Their plowshare. Their strength. Their sign. Extreme habitation. Desolate. Fortress.
Ethan (e'-than) - Firmness. Strength. Ancient. Perplexity. Strong. The gift of the island. Perpetuity. Firm. God as very ancient. Long lived.
Ethanim (eth'-a-nim) - Gifts. Strong. Valiant. The perineal. Permanent Flowing.
Ethbaal (eth'-ba-al) - Living with Baal. A man of Baal. With him is Baal. Baal's man. Toward the idol. With Baal.
Ether (e'-ther) - Abundance. Plenty. Talk.
Ethiopia (e-the-o'-pe-ah) - Same as Cush. A black countenance. Full of darkness. Region of burnt faces. Blackness. Heat. Country of burnt faces. Dark and swarthy countenance. Black. Burnt.
Ethiopians (e-the-o'-pe-ans) - Descendants of Cush. A black countenance. Full of darkness. Region of burnt faces. Blackness. Heat. Country of burnt faces. Dark and swarthy countenance. Black. Burnt.
Ethnan (eth'-nan) - A gift of a harlot. Hire. Hire of unchastity. Bountiful gift.
Ethni (eth'-ni) - Reward. Bountiful. My gift. My hire. Strong. Munificent. Gift of God. Giving. Jehovah rewards.

Eubulus (yu-bu'-lus) - Good counselor. Well advised. Prudent. Counseling wisely. Good counsel.

Eunice (yu-ni'- see) - Conquering well: Happy or good victory. Distinguished conqueror.

Euodias (yu-o'-de-as) - Success. Prosperous journey. Sweet scent. Prosperous course. Good journey.

Euphrates (yu-fra'-teze) - Fruitfulness. Fruitful. The fertile river. That makes fruitful. Flowing of waters. The good and abounding river. Inexhaustible. Out pouring. To break forth. Unlimited.

Euroclydon (yu-roc'-lid-on) - Storm from the East. A wind. An easterly tempest.

Eutychus (yu'-tik-us) - Fortunate. Happy. Well off.

Eve (eev) - Life. Life giving. Living. Mother of all who have life. Enlivening. Life giver. Alive. Human activity.

Evi (e'-vi) - Desire. Unjust. Dwelling.

Evil-merodach (e'-vil-mer'-o-dak) - The fool of Merodach. Foolish is your rebellion. A rebellious fool. The fool grinds bitterly. First. Sublime. The man of the god Marduk. Servant.

Exodus (ek'-so-dus) - Departure. Going out.

Ezar (e'-zar) - Treasure. Help.

Ezbai (ez'-bahee) - Spoil. Beautiful. My humblings. Hyssop like. Spirit of God. Shining. The man God strengthens. God is powerful. God strengthens.

Ezbon (ez'-bon) - Great beauty. Splendor. Hastening to discern. I will be enlargement. Hastening to understand. Great honor. Working, hearing or splendor of God.

Ezekias (ez-e-ki'-as) - Strength of the Lord. Jehovah is strength. Greek form of Hezekiah.

Ezekiel (e-zeke'-yel) - Strength of God. When God will strengthen. God is strong.

Ezel (e'-zel) - Departure. Running. Going abroad. Walk. Separation. Division.

Ezem (e'-zem) - Strength. Bone. Mighty. Same as Azem.

Ezer (e'-zur) - Treasury. Treasure. Help. A help. Union. God is a help.

Ezion-gaber (e'-ze-on-ga'-bur) - The backbone of a man (intense form). Counsel of a man. The word of the man. Giant's backbone.

Ezion-geber (e'-ze-on-ge'-bur) - Same as Ezion-gaber. The backbone of a man. Counsel of man. The word of the man. Giant's backbone.

Eznite (ez'-nite) - Whose pleasure is the spear. His bending of the spear. The stiff-backed. Spear. Sharpe. To be sharp or strong. Same as Adino the Eznite.

Ezra (ez'-rah) - Help. Assistance. My helper. Court. God is a help.

Ezrahite (ez'-rah-hite) - Sprung up. A native as arising out of the soil.

Ezri (ez'-ri) - Help of the Lord. God is a help. My help. Help of Jehovah. Helpful. Help of God. God is my help.

F

Fair Havens (fair hay'-vens) - Good harbor.
Felix (fe'-lix) - Delusive. Happy. Prosperous.
Festus (fes'-tus) - Joyful. Festal. Prosperous. Festival.
Fortunatus (for-chu-na'-tus) - Prosperous. Well freighted. Lucky. Fortunate. Prospered.
Frankincense (frank-in'-cense) - Whiteness.

G

Gaal (ga'-al) - Loathing. An abhorrence. Rejection. Contempt. Abomination. Miscarriage. A reward.
Gaash (ga'-ash) - Shaking. Earthquake. Tempest. Commotion. Quaking. Trembling.
Gaba (ga'-bah) - Hill. Highlander. A hill or hillock.
Gabbai (gab'-bahee) - An exactor of tribute. In-gatherer. Tax gatherer. My eminences. The book. He is exalted. Collective.
Gabbatha (gab'-ba-thah) - Height. Elevated. Platform. High. The knoll. Elevated spot or place.
Gabriel (ga'bre-el) - Man of God. God my strength. God is my strength. The mighty one. Hero of God. The manifestation of God. Man. God is great.

Gad (gad) - Good fortune. Good luck. A troop. A seer. A band. An assembly. Troop armed. Company prepared.
Gadara (gad'-a-ra) - Walls.
Gadarenes (gad-a-renes') - Reward at the end. Men of Gadara. Walled around. Trooped in. Fortified.
Gaddi (gad'-di) - Fortunate. Belonging to fortune. My troop. A kid. The troop of God. My fortune.
Gaddiel (gad'-de-el) - God is a fortune bringer. God has given fortune. My fortune. Troop of God. The Lord my happiness. Goat of God. Fortune of God. God is my fortune.
Gadi (ga'-di) - Fortune sent from God. Fortunate. Troop of God. My fortune.
Gadites (gad'-ites) - Descendants of Gad. Good fortune. Good luck. A troop. A seer. A band. An assembly. Troop armed. Company prepared.
Gaham (ga'-ham) - Having large and flaming eyes. Sunburnt. Flaming. Blackness. The devastator waxed hot. The valley was lost. To burn. Burning brightly. Swarthy. Having full eyes.
Gahar (ga'-har) - Hiding place. Prostration. The valley burned. Lurker. Concealment. Reddish. Lurking place.
Gaius (gah'-yus) - I am glad. On earth Lord. An earthly man. Weighty. I rejoice. The Lord.
Galal (ga'-lal) - He has rolled away the reproach of the parents. Worth. Influential. Rolling of one's day upon the Lord. A roll. Weighty. He rolled. Worthy. Great. Rolling.
Galatia (ga-la'-she-ah) - Land of the Gali or Gauls. Circuit. Milky. White. The color of milk. Rolling.

Galatians (ga-la'-she-uns) - Inhabitants of Galatia. Circuit. Milky. White. The color of milk. Rolling.

Galeed (ga'-le-ed) - Hill of witness. Witness. Heap of witnesses or testimony. The heap of witness.

Galilaean (gal-i-le'-un) - Same as Galilee. Circuit. Rolling. Revolving. A mound of earth. Circle. Wheel revolution.

Galilee (gal'-i-lee) - Circuit as enclosed or rolled around. Rolling. Revolving. A wheel. Revolution. Circle region. Turned around. A mound of earth.

Gallim (gal'-lim) - Fountains. Heaps. Billows as heaps of water. Who heaps up. Who covers. Many springs.

Gallio (gal'-le-o) - He that sucks. Who lives on milk. Giving suck.

Gamaliel (gam-a'-le-el) - Recompense of God. Benefit of God. God is the one who brings recompense. The gift or reward of God. Camel of God. Reward of God. God is my recompense.

Gammadims (gam'-ma-dims) - Warriors. Cutters. Additional garments. Dwarfs. Brave. Valiant. Warrior. Pygmies. Deserters.

Gamul (ga'-mul) - A recompense. Weaned. Matured. Recompensed. Rewarded. Retribution.

Gareb (ga'-reb) - Scabby. Leperous. Reviler. Rough. A scab. Despiser.

Garmite (gar-mite) - Bony.

Garmites (gar'-mites) - Men of Garmi. Bony.

Gashmu (gash'-mu) - Rain. Corporealness. Shower. Very fat.

Gatam (ga'-tam) - Great fatigue. Puny. Burnt valley. Reach thou the end. Their touch. Touch. Their lowing.

One puny and thin. The greatest fatigue.

Gath (gath) - Winepress. A wine-fat.

Gath-hepher (gath-he'-fer) - Winepress of the well. Digging up: Wine press

Gath-rimmon (gath-rim'-mon) - Winepress of the pomegranate. The high winepress. Very high. Pomegranate press.

Gaza (ga'-zah) - Strong. Fortified. Same as Azzah. A goat. Stronghold. Whole.   Complete.

Gazathites (ga'-zath-ites) - Inhabitants of Gaza. Strong. Fortified. A goat. Stronghold. Whole. Complete.

Gazabar (gaz'-a-bar) - A treasurer.

Gazer (ga'-zur) - Place cut off. Precipice. A dividing. A sentence. A portion.

Gazez (ga'-zez) - Shearer. A passing over. Cut off. Sheep shearer.

Gazites (ga'-zites) - Inhabitants of Gaza. Strong. Fortified. A goat. Stronghold. Whole. Complete.

Gazzam (gaz'-zam) - Violently torn off. Swaggerer. Devourer. Palmerworm - literally their shearing. The fleece of them. Devouring. Bird of prey.

Geba (ghe'-bar) - Same as Gaba. Hill. A drinking cup. Height. Hillock. Mountain.

Gebal (ghe'-bal) - Boundary. A border. Bound. Limit. A mountain.

Geber (ghe'bur) - Warrior. Hero. Strong. Manly. A man of power. A valiant man. Strong one.

Gebim (ghe'-bim) - Pits. Trenches. Grasshoppers. Height. Springs. Cisterns. Ditches.

Gedaliah (ghed-a-li'-ah) - Magnified of the Lord. Whom Jehovah has made great. Jehovah is great. Brought up by God. God is my greatness. Made great by Jehovah. Jah has become great. He was great.

Gedeon (ghed'-e-on) - The cutter down. Distinguished. Stock. A great trunk of a tree. Greek form of Gideon.

Geder (ghe'-dur) - A wall. A walled place. Hedges. Enclosure. Circumvallation. Fence.

Gederah (ghed'-e-rah) - Enclosure. Sheepfold. Sheepcote. A place hedged in.

Gederathite (ghed'-e-rath-ite) - Inhabitants of Gederah. Enclosure. Sheepfold. Sheepcote. A place hedged in.

Gederite (ghed'-e-rite) - Inhabitants of Geder. A wall. A walled place. Hedges. Enclosure. Circumvallation. Fence.

Gederoth (ghed'-e-roth) - Folds. Fortification. Sheepfold. Hedges. Places hedged in. Walls.

Gederothaim (ghed-e-ro-tha'-im) - Two-folds. Two fortified places. Two sheepfolds. Double wall. Places hedged in. Walls.

Gedor (ghe'-dor) - Fortified. A fortress. Wall. A hedged place. Inclosure.

Geharashim (ge-ha-ra'-shim) - Valley of craftsman.

Gehazi (ghe-ha'-zi) - Valley of vision. The valley of sight. Denier. Greatly exalted.

Gehenna (ge-hen'-na) - Hell (from the valley of Hinnom).

Geliloth (ghel'-il-oth) - Regions. Circles. Borders. Rolling. Circuits.

Gemalli (ghe-mal'-li) - Possessor of camels. Camel owner. Rider of a camel. Wares. A camel. Reward of God.

Gemariah (ghem-a-ri'-ah) - Perfected of the Lord. Whom Jehovah has completed. Jehovah has fulfilled. Accomplishment of the Lord. God has finished. God perfected. Jehovah has accomplished.

Genesis (jen'-e-sis) - Generation. Beginning.

Gennesaret (ghen-nes'-a-ret) - A harp. Harp shaped. Garden of the prince. Ten gardens. Garden of riches.

Gentiles (jen'-tiles) - A people or nation other than the Jews. Nations. Foreigners.

Genubath (ghen'-u-beth) - Theft. Robbery. Taken by stealth.

Gera (ghe'-rah) - Rumination. (the cud). Grain. Excitement. Enmity. Pilgrimage. Lengthening. Sojouner. Pilgrim.

Gerah (ghe-rah) - A piece. A bit. (The twentieth part of a shekel).

Gerar (ghe'-rar) - Sojourning. Journeying. A lodging place. To tarry. To sojourn. To dwell. To fear. To be a stranger. Annoyance. Dragging away. Pilgrimage. A rolling country. Halting place.

Gergesenes (ghur'-ghes-enes') - A stranger drawing near. Those who came from pilgrimage or fight. Potter's earth.

Gerizim (gher'-iz-im) - Cutters down. Fellers. Cuttings off. Divisions. Mount. Waste place. Disruptions. Cut up i.e., rocky wasteland.

Gershom (ghur'-shom) - A stranger there. Exile. Expulsion. A sojourner there. Banishment. Violent expulsion.
Gershon (ghur'-shon) - Same as Gershom. His banishment. The change of pilgrimage. Expulsion. Exile. A stranger there. A sojourner there. Banishment. Violent expulsion.
Gershonites (ghur'-shon-ites) - Inhabitants of Gershon. A stranger there. Exile. Expulsion. A sojourner there. Banishment. Violent expulsion.
Gesham (ghe'-sham) - Large clod. Firm. Strong. Filthy. Lumpy. A great flock.
Geshem (ghe'-shem) - Rain. Shower. Springs. River.
Geshur (ghe'-shur) - Expulsion. A bridge. Proud beholder. The vale of trial or searching. To join. Bridge. Banishment.
Geshuri (ghesh'-u-ri)- Exiles. The vale of trial or searching. To join. Bridge. Inhabitants of Geshur.
Geshurites (ghesh'-u-rites) - Inhabitants of Geshur. Exiles. The vale of trial or searching. To join. Bridge.
Gether (ghe'-ther) - Fear. A proud spy. The vale of trial or searching. Derivation. Uncertain. Dregs.
Gethsemane (gheth-sem'-a-ne) - Oil or olive press. A very fat or plentiful vale. Press for olives. Oil press. Yielding.
Geuel (ghe-u'-el) - Majesty of God. Salvation of God. Exalt ye God. God's redemption. Majesty. Redeemed of God.
Gezer (ghe'-zur) - Same as Gazer. Place cut off. Precipice. A piece or portion cut off. Dividing. A cutting off. A steep place. Portion. Division.

Gezrites (ghez'-rites)- Inhabitants of Gezer. Place cut off. Precipice. A piece or portion cut off. Dividing. A cutting off. A steep place. Portion. Division.
Giah (ghi'-ah) - Breaking forth of a fountain. Gushing forth. To draw out. Extend. To guide. Produce. A groan or sigh. Fountain. Issuing forth. Bubbling spring.
Gibbar (ghib'-bar) - Hero. Mighty. Mighty man. Strong. Very strong. Warrior. Manly.
Gibbethon (ghib'-be-thon) - A lofty place. A back. A high house. Height. Hill.
Gibea (ghib'-e-ah) - Hill. Highlander. High ground. Same as Gaba.
Gibeah (ghib'-e-ah) - The hill. A hill.
Gibeath (ghib'-e-ath) - The hill. Hilliness. Same as Gibeah.
Gibeathite (ghib'-e-ath-ite) - Hilliness. The hill. Inhabitant of Gibeah.
Gibeon (ghib'-e-on) - High hill. A dweller on a hill. Hill. Cup. Thing lifted up. Hill city. A great hill. Pertaining to a hill.
Gibeonites (ghib'-e-on-ites) - Inhabitants of Gibeon. High hill. A dweller on a hill. Hill. Cup. Thing lifted up. Hill city. A great hill. Pertaining to a hill.
Giblites (ghib'-lites) - Inhabitants of Gebal. Boundary. A border.
Giddalti (ghid-dal'-ti) - I have trained up. I have increased. I have magnified. I magnify God. I have made great. I have maintained. I have magnified God.
Giddel (ghid'-del) - He has become great. Very great. Gigantic. He has magnified. Great. Large. He has made great. Stout. Giant. Magnified.

Gideon (ghid'-e-on) - Feller. Cutter down. One who cuts down. A hewer down. A cutting down. He that bruises. Great warrior. A cutting of. A destroyer. He that bruises. Warrior. Great trunk of a tree. Tree-feller. Impetuous warrior.

Gideoni (ghid-e-o'-ni) - Same as Gideon. War like. Feller. Cutting down. One who cuts down. A hewer down. A cutting down. He that bruises. Great warrior. A cutting of. A destroyer. He that bruises or breaks. Warrior. Great stock of a tree. Tree feller. Impetuous. Warrior.

Gidom (ghi'-dom) - Cutting down. Desolating. Complete cutting off. Desolation.

Gihon (ghi'-hon) - Great breaking forth of waters. A river. Valley of grace. A fountain. Great bursting into. Irruption. Stream.

Gilalai (ghil'-a-lahee) - Rolled off the Lord. Weighty. A wheel. Rolling. God rolled over. Dungy.

Gilboa (ghil-bo'-ah) - Bubbling water of a fountain. Rolling or pouring out. A flow of joy. Revolution of inquiry. A spring of flowing. Fountain of ablution. Bare mountain.

Gilead (ghil'-e-ad) - Perpetual fountain. A heap of testimony. A witness. Mass of testimony. Strong. Spring perpetual. Heap of witness. Mound of stones.

Gileadites (ghil'-e-ad-ites) - Inhabitants of Gilead. Perpetual fountain. A heap of testimony. A witness. Mass of testimony. Strong. Spring perpetual. Heap of witness. Mound of stones.

Gilgal (ghil'-gal) - Liberty. Rolling away. Circle. Wheel. Rolling. Heap. Revolving continually. Circle of stones.

Giloh (ghi'-loh) - Exodus of a great multitude. His joy. He that rejoices. He that overturns. Exile. Circle.

Gilonite (ghi'-lo-nite) - Inhabitants of Giloh. Exodus of a great multitude. His joy. He that rejoices. He that over turns. Exile. Circle.

Gimzo (ghim'-zo) - Sycamores. Swallowing this. That bulrush. A grove of sycamores. Producing sycamores.

Ginath (ghi'-nath) - Protection. Similitude. Who arrives from pilgrimage. Shape a garden. Protection.

Ginnetho (ghin'-ne-tho) - Great protection. Garden. Gardener. Who arrives from pilgrimage. A roof. Covering.

Ginnethon (ghin'-ne-thon) - Same as Ginnetho. Great protection. Garden. Gardener. Who arrives from pilgrimage. A roof. Covering. Roof of a house.

Girgashites (ghur'-gash-ites) - Dwellers in a clayey soil. Driven out. A stranger drawing near. Who arrives from pilgrimage.

Girgasite (ghur'-ga-site) - Dwellers in a clayey soil. Driven out. A stranger drawing near.

Gispa (ghis'-pah) - Soothing. Flattery. Attentive. Banishment coming hither. An overseer. Soft attraction. Caress. Attentive listening.

Gittahhepher (ghit'-tah-he'-fer) - Winepress of the well. Digging. Winepress. To dig a winepress.

Gittaim (ghit-ta'-im) - Two winepresses. A winepress.

Gittites (ghit'-tites) - Inhabitants of Gath. Winepress.

Gittith (ghit'-tith) - Same as Gath. Winepress.

Gizonite (ghi'-zo-nite) - Stone quarrier. Shaving. Quarry. Pass. Ford.

Goath (go'-ath) - Fatigue. His touching. His roaring. Lowing.

Gob (gob) - Pit. Snare. The back. Cistern. Grasshopper. A deep hole.

God (god) - God. The supreme being. Good. Elohim. Jehovah. (See chapter on all revealed names of God).

Gog (gog) - Extension. A roof. A mountain. Covering. Golden ornament.

Golan (go'-lan) - Great exodus. Exile. Their captivity. Their rejoicing. Passage. Captive. Revolution. Great emigration. Circle.

Golgotha (gol'go-tha) - Place of the skull. A heap of skulls. Something skull shaped.

Goliath (go-li'-ath) - Exile. The exile. Soothsayer. Taken captive. Stripped as a captive. Passage. Revolution. Heap. Great. Thick. Fat.

Gomer (go'-mer) - Complete. Completion. Heat. Perfect. Conclusion i.e., filling up of. The measure of idolatry or ripeness of consummate wickedness. To finish. Perfection. Consuming.

Gomorrah (go-mor'-rah) - People of fear. Fear of the people. A rebellious people. Depression. Bondage. Submersion. Abundance of water. A ruined heap.

Gomorrha (go-mor'-rah) - Same as Gomorrah. People of fear. Fear of the people. Depression. Bondage. Submersion. Abundance of water. A ruined heap. A rebellious people.

Gopher (go'-pher) - Covered. Pitch - wood.

Goshen (go'-shen) - The place or temple of the sun. Approaching. Drawing near. Rain. Coat of maul. Mound of earth.

Gozan (go'-zan) - Cut through. A fleece. Pasture. Who nourisheth the body. Quarry. Great by cutting.

Grecia (gre'-sha) - A defrauder. Unstable. The miry one. Tender. Soft. Effervescing. This is a Hebrew definition.

Grecians (gre'-shuns) - Same as Greeks. Unstable. The miry one. Soft. Effervescing. A Greek speaking person. Supple. Clay. He that deceives. A defrauder. Tender.

Greece #1 (gres) - (Hebrew definition) Same as Grecia. A defrauder. Hot and active. Effervescing.

Greece #2 (gres) - (Greek definition) Unstable. The miry one. A stranger.

Greeks (greks) - Same as Greece. Unstable. The miry one. A stranger. Non-Jewish.

Gudgodah (gud-go'-dah) - Cavern of thunder. The slashing place. Cleft. Incision. Well of much. Water. Same as Horhagidgad.

Guni (gu'-ni) - My garden. Protected. Painted with colors. A garden. A covering. Colored. Dyed. Resemblance.

Gunites (gu'-nites) - Descendants of Guni. My garden. Protected. Painted with colors. A garden. A covering. Dyed. Resemblance.

Gur (gur) - Same as Gerar. Sojourning. Journeying. A lodging place. The young of a beast. A whelp. A cub still abiding in the lair. A place of abode. Lion's cub.

Gur-baal (gur-ba'-al) -Sojourning of Baal. The governor's whelp. A whelp of Baal. Abode of Baal. Dwelling place of Baal.

H

Haahashtari (ha-a-hash'-te-ri) - Muleteer. A runner. Messenger. Courier. One who runs. The messenger.

Habaiah (hab-ah'-yah) - Hidden of the Lord. The hiding of the Lord. Whom Jehovah protects. The Lord covered or protected. Jehovah has hidden.

Habakkuk (hab'-ak-kuk) - Embracing as a token of love. Ardently embraced. He that embraces. A wrestler. Embrace. Continually embracing. Embraced by God.

Habaziniah (hab-az-in-i'-ah) - Light of Jehovah. The hiding of Jah's thorn. A hiding of the shield of the Lord. Lamp of Jehovah. God's light. God covered with a shield.

Habor (ha'-bor) - Uniting together. A partaker. A companion. Joining together. United. Who is associated.

Hacerem (hak'-se-rem) - The vineyard. The vine.

Hachaliah (hak-a-li'-ah) - Dark flashing of the Lord. The waiting on Jah. Who waits for the Lord. Hoping in God. Whose eyes Jehovah enlivens. Jehovah is hidden. Darkness of Jehovah.

Hachilah (hak'-i-lah) - Dark. Dusky. Gloomy. My hope is in her. Obscurity. Darksome.

Hachmoni (hak'-mo-ni) - Very wise. Skillful. Wise. A wise man. Skilled.

Hachmonite (hak'-mo-nite) - Very wise. Skillful. Wise. A wiseman. Skilled. Same as Hachmoni.

Hadad (ha'-dad) - Chief. Most eminent. Most high. Sharpness. Joy. Noise. Clamor. Fierce. Powerful. Mighty. Thunderer.

Hadadrimmon (ha'-dad-rim'-mon) - (Hadad - chief. Most eminent. Most high. Rimmon - a pomegranate. Very high). Bursting of the pomegranate. Great shouting. Rending of the pomegranate. To rise. Exalt. Invocation to the God.

Hadadezer (had-a-de'-zer) - Whose help is Hadad. Mighty is the help. Hadar is a help. Beauty of assistance. Adad his help. Hadad is my help.

Hadah (had'-dah) - Sharpness. Swiftness. Joy. See Enhaddah.

Haddon (had'-don) - See Esarhaddon.

Hadar (ha'-dar) - Ornament. Honor. Privy chamber. Power. Greatness. Fierce. Revered. Honored. Esteemed. Magnificence.

Hadarezer (had-a-re'-zer) - Majesty of help. Whose help is Hadad. Honor of the helper. The assistance of Hadad. Hadad is my help.

Hadashah (had'-a-shah) - New. Renewal. News. A month. New city.

Hadassah (ha-das'-sah) - Myrtle. Joy. Hebrew name of Esther.

Hadattah (ha-dat'-tah) - Newness. Sharpness. New Hazor.

Hades (ha'-des) - Hell. The New Testament name for the Hebrew word Sheol.

Hadid (ha'-did) - Sharp. Painted. Peak. Rejoicing.

Hadlai (had'-la-i) - Forsaken of the Lord. Frail. Lax. Resting. Loitering. Hindering. Idle. Fat.

Hadoram (ha-do'-ram) - Noble generation or race: Their glory. Hadar is high. Their beauty. Their power. Distinguished honor. Exalted. Power. Hadad is exalted.

Hadrach (ha'-drak) - Spherical. Point. Joy of tenderness. Periodical return. Roundness. Periodical return of the sun.

Hagab (ha'-gab) - Grasshopper. A locust. Bent. A stranger. One that fears.

Hagaba (hag-a-bah) - Grasshopper. Leaper. A locust. A stranger. One that fears.

Hagabah (hag'-a-bah) - Same as Hagaba. Grasshopper. Leaper. A locust. A stranger. One that fears.

Hagar (ha'-gar) - Flight. Fugitive. Immigrant. The sojourner. Ensnaring. A stranger. One that fears. Mid-day. Same as Agar.

Hagarenes (hag-a-renes) - Fugitives. Sojourners. Ensnaring. Descendants for Hagar.

Hagarites (hag'-a-rites) - Same as Hagarenes. Fugitives. Sojourners. Ensnaring. Descendants of Hagar.

Haggai (hag'-ga-i) - Festival of the Lord. Festal. Born of a festival day. My solemn feast. Feast. Solemnity. Festive. Joy of the Lord.

Haggeri (hag'-gher-i) - Wanderer. Same as Hagarenes. Fugitives. Sojourners. Ensnaring. Descendent of Hagar. The Lord's feast.

Haggi (hag'-ghi) - Exultation of the Lord. Festive. Born of a festival. My feast. Very great joy. Born on a feast day. The Lord's feast.

Haggiah (hag-ghi'-ah) - Exultation. Festival of Jehovah. Feast of Jehovah. The Lord's feast. Joy of the Lord. Festival of Jah.

Haggites (hag'-ghites) - Same as Haggi. Exaltation of the Lord. Festive. Born of a festival. My feast. Very great joy. Born on a feast day. The Lord's feast.

Haggith (hag'-ghith) - Same as Haggi. Exaltation of the Lord. Festive. Born of a festival. Festival of the Lord. Festival. Dancer. A solemnity. Rejoicing. Joy. A dancer.

Hai (ha'-i) - Same as Ai. A heap of ruins. A ruin. A heap. As it overturned. Crookedness.

Hakkatan (hak'-ka-tan) - Little. Smallness. The younger. The little one. Little or junior. Small.

Hakkoz (hak'-koz) - Same as Coz. Thorn. Nimble. The thorn of the nimble. A thorn. Summer. An end. The thorn.

Hakupha (ha-ku'-fah) - Bent. Curved. Incitement. Decree on the month. Embracing.

Halah (ha'-lah) - Old age. Completion. Painful. Fresh anguish. A moist table. Signification unknown. Moist surface.

Halhul (hal'-hul) - Trepidation. Trembling. Grief. Looking for grief. Full of hollows. Fear. Contorted.

Hali (ha'-li) - Necklace. Ornament. Jewel. Sickness. A beginning. A precious stone. A trinket as polished. A necklace.

Hallelujah (hal-le-loo'-i-yah) - Praise ye the Lord.

Hallohesh (hal-lo'-hesh) - The whisperer. Enchanter. The charmer. Saying nothing.   A mutterer.

Halohest (hal-lo'-hest) - Same as Hallohesh. The whisperer. Enchanter. The charmer. Saying nothing. A mutterer.

Ham (ham) - Heat. Hot. Warm. Black. Dark. Brown. Swarthy. Crafty.

Haman (ha'-man) - Alone. Solitary. Well disposed. A rioter. The ragger. Their tumult. Celebrated. Magnificent. Noise. Tumult. Unique. Splendid. Troubling.

Hamath (ha'-math) - Defense. Citadel. Fortress. Furious. Enclosure of wrath. Warm. Hot springs. Anger. Heat. A wall. A garrison.

Hamathite (ham'-a-thite) - Same as Hamath. Defense. Citadel. Fortress. Furious. Warm. Enclosure of wrath. Hot springs. Anger. Heat. A wall. A garrison.

Hamath-zobah (ha'-math-zo'-bah) - Fortress of Zobah. Same as Hamath. The heat. A fortification. Pressing down. Warning.

Hammath (ham'-math) - Warm baths. Warm springs. Hot place. Hot springs. A bath.

Hammedatha (ham-med'-a-thah) - He that troubles the law. Double. A twin. Measure. Given by the god. Given by the moon.

Hammelech (ham'-me-lek) - The king. A king. A counselor.

Hammoleketh (ham-mol'-e-keth) - The queen or regent. She who reigns.

Hammon (ham'-mon) - Hot. Great hot baths. Heat. The sun: Hot or sunny. Hot spring. Warm springs. A great bath.

Hammoth-dor (ham'-moth-dor') - Same as Hamath. Defense. Citadel. Fortress. Warm springs of Dor. Hot places of the dwelling or generation. Warm springs dwelling. Baths.

Hamonab (ham'-o-nab) - Multitude. His multitude. His uproar. A great multitude.

Hamon-gog (ha'-mon-gog') - Multitude of Gog. A crowd upon the roof. Foster child. Extension. Gog's multitude.

Hamor (ha'-mor) - Ass. An ass. Clay. Dirt. A he ass. Wine. Donkey.

Hamoth (ha'-moth) - Indignation.

Hamuel (ham-u'-el) - Heat or wrath of God. God is a sun. Warmth of God. They were heated of God. The pity of God. The wrath of God. God protects.

Hamul (ha'-mul) - Who has been favored. Who has experienced mercy. Pitied. Pity. Godly. Merciful. Spared. He who has been spared or pitied. Spared by God.

Hamulites (ha'-mu-lites) - Descendants of Hamul. Who has been favored. Who has experienced mercy. Pitied. Pity. Godly. Merciful. Spared. He who has been spared or pitied. Spared by God.

Hamutal (ha'-mu'-tal) - Akin to the dew. Refreshing like dew. Kinsman of the dew. Father-in-law of dew. The shadow of his heat. Father-in-law is protection.

Hanameel (ha-nam'-e-el) - Gift of God. The grace of God. God has pitied. Place of God's favor. The grace that comes from God. God has given. God is a rock or safety. God is merciful. God is gracious.

Hanan (ha'-nan) - Compassionate. Merciful. Gracious. A gracious giver. Full of grace. Favored. He gave gratuitously.

Hananeel (ha-nan'-e-el) - Graciously given of God. Whom God graciously gave. God was gracious. God is gracious. The mercy of God. Grace. God has favored. God has bestowed gratuitously. God is merciful.

Hanani (ha-na'-ni) - Graciously given of the Lord. Gracious to me. Gracious. The mercy of God. My grace. My mercy. He has graciously given me. Gracious gift of the Lord.

Hananiah (han-a-ni'-ah) - Jehovah is gracious. Gift of the Lord. Graciously given of the Lord. Grace. Mercy. The Lord has graciously given. Jehovah's goodness.

Hanes (ha'-nees) - Grace has fled. To bring down. To lead down. Banishment of grace. Mercury.

Haniel (ha'-ne-el) - Favor of God. Grace of God. The gift of God.

Hannah (han'-nah) - Gratuitous gift. Grace. Mercy. Gracious. Graciousness. Favor. Bestowed. She was gracious. He that gives. Free gift. Prayer.

Hannathon (han'-na-thon) - Extraordinary free gift. Graciously regarded. The gift of grace. Favored. Precious gift. Dedicated to grace.

Hanniel (han'-ne-el) - Same as Haniel. Favor of God. Grace of God. The grace or mercy of God. Favor.

Hanoch (ha'-nok) - Same as Enoch. Dedicated. Initiated. Initiating. Experienced.

Hanochites (ha'-nok-ites) - Descendants of Enoch. Initiated. Dedicated. Initiating. Experienced.

Hanun (ha'-nun) - Giving for naught. Enjoying favor. Gracious. He that rests. Whom God pities. Merciful. Favored. Given freely. Graciously given.

Haphraim (haf-ra'-im) - Two wells. Two pits. Double digging. Searching. Digging. Double pit. Double wells.

Happizzez (hap-piz'-zez) - Scattering. The dispersion.

Hara (ha'-rah) - Mountainous. A hill. Showing forth. Mountain. Hill country. A mountain. Mountainous land. Mountains.

Haradah (har'-a-dah) - Fear of a host. Well of great fear. Place of terror. Great fear. Anxiety. Trembling. Fear.

Haran #1 (ha'-ran) - Mountaineer. Very high. Enlightened. Strong (generally refers to a man). Mountainous. Country. Very noble. Hilly. Parched.

Haran #2 (ha'-ran) - Very dry. Place parched with the sun. Grievous (generally refers to a place). Parched. Dry.

Hararite (har'-a-rite) - Same as Haran. Mountaineer. Very high. Enlightened. Strong.

Harbona (har-bo'-nah) - Warlike. Martial. A destroyer. Ass driver. The anger of him who builds. Very warlike. Donkey driver.

Harbonah (har-bo'-nah) - Same as Harbona. Warlike. Martial. Very warlike. His sword. Ass driver. His destruction. Donkey driver.

Hareph (ha'-ref) - Maturity i.e., the flower of life. Plucking. Plucking off. Early born. Reproachful. Winter. Reproach. To expose by stripping. Autumn.

Hareth (ha'-reth) - A cutting. Thicket. Forest.

Harhaiah (har-ha-i'-ah) - Anger of the Lord. Jehovah is protecting. Dried up.

Kindled of Jah. Jah is protecting. Jah is kindled with anger. Fearing Jah. Heat.

Harhas (har'-has) - Glitter. Splendor. He burned. He pitied. Anger. Heat of confidence. Complete poverty. Shining. Glittering.

Harhur (har'-hur) - Extreme burning. Inflammation. Nobility. Distinction. Made warm. The greatest heat.

Harim (ha'-rim) - Snub nosed. Flat nosed. Bent upwards. Consecrated. Destroyed. Dedicated to God. Compassion.

Hariph (ha'-rif) - Early born. Autumnal rain or showers. Strong. One early born. Autumn.

Harnepher (har-ne'-fur) - Panting. The frustrater. Burnt. The anger of a bull. Increasing heat. Making a noise. Snorting or panting. Horus is merciful.

Harod (ha'-rod) - Trembling. Fear. Terror. Astonishment. Fountain of trembling.

Harodite (ha'-ro-dite) - Inhabitants of Harod. Fear. Terror. Trembling.

Haroeh (ha-ro'-eh) - Seeing. Seer. Vision. The seer. Prophet. He looked upon.

Harorite (ha'ro-rite) - Same as Hararite. Mountaineer. Very high. Enlightened.

Harosheth (har'-o-sheth) - Manufactory. Carving i.e., cutting, carving and working in stones, wood or iron. A plowed field. A forest. Agriculture. Workmanship. Deafness. Silence. City of crafts. Handicraft. Mechanical work.

Harosheth Hagoyim (ha'ro-sheth-hag'-o-yim) - Forest of the Gentiles.

Harsha (har'-shah) - Enchanter. Magician. Artifice. Deviser. Secret work. A wood. Workmanship. Worker. Hidden. Silent.

Harum (ha'-rum) - High i.e., illustrious, exalted, elevated. High. Throwing down from a height.

Harumaph (ha-ru'-maf) - Flat nose. Flat nosed. Destruction. Slit nosed. Snub nosed. Mutilated nose.

Haruphite (ha'-ru-fite) - Matured. Slender. Sharp. Descendants of Horuph or Hariph.

Haruz (ha'-ruz) - Sharpened. Decided. Industrious. Careful. Earnest. Sharp. Valley of decision. Eager. Active. Cutting off. Gold.

Hasadiah (has-a-di'-ah) - Love of the Lord. Whom Jehovah loves. Jehovah is kind. Jehovah has shown kindness. The mercy of the Lord. Jehovah loves. He was merciful. Jehovah is faithful.

Hasenuah (has-e-nu'-ah) - Light. She that is hated. The violated. The thorny. Pointed. Bristling.

Hashabiah (hash-a-bi'-ah) - Esteemed of the Lord. Whom Jehovah esteems. Jehovah is associated. Jehovah has devised. The estimation of the Lord. God has bound. Jehovah regards. Jehovah has taken account.

Hashabnah (hash-ab'-nah) - Jehovah is friend. Same as Hashabiah. Named. A putting to. Jah is friend. God built inventiveness. Jehovah has considered.

Hashabniah (hash-ab'-ni'-ah) - Jehovah is friend. Named. A putting to. God built. Silence of God. Jehovah has considered. Same as Hashabiah.

Hashbadana (hash-bad'-a-nah) - Reason. Thought in judging. Wise judge. Thought. He hasted in the judgment. Considerate in the judgment. Wise judgment. Choice linen girdle. Thoughtful judge. Judge.

Hashem (ha'-shem) - Astonished. Shining. Dull. Sleepy. To make desolate. Named. A putting to. Lay waste. Putting to wealthy. Fat.

Hashmonah (hash-mo'-nah) - Very fat. Fatness. Fat soil. He hastened the numbering. Great fatness. Fertile. Fruitfulness.

Hashub (ha'-shub) - Much esteemed. Thoughtful. Associated. Esteemed. Numbered. Intelligent. Informed. Thinking. Considerate.

Hashubah (hash-u'-bah) - Highly esteemed. Esteemed. Association. Consideration. Estimation. Thought. Jehovah has considered. Binding.

Hashum (ha'-shum) - Great. Wealth. Rich. Shining. The desolate hasted. Silence. Their hasting. Distinguished. Great silence. Opulent. Enriched. Broad-nosed.

Hashupha (hash-u'-fah) - Exhaustion. Made bare. Nakedness. Stripped. Spent. Made base. Naked. Uncovered.

Hasrah (has'-rah) - Extremely poor. Extreme poverty. Wanting. Glittering. Splendor. Poverty. Want.

Hassenaah (has-se-na'-ah) - Elevated (idea of lifting up). Thorny. Thornhedge. Pointed.

Hassenuah (has-se-nu'-ah) - Thorny. Hated.

Hasshub (hash'-ub) - Same as Hashub. Much esteemed. Thoughtful. Associated. Intelligent. Thinking. Considerate.

Hasupha (has-u'-fah) - Same as Hashupa. Exhaustion. Made bare.

Nakedness. Swift. Spent. Made base. Naked. Uncovered.

Hatach (ha'-tak) - Gift. A gift. Why will you smite? He that strikes. Verity. Good.

Hathath (ha'-thath) - Terror. Casting down. Bruised. Fear. Dismay.

Hatipha (hat'-if'-ah) - Seized. Captivated. Captive. Robber. Injury. Robbery. Taken.

Hatita (hat'-it-ah) - Exploring. Digging. My sin removed. A bending of sin. Exploration. Joining. Binding of sin.

Hattil (hat'-til) - Inquietude. Wavering. Decaying. Vacillating. Sin cast out. Howling for sin. Uneasiness. Fluctuating. Talkative. Waving. Shaking.

Hattush (hat'-tush) - Assembled. Gathered together. Contender. Sin was hated. Forsaking sin. Extension. Enlargement.

Hauran (hau'-ran) - Very white. Whiteness. A hole. Liberty. Caves. Cavernous. Black land.

Havilah (hav'-il-ah) - Bringing forth. Trembling with pain. Circle. To declare to her. That suffers pain. Circular. Trouble. Pain. District.

Havoth-jair (ha'-voth-ja'-ir) - Villages of the enlightener. Living places. Producers. The villages that enlighten. Huts or hamlets. Hamlets of Jair.

Hazael (ha'-za-el) - He who sees God. Whom God watches over. God sees. God has seen. That sees God. God beheld or has seen. God cares for. Vision of God.

Hazaiah (ha-za-i'-ah) - Seen of the Lord. Whom Jehovah watches over. Jehovah has seen. Jehovah is seeing.

Seeing the Lord. God beheld. Jah has seen. Jehovah sees.

Hazar (ha'-zar) - An enclosure.

Hazar-addar (ha'zar-ad'-dar) - Village of greatness. Enclosures of glory. An imprisoned generation.

Hazar-enan (ha'-zar-e'-nan) - Village of fountains. Enclosure of their fountains. Imprisoned village of the great fountain. Village of springs. Cloud.

Hazar-gaddah (ha'-zar-gad'-dah) - Village of fortune or luck. Enclosure of conflict. Enclosure of fortune. Imprisoned band. The village of the multitude. Village of Gad.

Hazar-hatticon (ha'-zar-hat'-ti-con) - The middle village. The middle enclosure. Preparation.

Hazar-maveth (ha'-zar- ma'-veth) - The court of death. Death town. The enclosure of death. Dwelling of death. Village of death. Death was near.

Hazar-shual (ha'-zar-shoo'-al) - Village of the fox or jackal. Enclosure of the jackal. A wolf's house. Village of jackals. Village of the wolf.

Hazar-susah (ha'zar-soo'-ah) - Village of the houses. More enclosure. A wolf's house. Village of horses. Village of the horse or Calvary.

Hazar-susim (ha'-zar-soo'-sim) - Village of the houses. Enclosure of the horses. A wolf's house. Village of horses. Court of the horses. Villages of the horses. Same as Hazarsusah.

Hazazon-tamar (haz'-a-zon-ta'-mar) - Pruning of the palm. Drawing near to bitterness. The palm tree.

Hazelelponi (haz-el-el-po'-ni) - The shadow looking upon me. The shade turns toward me. Sorrow of

countenance. Shade of the face. Deliverance of God looking on me. Give shade.

Hazerim (haz'-e-rim) - Villages. Country village. Inclosures. Courts. Palaces.

Hazeroth (haz'-e-roth) - Same as Hazerim. Villages. Enclosures. Palaces. Yards.

Hazezon-tamar (haz'-a-zon-ta'mar) - Same as Hazazon-tamar. Pruning of the palm. Copious cutting of the palm tree. Drawing near to bitterness.

Haziel (ha'-ze-el) - The vision of God. God is seeing.

Hazo (ha'-zo) - Vision. Seer. Village. Seeing. Prophesying. Visionary. Sight.

Hazor (haz'-or) - Fence. Castle. A court. To trumpet. Enclosure. Village enclosure. Inclosed. Hay.

Hazor-hadattah (ha'-zor'-ha-dat'-tah) - New castle. Enclosure of rejoicing. New enclosure. New village.

Heber (he'-bur) - Fellowship. A companion. Production. One that passes. A company. Enchantment. Alliance. Anger. Associate. Passenger. Community.

Heberites (he'-bur-ites) - Same as Heber. Fellowship. A companion. Production. One that passes. Descendants of Heber.

Hebrew (he'-broo) - He who passed over. From the other side. Passes over. Further bank of the river. On the other side.

Hebrewess (he'-broo-ess) - One who passes over. A Jewess. A Jewish woman who is a believer.

Hebrews (he'-broos) - Passing beyond. A region across. He who passed over. From the other side.

Passes over. Further bank of a river. On the other side.

Hebron (he'-brun) - Confederation. Conjunction. Alliance. Associating. Joining together. Union. Company. Society. Friendship. Sure alliance.

Hebronites (he'-brun-ites) - Same as Hebron. Confederation. Conjunction. Alliance. Associating. Joining together. Union. Company. Society. Friendship. Sure alliance. Descendants of Hebron.

Hegai (he'-gahee) - Venerable. A speaker. My meditations. A eunuch. Their army. Their trouble. Thorn. Briar. Grooming.

Hege (he'-ghe) - Same as Hegai. Venerable. A speaker. Meditation. A eunuch. Their army. Their trouble. Thorn. Briar. Grooming.

Helah (he'-lah) - Scum. Sick. Rust. Disease. Necklace.

Helam (he'-lam) - An army. Their strength. Stronghold. Place of abundance. Their army. Their trouble. A great army. Fortress. Dreams.

Helbah (hel'-bah) - Fatness i.e., fertile. Fertile region. Part. Portion. Fatness. Fertility.

Helbon (hel'-bon) - Fat i.e., fertile. The fat one. Part. Portion. Fruitful. Very fat. Milk.

Heldai (hel'-dahee) - Life. Age. My endurance. Enduring. Durable. My time. Part. Portion. Worldliness. Worldly. Thick. Fleshy. Enduring. Long-lived.

Heleb (he'-leb) - Fat i.e., fertile. Fatness. Endurance. Part. Portion.

Heled (he'-led) - Life. Duration. Enduring. Durable. The age. Portion of time. Brawny. Fleshy. The world as transient. Worldly.

Helek (he'-lek) - Portion. Smoothness. A portion or part. Part. Possession.

Helekites (he'-lek-ites) - Same as Helek. Portion. Smoothness. A portion or part. Possession.

Helem (he'-lem) - One who hammers. Hammer. Dream. Dreaming. Healing. Battering. Bruising. Strength. Robust. Manly. Vigor.

Heleph (he'-lef) - Exchange. Change. Changing. Passing over. Place of rushes.

Helez (he'-lez) - Liberation. Strength. Alertness. Stripped as for battle. Armed. Set free. Delivered. God has saved.

Heli (he'-li) - Elevation. Ascending. Greek form of the Hebrew name Eli. Climbing up. Lofty. High. God is high.

Helkai (hel-kahee) - Portion of the Lord. Jehovah is a portion. Apportioned. Part. Portion. The Lord's portion. Jehovah is my portion.

Helkath (hel-kath) - Portion. Smoothness. A field. Dividing.

Helkath-hazzurim (hel-kath-haz'-zu-rim) - Field of swords. The portion of the rocks. Possession of the besieger. Smoothness of the rocks. The field of strong men. Field of sharp swords. Barrenness of rocks.

Helon (he'-lon) - Very strong. Strong. Window. Grief. Very persevering or brave. Strength.

Hell (hell) - Hades. The New Testament name for the Hebrew word Sheol. Gehenna - the valley of Gehenna.

Hemam (he'-mam) - Destruction. To destroy. The south. Exterminating. Commotion. Raging.

Heman (he-man) - Faithful. Raging. Right-handed. Their trouble. Tumult. Much. In great number. Great multitude.

Hemath (he'-math) - Warmth. Furious. A garrison. A wall.

Hemdan (hem-dan) - Desire. Desirable. Delight. Pleasant. Very red.

Hen (hen) - Gracious gift. Grace. Favor. Quiet. Rest. Free gift.

Hena (he'-nah) - Depression. Low land. The shaken. Troubling. Low ground.

Henadad (hen'-a-dad) - The favor of Hadad. Hadad is gracious. Grace of the beloved. He showed favor.

Henoch (he'-nok) - Initiated. Initiating. Dedicated. Experienced. Same as Enoch. Consecrated. Disciplined.

Hepher (he'-fer) - Well. Pit. Digging. A digger. Digging of the well.

Hepherites (he'-fer-ites) - Well. Pit. Digging. Descendants of Hepher.

Hephzibah (hef'-zi-bah) - My delight is in her. In whom is my delight.

Heres (he'-res) - Sun. The son. An earthen pot. Mountain of the sun. Peak. A magician. Shining.

Heresh (he'-resh) - Silence. Artificer. Work. A carpenter. Tillage. To scratch. Engrave. Silent.

Hereth (he'-reth) - Thicket.

Hermas (her'-mas) - Interpreter. Mercury i.e., herald or messenger of the gods. Sand bank. Begotten of Mercury.

Hermes (her'-mees) - Gain. Bringer of good luck. Teacher for gain. Begotten of Mercury. Mercury. Refuge.

Hermogenes (her-moj'-e-nees) - Begotten of Mercury. Generation of lucre. Born lucky. Born of Hermes.

Hermon (her'-mon) - Devoted. A prominent summit of a mountain. Anathema. Devoted to destruction. The peak. A sure fortress. A rugged mountain. Abrupt. Sacred mountain.

Hermonites (her'-mon-ites) - Same as Hermon. Devoted. A prominent summit of a mountain. Anathema. Devoted to destruction. The peak. A sure fortress. A rugged mountain. Abrupt. Sacred mountain.

Herod (her'-od) - Heroic. Son of the hero. The glory of the skin. Mount of pride.

Herodians (he-ro'-de-uns) - A political party active during the time of the Herodian dynasty of the sect of Herod.

Herodias (he-ro'-de-as) - Heroic. Feminine form of Herod. Daughter of a hero.

Herodian (he-ro'-de-un) - Conqueror of heroes. Valiant. Son of Juno. Imitation of heroes. Heroic.

Hesed (he'-sed) - Mercy. Kindness. Pity. Grace. Favor.

Heshbon (hesh'-bon) - Reason. Device. Counting. An account. Invention. Industry. Firm binding. Strong reason. Intelligence. Stronghold.

Heshmon (hesh'-mon) - Very fat. Fatness i.e., fruitful soil. Hasting the separation. A hasty messenger. Opulent. Fruitfulness.

Heshvan (hesh'-van) - Eighth Jewish month (October-November).

Heth (heth) - An annoyance. An annoyer. Dread. Fear. Terrible. Terror. Trembling. Great fear or dread.

Hethlon (heth'-lon) - Hidden place. A place wrapped up. Swaddled. A fearful dwelling. Hiding place. Wrapped up. Safe wrapping.

Hezeki (hez'-e-ki) - Strength or might of Jehovah. Jehovah is strength. My strong one. Strong.

Hezekiah (hez-e-ki'-ah) - The Lord my strength. The might of Jehovah. Strength of the Lord. A strong support is Jehovah. Strengthened of Jehovah. Jehovah is strength.

Hezion (he'-zi-on) - Vision. Gracious sight.

Hezir (he'-zur) - Returning home. A swine. An entry or vestibule. Insight. Intuition. Protected.

Hezrai (hez-rahee) - Bulwark of the Lord. Enclosed wall. Enclosed. Beautiful. Walled in. An entry or vestibule. Inclosed.

Hezro (hez'-ro) - Bulwark of the Lord. Enclosed wall. Enclosed. Beautiful. Enclosures. Inclosure.

Hezron (hez-ron) - Enclosed. Surrounded by a wall. Shut in. Blooming. Dart of joy. His court. The division of the song. The dart of joy. A place securely trenched. Courtyard. Enclosure. Walled.

Hezronites (hez'-ron-ites) - Descendants of Hezron. Enclosed. Surrounded by a wall. Shut in. Blooming. Dart of joy. His court. The division of the song. The dart of joy. A place securely trenched. Courtyard. Enclosure. Walled.

Hiddai (hid'-dahee) - Echo of the Lord. The rejoicing of Jehovah. Joyful. Mighty. My noises. My echoes. A praise. A cry. Goodness of God. Chief.

Hiddekel (hid'-de-kel) - The rapid swift. The rapid Tigris. Riddle of the date palm. Riddle of lightness. Sharp voice. Sound. Quick flowing. An influx. To spread. To crown.

Hiel (hi'-el) - God lives. The life of God. Life from God. God is animation. God is living.

Hierapolis (hi-e-rap'-o'-lis) - Sacred city. Temple city. Holy City. A holy city. Priestly.

Higgaion (hig-gah'-yon) - Meditation. To murmur. To meditate. Reflection. Consideration. Murmur or gentle sound.

Hilen (hi'len) - Sandy. Pain them. Fortress. A window. Grief. The abode of tarrying. Place of caves. Strong place.

Hilkiah (hil-ki'-ah) - Portion of the Lord. The Lord my portion. Jehovah is protection. Portion of Jehovah. God is my portion.

Hillel (hil'-lel) - Praise of God. Praised greatly. To make bright. Clear. To make mad. Foolish. Praising. He that praises. Praise. He has praised.

Hinnom (hin'-nom) - Lamentation. Gratis. Behold them. To make self-drowsy. Abundant. There they are. Their riches. Sorrow. Full of goodness.

Hirah (hi'-rah) - Nobility. Noble race. Destination. Paleness. Hollowness. Splendor. Liberty. Anger.

Hiram (hi'ram) - Consecration. Their paleness. Exalted in life. Most noble. High born. Exaltation of life. A destroyer. Height of life. My brother is exalted.

Hittite (hit'-tite) - An annoyance. An annoyer. Dread. Fear. One who is broken. Who fears. Terror. Patron. Broken asunder. Descendants of Heth.

Hittites (hit'-tites) - An annoyance. Broken asunder. An annoyer. Dread. Fear. One who is broken. Who fears. Terror. Patron. Descendants of Heth.

Hivites (hi'-vites) - A declarer. Pronouncer. Villagers. Showers of life. Lives. Life giving. A villager. Wicked. Wickedness. Peasants.

Hizkiah (hiz-ki'-ah) - Jehovah is strong. Same as Hezekiah. The Lord my strength. The might of Jehovah. Strength of the Lord. Strengthened of Jah. The strength of God. Jehovah is strength.

Hizkijah (hiz-ke'-jah) - Jehovah is strong. Same as Hezekiah. The Lord my strength. The might of Jehovah. Strength of the Lord. Strengthened of Jah. The strength of God. Jehovah is strength.

Hobab (ho'-bab) - Beloved. Most beloved. Lover. Favored. Cherished. Much beloved.

Hobah (ho'-bah) - Hiding place. Affectionate. Love. Friendship. Secrecy. A cave or hiding place.

Hod (hod) - Glory. Majesty. Splendor. Praise. Confession. Grandeur.

Hodaiah (ho-da-i'-ah) - Praise of the Lord. The splendor of Jehovah. Honored of Jehovah. Majesty of Jah. The glory of the Lord.

Hodaviah (ho-da-vi'-ah) - Praise of the Lord. Jehovah is his praise. A table. News. Praise of Jehovah. The glory of the Lord. Praise ye Jehovah. Give honor to Jehovah.

Hodesh (ho'-desh) - The new moon. Beautiful as the new moon. A month. A table. News. The beginning of the moon.

Hodevah (ho-de'-vah) - Jehovah is honor. Same as Hodeviah. Praise of the Lord. Jehovah is his praise. Majesty of Jah. A table. News.

Hodiah (ho-di'-ah) - Same as Hodaiah. Praise of the Lord. The splendor of Jehovah. Honored of Jehovah. A table. News.

Hodijah (ho-di'-jah) - Praise of the Lord. The splendor of Jehovah. Honored of Jehovah. Majesty of Jehovah. Praise or glory of God.

Hoglah (hog'-lah) - Partridge. The feast has languished. His festival or dance.

Hoham (ho'-ham) - A multitude of a multitude. A great multitude. Jehovah protects the multitude. He crushed. Whom Jehovah incites. Woe to them. Jehovah impels. Multitude of multitudes.

Holon (ho'-lon) - Sandy. Anguished. A window. Grief. Abode of continuance. Place of caves. Round or whirling.

Homam (ho'-mam) - Destruction. Raging. Destroyer. Strong. Making an uproar.   A crowd.

Hophni (hof-ni) - Boxer. A pugilist. A little fist. A handful. Strong. He that covers my fist. A fighter.

Hophra (hof'-rah) - Priest of the sun. To cover evil. The heart of Ra endures.

Hor (hor) - Mountain. Who conceives. Elevated. Who shows. Hill.

Horam (ho'-ram) - High spirited. Elevated. Lofty. Their progenitor. Their hill. Very elevated. Height. High.
Horeb (ho'-reb) - Arid. Desert. Desolation. Solitude. Destruction. Parched. Desolate. Waste.
Horem (ho'-rem) - Devoted. Banned: an offering dedicated to God. Sacred. Dedication.
Horesh (ho'-resh) - Forest.
Horhagidgad (hor'-hag'-id'-gad) - A mount of Galgad. Cavern of thunder. The slashing hole. The hill of felicity. Hole of the cleft. Cave. Well of much water. Cleft mountain.
Hori (ho'-ri) - Cave dweller. A caveman. Free. Noble. A prince. Freeborn. Chief.
Horims (ho'-rims) - Descendants of Hori. Cave dweller. A caveman. Free. Noble. A prince. Freeborn. Chief. Princes. Being angry.
Horites (ho'-rites) - Same as Hori. Cave dwellers. A caveman. Free. Noble. A prince. Freeborn. Chief.
Hormah (hor'-mah) - Anathema. Devoted to destruction. A devoting. A place laid waste. Excommunication. Utter destruction. Devoted or consecrated to God. A curse. Complete destruction.
Horonaim (hor-o-na'-im) - Grievous. Vexatious. Two caverns. Double caves. Double cave town. Angers. Ragings. Great caves. Two caves.
Horonite (ho'-ron-ite) - Grievous. Vexatious. Two caverns. Men of anger. Same as Horonaim. Double cave town. Great caves. Angers. Ragings. Indignation. Anger.

Hosah (ho'-sah) - A place of refuge. Fleeing for refuge. Fleeing to Jehovah for refuge. Hopeful. Trusting. Refuge.
Hosanna (ho-zan'-nah) - Greek - Save us we pray. Hebrew - God make it rain. Save I pray thee. Keep. Preserve.
Hosea (hose'-ah) - Jehovah is help or salvation. Salvation. Causing to save. Deliverer. The salvation of the Lord. He has liberated.
Hoshaiah (ho-sha-i'-ah) - Whom Jehovah has set free. Set free of the Lord. God has saved. Saved of Jah. Jehovah has saved. The salvation of the Lord. Jah has saved.
Hoshama (ho-sha'-mah) - The Lord has heard i.e., his parents' prayers. Jehovah has heard. Whom Jehovah hears. Heard. He obeys. The Lord heard.
Hoshea (ho'-she'-ah) - Jehovah is help or salvation. Salvation. Causing to save. God is help. The salvation of the Lord. He has saved. Deliverance. Same as Hosea.
Hotham (ho'-tham) - Signet ring. Determination. A seal.
Hothan (ho'-than) - Same as Hotham. Signet ring. Determination. A seal.
Hothir (ho'-thur) - Abundance. A surplus. Preserver. Excelling. Remaining. He kept surviving. He has caused to remain.
Hozai (ho'-za-i) - Jehovah is seeing.
Hukkok (huk'-koh) - Appointed portion. Decreed. Engraver. Scribe. Lawyer. Appointed. What is cut in. Ditch.
Hukok (hu'-kok) - Same as Hukkok. Appointed portion. Decreed. Engraver. Scribe. Lawyer. Appointed. What is cut in. A ditch. Hewn.

Hul (hul) - Writhing. Trembling. Circle. Pain. Infirmity. Fear. Sorrow. Childbirth.

Huldah (hul'-dah) - Weasel i.e., from its quickness getting into holes. Endurance. Perpetuity. The world. Circle of the world.

Humtah (hum'-tah) - A place of lizards. Fortress. Lizard. Snail. Bulwark.

Hupham (hu'-pham) - Inhabitants of the seashore. Protected. A covering. Coast man. Their bank. Their chamber. Complete covering. Protection. Coast inhabitants.

Huphamites (hu'-fam-ites) - Descendants of Hupham. Inhabitants of the seashore. Protected. A covering. Coast man. Their bank. Their chamber. Complete covering. Protection. Coast inhabitants.

Huppah (hup'-pah) - Nuptial bed. Covering. Protected. Protection. Chamber.

Huppim (hup'-pim) - Same as Hupham. Inhabitant of the seashore. Protected. A covering. Coast man. Their bank. Their chamber. Complete covering. Protection. Coast inhabitants. Seashore. A chamber. Covered.

Hur (hur) - Cavern. Noble. Splendor. White. A prison. Hole. Liberty. Whiteness. Free. Immaculateness.

Hurai (hu'-rahee) - Linen worker. Linen weaver. Noble. My caves. He was propitious.

Huram (hu'-ram) - Exalted in life. Most noble. Ingenious. Their whiteness. High born. Lofty brother. Their liberty. Their hole.

Huri (hu'-ri) - Linen worker. Linen weaver. Nobleman. My whiteness. Being angry. Weaver. Born of noble descent.

Hushah (hu'-shah) - Haste in being born. Passion. Hasting. Holding peace.

Hushai (hu'-shahee) - Hasting of the Lord. Hasting. Quick. Rapid. Their haste. Their silence. Their sensuality. Haste of the Lord.

Husham (hu'-sham) - Great haste i.e., a son born prematurely. Haste. Passion. Hostility. Quickest haste.

Hushathite (hu'shath-ite) - Inhabitants of Hushah. Haste. Counsel. Woods. Fastened. Hasting. Sensuality.

Hushim (hu'-shim) - Those who hasten their birth. Those who make haste. To hasten. Hasting. Opulent. Hasters. Counsel. Woods. Fastened. Hastily. Repeated haste.

Huz (huz) - Firm. Counselor. Trees. Counsel. Woods. Fastened. Consultation. Firmness.

Huzath (huz'-oth) - Streets. Populous.

Huzzab (huz'-zab) - It is decreed. He was established. To establish. Molten. Fixed or determined. Beautifully beaming.

Hymenaeus (hy-men-e'-us) - Nupital. Belonging to marriage. From Hymen the god of marriage. A wedding song. Marriage.

I

Ibhar (ib'-har) - Whom God elects. God does choose. Chosen. Chooser. He will choose. Choice. Jehovah chooses. Election. He that is chosen. He chose. Whom God chooses.

Ibleam (ib'-le-am) - Devouring the people. He destroys the people. Devouring people. Ancient people. People decreasing. He conquered the people. People devouring.

Ibneiah (ib-ne-i'-ah) - He will be built up of the Lord. Whom Jehovah will build up. Jehovah does build. Jah will build. Built by Jah. Passing over. Being angry. Being with young. God hears.

Ibnijah (ib-ni'-jah) - He will be built up of the Lord. Whom Jehovah will build up. Jehovah does build. Jehovah is builder. He will be built of Jah. Building of Jah. Jah is builder. God hears. Jehovah builds.

Ibri (ib'-ri) - Beyond at the river i.e., born beyond the river. Passes over. One who has crossed. A Hebrew. Being with young. Being angry. Beyond the river.

Ibzan (ib'-zan) - Great fatigue i.e., of the mother at birth. Active. Splendid. Their witness. Shining. Swift. Father of a target. Father of coldness. Toil. Suffering. Beautiful.

Ichabod (ik'-a-bod) - Inglorious. The glory is departed. The glory is not. Where is the glory? Woe. Where is honor? Without glory.

 Iconium (i-co'-ne-um) - Little image. Yielding. The comer. Coming. Breast of sheep. Image-like.

Idalah (id'-a-lah) - Place of execration. Snares. He will fly to her. Hand of imprecation. Exalted. Memorial to God. Memorial of God. The hand of slander. He extols. Sublime. What God exalts. Memorial.

Idbash (id'-bash) - He will be as agreeable as honey. Honeyed. Honey sweet. Corpulent. Hand of shame. Sweet. Flowing with honey. The land of destruction. He was as sweet as honey. A stout fat one.

Iddo #1 (id'-do) - Ezra 8:17 - Great calamity. Misfortune. Powerful. His bond. Power.

Iddo #2 (id'-do) - I Chron. 27:21 - Son of Zechariah and ruler of the half tribe of Manasseh. Love of Him i.e., the Lord affectionate. Festal. Favorite. His power. An ornament. Festa. Loving favorite.

Iddo #3 (id'-do) - II Chron. 9:29 - Time of Him i.e., the Lord. A prophet of God. Seasonable. His band. Praise. Timely.

Idumaeu (i-doo-me'-ah) - Same as Edom. Red. Earthy. Bloody. Land of the Edomites.

Idumea (i-doo-me'-ah) - Same as Edom. Red. Earthly. Bloody. Land of the Edomites.

Igal (i'-gal) - He will redeem i.e., God His people. Whom God will avenge. Deliverer. He will vindicate. Avenger. Jehovah redeems. Redeemed. Defiled. God will revenge. He redeems.

Igdaliah (ig'-da-li-ah) - Whom Jehovah shall make great. Great is Jehovah. Greatness of the Lord. Jehovah is great. God is magnified.

Igeal (ig'-e-al) - Same as Igal. He will redeem His people. Whom God will avenge. He will vindicate. Deliverer. Avenger. A redeemer. Redeemed. Defiled.

Iim (i'-im) - Ruinous heaps. Heaps. Ruins. Heaps of Hebrews.

Ije-abarim (i'-je-ab'-a-rim) - Ruinous heaps of Abarim. Heaps of the regions beyond or those who have crossed. Ruins. Heaps of Hebrews.

Ijon (i'-jon) - A great heap. Ruin. Look. Eye. Fountain.

Ikkesh (ik'-kesh) - Perverse. Deceitful. Subtle. Perverseness of mouth. Twisted. Forward. Wicked.

Ilai (i'-lahee) - Most high. Elevated. Supreme. The shade of the Lord.

Illyricum (il-lir'-ic-um) - The lyric band. Joy. Rejoicing. High.

Imla (im'-lah) - He will fill up. Whom God will fill up. God does fill. Fulfilling. Plentitude. Full. God fulfills. He fulfills.

Imlah (im'-lah) - Same as Imla - He will fill up. Whom God fills up. God does fulfill. Fulfilling. Full. Plentitude. God fulfills. He fulfills.

Immanuel (im-man'-u-el) - God with us.

Immer (im'-mur) - He promised i.e., of the Lord. Talkative. Prominent. Saying. Speaking. A lamb. Promise.

Imna (im'-nah) - He will retain. Whom God assigns. God does restrain. Holding back. Withdrawing: May he preserve. He hindered. He will restrain. Restrained. God does restrain.

Imnah (im'nah) - Prosperity. He allots. Success. Right-handed. The right side. He will number. Good fortune. God doth restrain. Restrained.

Imrah (im'-rah) - He will extol himself. Stubborn. Height of Jehovah. A rebel. Waxing bitter. Changing.

Imri (im'-ri) - Promised of the Lord. Eloquent. Projecting. My saying. Jehovah has promised. Eloquently. Speaking. Exalting. Bitter. A lamb. Word or promise. Wordy.

India (in'-de-ah) - Praise ye. Give ye thanks. Flee ye away. Praise. Law. He murmured in a whisper.

Iphedeiah (if-e-di'-ah) - The Lord will redeem him. Whom Jehovah frees. Jehovah does deliver. Redemption of the Lord. Jah will redeem. Jah will liberate. Jehovah redeems.

Ir (ur) - Citizen. Watcher. Flowing together. Watchful. Watchman. City. Vision. Donkey's colt.

Ira (i'-rah) - Watchful. Watcher. City watch. A crowd. A watchman. Watchfulness. Citizen. Making bare. Pouring out.

Irad (i'-rad) - City of witness. Wild ass. A descent to a valley. Ornament of a city. Fugitive. Heap of empire. Dragon. Wild donkey.

Iram (i'-ram) - Belonging to a city. Watchful. Their city. Congregation. City wise. A high heap. The effusion of them.

Iri (i'-ri) - Same as Ir. Citizen. Watcher. Jehovah is watcher. My city. A crowd. Urbane. Fire. Light. Donkey's colt.

Irijah (i-ri'-jah) - Whom Jehovah looks on. He will see the Lord. God does see. Fear of the Lord. My fear of the Lord. Fear thou Jah. Jah will see me. Reverence toward God. Protection of the Lord. The fear of the Lord. Jehovah sees.

Ir-nahash (ur-na'-hash) - City of serpents. Snake town. Serpent city. Magic city. City of the serpent.

Iron (i'-ron) - Reverence. Pious. Tearful. Great fear. Piety. Place of alarm. Place of terror.

Irpeel (ur'-pe-el) - God will restore. Which God heals. The health. Medicine or exalting of God. God will heal. God heals.

Irshemesh (ur-she'-mesh) - City of the sun. Sun town. A city of bondage.

Iru (i'-ru) - Same as Iram - Belonging to a city. Watch. They were awake. Awake ye. Citizen. Young donkey. Roused up. City wise.

Isaac (i'-za-ak) - Laughing. Laughter. He laughs. Laughing one. He laughed. Happiness. Pleasure. He will laugh in mockery.

Isaiah (i-za'-ak) - Salvation of the Lord. Jehovah is helper. Salvation is of the Lord. Save thou Jehovah. Rescue. Defend. Deliver. Preserve. Salvation. Salvation of Jehovah. The Lord saved. Salvation of Jah.

Iscah (is-cah) - She will look out, as to God. She will see. Sheltered. Protected. He will pour out. He will anoint her. He will screen her. Watchful. He that anoints. A covering. To watch a servant.

Iscariot (is-car'-e-ot) - Man of Kerioth. A man of murder. He will be hired. A hireling.

Ishbah (ish'-bah) - He will praise God. Praising. He praises. Appeaser. He will praise.

Ishbak (ish'-bak) – Free. empty. Exhausted. He releases. He will leave alone. Leaving. Who is empty or exhausted. He excels. He will leave.

Ishbi-benob (ish'-be-be'-nob) - Dweller on the mount. He that predicts. One who dwells at Nob. His seat is in the high places. My seat is at Nob. Respiration. Conversion. Taking captive. Whose seat is on high.

Ish-bosheth (ish-bo'-sheth) - Man of shame. Bashful.

Ishi (i'-shi) - Salvation. My husband. My help. Saving. Literally, My man (Hosea 2:16). Salutary. God has saved.

Ishiah (i-shi'-ah) - Gift of the Lord. Whom Jehovah lends. Jehovah exists. Forgiven. Jah will lend. Forgotten of Jah. Jehovah will lend. It is the Lord.

Ishijah (i-'shi'-jah) - Gift of the Lord. Whom Jehovah leads. Jehovah exists. Forgiven. Jah will lend. Forgotten of Jah. Jehovah will lend. It is the Lord.

Ishma (ish'-mah) - Desolateness i.e., unfortunate. Distinction. Elevated. Desolate. Named. Marveling. Desolation. May God hear. Astonishment.

Ishmael (ish'-mael) - He will hear God. He will be heard of God. Whom God hears. The Lord hears. God hears. God that hears. The hearing God.

Ishmaelites (ish'ma-el-ite) - Descendants of Ishmael - He will hear God. He will be heard of God. Whom God hears. The Lord hears. God hears.

Ishmaiah (ish-ma-i'-ah) - He will hear the Lord. Whom Jehovah hears. Jehovah hears. Jah will hear. Hearing or obeying the Lord. God will hear.

Ishmeelites (ish'-me-el-ites) - Same as Ishmael. He will hear God. He will be heard of God. Whom God hears. The Lord hears. God hears. Descendants of Ishmael.

Ishmerai (ish'-me-rahee) - He will be kept of the Lord. Whom Jehovah keeps. God keeps. They will be my keepers. Preservative. Keeper. Jehovah is protector. Jehovah keeps.

Ishod (i'-shod) - Man of beauty. Man of splendor. Man of glory. Man of honor. Man of renown. A comely man. Man of vitality.

Ishpan (ish'-pan) - He will hide. Cunning. Firm. Strong. He will make them prominent. He will lay them bare. Hid. Broken in two. He shall rule. A firm, strong one. He shall hide.

Ish-tob (ish'-tob) - Man of Tob. Distinguished. Good man.

Ishuah (ish'-u-ah) - He will be equal. Equal. Alike. Level. Self-satisfied. He will level. Plainness. To be like. Equality. Likeness. Self-satisfying.

Ishuai (ish'-u-ahee) - Level. Equality. He will justify me. Equal. Resemblance.

Ishui (ish'-u-i) - Level. Equality. He will justify me. Equal. Resemblance. Same as Ishuai.

Ismachiah (is-ma-ki'-ah) - Supported of the Lord. Jehovah supports. Whom Jehovah upholds. Jah will sustain. Cleaving to the Lord. God supported. Joined to.

Ismaiah (is-ma-i'-ah) - He will hear the Lord. Whom Jehovah hears. Jehovah hears. Jah will hear. God will hear.

Ispah (is'-pah) - He will be eminent. Strong. He will lay bare. Bold. He will scratch. A jasper stone. He will excel.

Israel (iz-ra-el) - He will be a prince with God. Prince with God. Contender of God. He strives with God. Soldier of God. God will rule. God ruled man. Ruling with God. One that prevails with God. He who prevails with God. He struggles with God. A prince prevailing with God. Greek - as a prince he prevailed with God.

Israelite(s) (iz'-ra-el-ite(s)) - Descendants of Israel - He will be a prince with God. Prince with God. Contender of God. He strives with God. Soldier of God. God will rule.

God ruled man. Ruling with God. One that prevails with God. He who prevails with God. He struggles with God. A prince prevailing with God. Greek - as a prince he prevailed with God.

Israelitish (iz-ra-el-i-tish) - Referring to Israel - He will be a prince with God. Prince with God. Contender of God. He strives with God. Soldier of God. God will rule. God ruled man. Ruling with God. One that prevails with God. He who prevails with God. He struggles with God. A prince prevailing with God. Greek - as a prince he prevailed with God.

Issachar (is'-sa-kar) - He is wages. He brings wages. He is hired. Reward. There is here. He will bring reward. Recompense. He brings a reward. Punishment. Price.

Isshiah (is-shi'-ah) - Gift of the Lord. Whom Jehovah lends. Jehovah exists. Forgiven. Jehovah will lend. May Jehovah forget. It is the Lord.

Isuah (is'-u-ah) - Level. He will level. Equality. Likeness. Plainness. Equal.

Isui (is'-u-i) - Level. Equality.

Italian (it-al'-yan) - Belonging to Italy. Calf-like.

Italy (it'-a-lee) - Calf-like. Island of the fish or lamb. Abounding with calves or heifers.

Ithai (ith'-a-i) - Ploughman. Being. Existing. With me. Timely. Strong. My sign. A plowshare.

Ithamar (ith'-mah) - Land of palm. Island of palms. Palm coast. Palm tree. Palm island. Like to the palm tree. Oasis of palms.

Ithiel (ith-e-el) - God is with me. God is. The Lord comes. God with me. Sign. With God. God has arrived.

Ithmah (ith'-mah) - Bereavement. Loneliness. Purity. Orphanage. Orphanhood. An orphan. Admiration.

Ithnan (ith'-nan) - Stable i.e., Firm. He will hire them. He will stretch out. Extensive. Constant. Firm consistence. Bestowed.

Ithra (ith'-rah) - Excellence. A remnant.

Ithran (ith'-ran) - Exalted. Very eminent. Excellent. Abundance. Remaining. Searching out diligently. Very excellent.

Ithream (ith'-re-am) - Exalted of the people. Abundance of the people. Rest of the people. Remainder of the people. Remnant. Residue of the people. Excellence of the people. Remnant of the people.

Ithrite (ith'-rite) - Descendants of Jether. Same as Ithra. Excellence. Remaining.

Ittah-kazin (it'-tah-ka'-zin) - Time of the judge. Time of the chief. To the due time of the prince. Time of a judge. Hour. Abode of a prince.

Ittai (it'-ta-i) - Nearness of the Lord. Plowman. Living. With me. Timely. With the Lord. Near. Living being.

Ituraea (i-tu-re'-ah) - Past the limits. A province so named from Jetur. Guarded. Mountainous. To keep guarded. Encircled.

Ivah (i'-vah) - Overturned. Produced. He is a perverter. Overthrow. Iniquity. Ruin. Sky.

Iyyar (e'-yar) - Second Jewish month (April-May).

Izehar (iz'-e-har) - Anointed. Oil. Bright one. Olive oil. Anointing. The Lord ariseth. The clearness of the Lord. May the deity shine. As producing light. Olive tree.

Izeharites (iz'-e-har-ites) - Descendants of Izehar - Anointed. Oil. Bright one. Olive oil. Anointing. The Lord ariseth. The clearness of the Lord. May the deity shine. As producing light. Olive tree.

Izhar (iz'-har) - Same as Izehor. Anointed. Oil. Bright one. Olive oil. Anointing. The Lord ariseth. The clearness of the Lord. May the deity shine. As producing light. Olive tree. Always green.

Izhorites (iz'-har-ites) - Same as Izehorites. Descendants of Izehar. Anointed. Oil. Bright one. Olive oil. Anointing. The Lord ariseth. The clearness of the Lord. May the deity shine. As producing light. Olive tree. Always green.

Izrahiah (iz'-ra-hi'-ah) - Brought to light of the Lord. Whom Jehovah brought to light. Jehovah is appearing. Jehovah does arise. Jah will arise as the sun. Jah will bring forth. The Lord ariseth. The clearness of the Lord. Jehovah will appear. God is risen. Whom Jah brings forth.

Izrahite (iz'-ra-hite) - He will be bright. He will arise.

Izri (iz'-ri) - Jehovah creates. Balm. My imagination. My thought. A form. Conception. Fasting. Tribulation. Formative. Creative.

J

Jaakan (ja'-a-kan) - Intelligent. One who turns. Let him oppress them. Wrestler. Tribulation. Labor. Violently taking away possessions.

Jaakobah (ja-ak'-o-bah) - A helper. Supplanter. Supplanting. To Jacob. He will seek to overreach. Deceiver. The heel. Another Jacob.

Jaala (ja'-a-lah) - Same as Jael - Climber. A wild goat. Chamois. Gazelle. Doe. Elevation. Ascending. A little doe or goat.

Jaalah (ja'-a-lah) - Same as Jaala. Climber. A wild goat. Chamois. Gazelle. Doe. Elevation. Ascending.

Jaalam (ja'-a-lam) - He will be hid. He will hide. Whom God hides. Hidden. Young man. Heir. Ascender of mountains.

Jaanai (ja'-a-nahee) - The Lord hears. Whom Jehovah answers. Jehovah answers. He will give my answers. Responsive. Answerer. Answering. Afflicting. Making poor. The Lord answers.

Jaare-oregim (ja'-a-re-or'-eg-im) - Tapestry of the weavers. Forests of the weavers. Words of weavers. Foresters. The curtains of the webs.

Jaasau (ja-a'-saw) - Made of the Lord. Jehovah makes. They will make him. They will perform. They will do. To make. Doing. My doing. Jehovah is maker. The Lord hears. The Lord will do. Whom Jehovah has made.

Jaasiel (ja-a'-se-el) - Made of God. Whom God created. God is maker. It will be done of God. God's work. Created. The work of God.

Jaazaniah (ja-az-a-ni'-ah) He will be heard of the Lord. Whom Jehovah hears. Jehovah does hearken. Whom the Lord will hear. Jehovah is hearing. The Lord hears. Heard of Jah.

Jaazer (ja-a'-zer) - Whom the Lord helps. Whom God aids. Let him help. Helpful. Which glides away. God helps. He bringeth help. Place hedged about.

Jaaziah (ja-a-zi'-ah) - He is comforted of the Lord. Whom Jehovah strengthens. God consoles. God determines. Whom Jehovah consoles. Which glides away. The Lord comforts or consoles. Emboldened of Jah. Jehovah is determining.

Jaaziel (ja-a'-ze-el) - He is comforted of God. Whom God strengthens. God is determining. God is consoling. Comforted by God. Which glides away. God comforts. God consoles. Emboldened of God.

Jabal (ja'-bal) - Leading. Flowing river. A river moving or which glides away. A stream which glides away. Flowing easily. A stream. Wanderer. Nomad. Moving.

Jabbok (jab'-bok) - Emptying. Pouring out. Running out. Pouring forth. Evacuation. Dissipation. Wrestling. Flowing. With the constant murmur of the water.

Jabesh (ja'-besh) - Dry. A dry place. Arid. Parched. Dryness. Confusion. Shame. Dry place.

Jabesh-gilead (ja'-a-re-or'-eg-im) - Jabesh of Gilead. (Jabesh - Dry. A dry place. Arid. Gilead - Perpetual fountain). Dry. Dried. Jabesh in the territory of Gilead.

Jabez (ja'-bez) - He will cause pain to his mother in his birth. Causing pain. Sorrow. Trouble. He makes sorrow. Height. Whiteness swept away. Mire swept away. Shovel of mire. Who causes sorrow. Height. Sorrow. He produced sorrow.

Jabin (ja'-bin) - God discerns. He will understand. Whom God considered. He that understands. Intelligent. Discerner. Observed. Building of God. He shall be intelligent.

Jabneel (jab'-ne-el) - Will be built. Will be prospered. Which God causes to be built. Built of God. God buildeth. The building of God.

Jabneh (jab'-neh) - Will be built. Will be prospered. Which God causes to be built. A building. Building of God. God lets build. Building. Understanding.

Jachan (ja'-kan) - He will stir up. Troubled. Troublous. Afflicting. Troublesome. Wearing out. Oppressing. He shall be fat. Afflicted.

Jachin (ja'-kin) - He will establish. Founding. Whom God strengthens. Prepared. He shall establish. He that strengthens and makes steadfast. God establishes.

Jachinites (ja'-kin-ites) - Descendants of Jachin - He will establish. Founding. When God strengthens. Prepared. He shall establish. He that strengthens and makes steadfast. God establishes.

Jacinth (ja'-cinth) - Hyacinth. Blue.

Jacob (ja'-cub) - He will supplant. He that supplants. He that follows after. A heeler. One who trips up. Takes hold by the hand. Supplanter. A detainer. He that held the heel.

Jada (ja'-dah) - He knows. Wise. Knowing. The knower i.e., the one who knows. He knew.

Jadau (ja'-daw) - Beloved of the Lord. Favorite. Friend. My loves. Knowing. His hand. His confession. Praised.

Jaddai (ja'-di) - Friend.

Jaddua (jad'-du-ah) - Celebrated. Known of God. Skilled. Very knowing. Known. Well distinguished.

Jadon (ja'-don) - Whom God will judge. He that rules. He that abides. He will strive or judge. Judge. He judged. Thankful. Judging.

Jael (ja'-el) - Climber A wild goat. Chamois. Gazelle. To help. Benefit. He that ascends. A kid.

Jagur (ja'-gur) - Lodging. Lodging place. Husbandman. Stranger. Settled abode.

Jah (jah) - Poetic form of Jehovah. He will be i.e., the Eternal who always is. The Eternal One. The name of the Lord everlasting. The Independent One (shortened form of Jehovah). Name signifies He is. Used in the sense of victor. Lord. The Everlasting. Eternal. The Self Existent Everlasting God.

Jahaleel (ja-ha'-le-el) - Praising God. Light of God.

Jahath (ja'-hath) - He will carry away. He will be broken. Revival. Grasping. Union. Oneness. He took away. Unity. Comfort.

Jahaz (ja'-haz) - A round depressed place. A place trodden down. Threshing floor. Earth pressed down and round. A place trodden under foot. The vision of the Lord.

Jahaza (ja-ha'-zah) - A round depressed place. A place trodden down. Threshing floor. Earth trodden down and round. A place trodden under foot.

Jahazah (ja-ha'-zah) - Same as Jahaz - A round depressed place. A place trodden down. Threshing floor. Earth pressed down and round. A place trodden under foot. The vision of the Lord.

Jahaziah (ja-ha-zi-ah) - He will see the Lord. Whom Jehovah watches over. Jehovah reveals. Jehovah sees. Jah will see. Whom Jehovah beholds. The Lord looked. Jah beholds. The vision of the Lord.

Jahaziel (ja-ha'-ze-el) - He will be seen of God. Whom God watches over. God sees. God reveals. Beheld by God. God looks. Seeing God.

Jahdai (jah'-dahee) - He will be directed of the Lord. Who Jehovah directs. God directs. Guide. He will be gladdened of God. Celebrated. A leader. The Lord leads. The Lord directs.

Jahdiel (jah'-de-el) - He will be made glad of God. Whom God makes glad. God makes glad. Union of God. Unity of God. The joining or unity of God. God gives joy. The unity.

Jahdo (jah'-do) - His union. Union. His enmity. I alone. His joy. His sharpness of wit. His newness. His joining. One together.

Jahleel (jah'-le-el) - Hope of God. Hoping in God. God waits. God does grievously afflict. Waiting for. Expectation of God. Wait for God.

Jahleelites (jah'-le-el-ites) - Descendants of Jahleel. Hope of God.

Hoping in God. God waits. God does grievously afflict. Waiting for. Expectation of God. Wait for God.

Jahmai (jah'-mahee) - He will be guarded of the Lord. Whom Jehovah protects. He will be my defenses. He will be my conceivings. Hot. Warm. Making warm. God keeps or guards. Jehovah protects.

Jahzah (jah'-zah) - Same as Jahaz. A round depressed place. A place trodden down. Threshing floor. Trodden down. Earth pressed down and round.

Jahzeel (jah'-ze-el) - He will allot of God. Whom God allots. God apportions. God distributes. God hasteneth. Hasteth

Jahzeelites (jah'-ze-el-ites) - Descendants of Jahzeel. He will allot of God. Whom God allots. God apportions. God distributes. God hasteth.

Jahzerah (jah'-ze-rah) - He will be caused to return. May he bring back. May he lead back. Jehovah protects. He will be led to the crown. He will be narrow-eyed. He leads back. Protection.

Jahziel (jah'ze-el) - Same as Jahzeel - He will allot of God. Whom God allots. God apportions. God distributes. God hasteth. Hoping in God. God dividedth. Allotted of God.

Jair #1 (ja'-ur) - He will enlighten. Diffuse. Light. Enlightens. Shining. Lightener. Jehovah enlightens; arouses or diffuses light. Enlightener. Same as Achan. He shone brightly. Illuminated.

Jair #2 (ja'-ur) - He will embroider. He will stir up. The father of Elhanan.

Jairite (ja'-ur-ite) - Descendants of Jair - He will enlighten. Diffuse. Light. Enlightens. Shining. Lightener. Jehovah enlightens, arouses or diffuses light. Enlightener. He shone brightly. Illuminated.

Jairus (ja-i'-rus) - He will enlighten or diffuse light. Same as Achan. He shall shine. Running water. Enlightened.

Jakan (ja'-kan) - Same as Akan. Torques. Wrestler. It binds like a chain.

Jakeh (ja'-keh) - Pious. Fearing God. Hear meaning. Obedience. Obedient.

Jakim (ja'-kim) - God sets up. A setter-up he raises up. Rising. Confirming. He makes to subsist. May God establish. Whom God lifts up. Establishing.

Jalon (ja'-lon) - Jehovah abides. Abiding. Passing the night. Obstinate. Tarrying. Murmuring. A sure abode. Lodging.

Jambres (jam'-brees) - Opposer. The sea with poverty. Bitter. A rebel. Poverty. A diviner. Wiseman. Soothsayer. He who is rebellious.

James (james) - Supplanter. Same as Jacob. He held the heel. Greek form of Jacob.

Jamin (ja'-min) - Right hand. Prosperity. South wind. Dexterous. Favor.

Jaminites (ja'-min-ites) - Descendants of Jamin. Right hand. Prosperity. South wind. Dexterous. Favor.

Jamlech (jam'-lek) - He will be made to reign. Jehovah rules. Let him constitute. God makes king. Reining. Asking counsel. He appoints a king.

Janna (jan'-nah) - He will answer. Sleeping. He afflicts. Poor answering.

Jannes (jan'-nees) - Full of pleasure. Favor. Impoverished. Be vexed. Be oppressed. Sleeping. He mocked. He deceived. He who seduces.

Janoah (ja-no'-ah) - Rest. He will give rest. Quiet. Sleeping. Constant rest. Resting.

Janohah (ja-no'-hah) - Same as Janoah. Rest. He will lead to rest. Quiet. Sleeping. Tarrying. Resting.

Janum (ja'-num) - Sleep. He will slumber. Asleep. Sleeping. Fixed seat.

Japheth (ja'-feth) - Enlargement. Extension. Let him enlarge. He that persuades. Beauty. Widespread. Enlarged. Fair. Persuading. Increase. Expansion. Widely spreading. Unfoldment. The extender.

Japhia (ja-fi'-ah) - Illustrious. Splendid. Shining. Gleaming. Which enlightens. Bright. Enlightening. Appearing. May God enlighten.

Japhlet (jaf'-let) - Jehovah causes to escape. Whom God will free. May He deliver. Whom God delivers. Fairness. Comeliness. He has set free. God delivers. May God deliver.

Japhleti (jaf'-let-i) - Will be liberated by the Lord. Let him escape. He will deliver. Fairness. Comeliness. Set free. Delivered. The descendants of Japhlet.

Japho (ja'-fo) - Beautiful. Beauty. To be fair to him. Fairness. Comeliness. A beautiful gate.

Jarah (ja'-rah) - Same as Jehoadah - Whom Jehovah adorns. The Lord will adorn. Honey. One who unveils. Forest. Honey wood. Honeycomb. A wood. Watching closely. Pouring out. Unveiler.

Jareb (ja'-reb) - He will plead. Adverse. One who is contentious. Avenger. Revenger. Wrangler. Let him contend. Adversary. Contender.

Jared (ja'-red) - Descent. Descending. He that descends. A descender. Low down. Commanding. A ruler. Coming down. Descended. Servant.

Jaresiah (ja-re-si-'ah) - He will be nourished of the Lord. Whom Jehovah nourishes. God does nourish or plant. Jehovah gives a couch. Honey which is of Jah. Jah the Lord. The bed of the Lord. The Lord hath taken away. Poverty. The bed of God. God has taken away poverty. Jehovah plants.

Jarha (jar'-hah) - Increasing moon. An adversary. The month of sweeping away. Jah. Adoption.

Jarib (ja'-rib) - He will plead the cause. He does contend. Adversary. Fighting. Chiding. Multiplying. Avenging. He gave cause. An adversary. May God strive.

Jarmuth (jar'-muth) - High. Height. Hill. Fearing. Seeing. Casting down death.

Jaroah (ja-ro'-ah) - New moon. To lunate or shine as the moon. The moon. Breathing. Making a sweet odor.

Jarvah (jar'-vah) - Breathing.

Jashem (ja'-shem) - Righteous. Upright.

Jashen (ja'-shen) - Sleeping. Shining. Righteous. Upright. Drowsy. Sleepy. Ancient.

Jasher - (ja'-shur) Same as Jesher - Uprightness. Upright. Just. The book of the righteous. Righteousness. Upright. Straight.

Jashobeam (jash-o'-be-am) - He will return among the people. The people return to God. Returning people. The people sitting. The captivity of the people. He dwelt among the people. The people return.

Jashub (ja'-shub) - He will return. Turning back. He returns. He who returns. A returning. A controversy. Dwelling place. He brought back.

Jashubi-lehem (jash'-u-bi-le'hem) - He is restored by bread. Giving bread. Bread returns. Returning to bread. Turning back to Bethlehem. He will be restorer of bread or of war. Returner of bread. He brought back bread. Turning back for food.

Jashubites (jash'-u-bites) - Descendants of Jashub - He will return. Turning back. He returns.

Jasiel (ja'-se-el) - Same as Jaasiel - Made of God. Whom God created. God creates. The strength of God. God has made.

Jason (ja'-sun) - Healing. He that cares. He that cures. About to give health. The healer.

Jasper (jas'-per) - He will be made bare. He will be made prominent.

Jathniel (jath'-ne-el) - He will be given of God. God gives. God bestows gifts. God is giving. Whom God bestows. Gift of God. Continued of God.

Jattir (jat'-tur) - Pre-eminent. Lofty. Excelling. Redundant. Excellent. A remnant. Very excellent. Pre-eminence.

Javan (ja'-van) - Supple. Clay. He that deceives. A defrauder. The effervescing one mired. Youthful. Effervescing. Deceiver. One who makes sad. Soft. Tender. Young. He who deceives. Ionians.

Jazeel (ja-ze'-el) - Strength of God.

Jazer (ja'-zur) - Same as Jaazer - Whom the Lord helps. Whom God aids. Helpful. Fortified. Assistance. Helper. He brings help.

Jaziz (ja'-ziz) - He will bring abundance. He will shine. He moves about. Shining. Wanderer. Prominent. Brightness. Departing. He shone greatly. He gives life and motion. Made prominent.

Jearim (je'-a-rim) - Forests. A leap. Woods.

Jeaterai (je-at'-e-rahee) - He will abound of the Lord. Steadfast. My profit. My steps. My remainders. Whom Jehovah leads. Searching out. The Lord may make. Following. The track of one.

Jeberechiah (je-ber'-e-ki'ah) - He will be blessed of the Lord. Whom Jehovah blesses. Jehovah does bless. Jehovah is blessing. Speaking well of. He blessed with the blessing of God. Jah blesses.

Jebus (je'-bus) - Treading down. A place trodden down. Trodden. Treading under foot. Mangers. Trampling. Threshing floor. Manger.

Jebusi (jeh'-u-si) - One trodden. Trodden under foot. Mangers.

Jebusites (jeb'-u-sites) - Descendants of Jebus - Treading down. A place trodden down. Trodden. Treading under foot. Trampling. Threshing floor. Manger.

Jecamiah (jek-a-mi'-ah) - Same as Jekamiah - He will be gathered of the Lord. Jah will establish. Let Jah arise. He who assembles the people.

Resurrection. May Jehovah establish. Flock of God. Jah will rise.

Jecholiah (jek-o-li'-ah) - Same as Jecoliah. Made strong of the Lord. Jehovah is strong. Is powerful. The prevailing of Jehovah. Able through Jehovah. Perfection. He was powerful. Jah enables.

Jechonias (jek-o-ni'-as) - Established of the Lord. Greek way of spelling Jeconiah. He will be established of the Lord. Jehovah establishes. Jah establishes. Preparation. Whom God establishes.

Jecoliah (jek-o-li'-ah) - Same as Jecholiah - Made strong of the Lord. Jehovah is strong. Is powerful. Jehovah establishes. Able through Jehovah. Perfection. The power of God.

Jeconiah (jek-o-ni'-ah) - Preparation. He will be established of the Lord. Jehovah establishes. Preparation. Whom god establishes.

Jedaiah #1 (jed-a-i'-ah) - Praise of the Lord. Jehovah is praise.; Jehovah knows. Praise thou Jah. Praised of Jehovah. The hand of the Lord. Confessing the Lord. The praise of God. (Nehemiah 3:10)

Jedaiah #2 (jed-a-i'-ah)- Known of the Lord. The Lord knew. Jehovah has favored. Jah has known. (I Chronicles 9:10)

Jedeiah (jed-e-a'-el) - One Lord. The joy of the Lord.

Jediael (jed-e-a'-el) - Known of God. God knows. Know thou Jah. The science. The knowledge of God. Known by God.

Jedidah (je-di'-dah) - Beloved. Darling of Jehovah. Will be made known of

God. Well beloved.
Amiable.
Jedidiah (jed-id-i'-ah) - Beloved of
Jehovah. Jehovah is a friend. The
beloved of Jah. Darling of Jehovah.
Beloved of the Lord. Peaceful.
Jediel (jed-i-el') - The knowledge.
Jeduthun (jed'-u-thun) - A choir of
praise. One who gives praise. Praising.
Celebrating. Friendship. Full of love.
He who praises. The law. Giving
praise. The praising one. Great love.
Jeezer (je-e'-zur) - Help. Helpless.
Island of help. Father of help. My
Father will help. Father of helps. Cost
of help.
Jeezerites (je-e'-zur-ites) -
Descendants of Jeezer - My Father
will help. In help. Father of helps.
Island of help.
Jegar-sahadutha (je'-gar-sa-ha-du'-
thah) - The heap of witness. The heap
of testimony. Heaps of witness or
testimony.
Jehaleleel (je-hal-e'-le-el) - He will
praise God. He praises God. Praiser of
God. Seeing God. May God shine
forth.
Jehalelel (je-hal'-e'-lel) - Same as
Jehaleleel - He will praise God. He
praises God. Praiser of God. Seeing
God. May God shine forth.
Jehdeiah (jeh-di-ah) - He will be
gladdened of the Lord. Whom
Jehovah makes glad. Jehovah inspires
with joy. Union of Jehovah. Unity of
God. Joy together. May Jehovah
rejoice. One Lord.
Jehezekel (je-hez'-e-kel) - God does
strengthen. God is strong. Same as
Ezekiel. God will strengthen. The
strength of God. Jehovah strengthens.

Jehiah (je-hi-ah) - He lives of the Lord
i.e., by the mercy of Jehovah. Jehovah
lives. God is living. Jah liveth. Jehovah
is living. God lives. Jah will live. The
Lord liveth.
Jehiel (je-hi'-el) - God lives. He lives of
God i.e, the mercy of God. Jah shall
save alive. God liveth. Carried away of
God. Treasured. To snatch away.
Jehieli (je-hi'-el-i) - He lives by mercy.
Same as Jehiel. Serving the living God.
Jehovah lives.
Jehizkiah (je-hiz-ki'-ah) - Jehovah is
strong. Jehovah has strengthened.
Same as Hezekiah. Whom Jehovah
strengthens. Strength of God. God
shows Himself strong. Strengthened
of Jah.
Jehoadah (je-ho'-a-dah) - Jehovah
unveils. Jehovah has adorned. Same
as Jarah. Whom Jehovah adorns.
Passing over. Testimony of the Lord.
God held up. Jehovah has numbered.
Jehoaddan (je'-ho-ad'-dan) - Lord of
pleasure. Jehovah is beauteous.
Jehovah is her ornament. Jehovah
pleased. Pleasure. Jehovah gives
delight. Delight of God.
Jehoahaz (je-ho'-a-haz) - Whom
Jehovah holds fast. Jehovah upholds.
Jehovah has laid hold. The Lord that
sees. Jehovah sees. Jehovah holds.
God has taken. Jehovah seized.
Possession of the Lord.
Jehoash (je-ho'-ash) - Jehovah
supports. Jehovah has laid hold.
Jehovah is strong. Jehovah hastens to
build. The Lord gave. Whom Jehovah
supports. The substance of the Lord.
Jehovah given: Fire of the Lord. God
has given. Jehovah bestowed.

Jehohanan (je-ho'-ha-nan) - The Lord graciously gave. Jehovah is gracious. Bestowed by the Lord. Jehovah favored. Grace.

Jehoiachin (je-hoy'-a-kin) - The Lord will establish. Jehovah has established. Jehovah will establish. Preparation. Jehovah appointed. God establishes. Jehovah establishes.

Jehoiada (je-hoy'-a-dah) - The Lord knows. Jehovah knows. Knowledge of the Lord. God known. God has known.

Jehoiakim (je-hoy'-a-kim) - The Lord will set up. Jehovah has set up. The Lord will rise up. Jehovah established. God confirms. Jehovah will raise. Avenging.

Jehoiarib (je-hoy'-a-rib) - The Lord will contend. Jehovah will contend. Jehovah a defender. God has pleaded my cause. Jehovah defended. Fighting.

Jehonadab (je-hon'-a-dab) - The Lord gave spontaneously. Jehovah is bounteous. The Lord willing. Jehovah is liberal. Jehovah impels. Gift of the Lord. Gift of a dove. God gave freely. Jehovah-largest.

Jehonathan (je-hon'a-than) - Jehovah has given. The Lord gave. Lord of giving. Whom Jehovah gave. Jehovah given. Gift of the Lord. Gift of a dove. The gift of God. Jehovah gives.

Jehoram (je-ho'-ram) - The Lord exalts. Jehovah is high. Jehovah is exalted. The Lord celebrated. Exalted by Jehovah. Exaltation of the Lord. Jehovah is exalted. Jehovah raised. God is exalted.

Jehoshabeath (je-ho-shab'-e-ath) - Same as Jehosheba - The Lord's oath.

Jehovah is the oath. Jehovah is her oath. Jehovah Sworn. Oath of God.

Jehoshaphat (je-hosh'-a-fat) - The Lord judges i.e., pleads for him. Whom Jehovah judges. Jehovah is judge. Jehovah judged.

Jehosheba (je-hosh'-e-bah) - Same as Jehoshabeath - The Lord's oath. Jehovah is the oath. Jehovah is her oath. Worshiper of Jehovah. Fullness. Oath of God. Jehovah sworn.

Jehoshua (je-hosh'-u-ah) - Jehovah saves. Same as Joshua. Saved by Jehovah. Jehovah saved. Salvation of God. Jehovah is salvation. The Lord is his salvation. The Lord saves. Lord of salvation.

Jehoshuah (je-hosh'-u-ah) - Same as Joshua - Jehovah is salvation. The Lord is his salvation. Lord of salvation. The Lord saves. Salvation of God. Jehovah his help. Saved by Jehovah. Jehovah saved.

Jehovah (je-ho'-vah) - He will be i.e., the Eternal who always is. The Eternal One. The existing one. Self-subsisting. I am who I am or I will be who I will be. Who is forever. Self-existent.

Jehovah-Jireh (je-ho'-vah-ji'-reh) - The Lord will see. The Lord will provide i.e., give a means of deliverance. The Lord has seen. God will provide. Jehovah will see, behold, discern.

Jehovah-M'Kaddesh (je-ho'-vah m-ked-desh') - The Lord is our (my) sanctification.

Jehovah-Nissi (je-ho'-vah-nis'-si)- The Lord is our (my) banner or ensign. God is my banner. Jehovah is my banner.

Jehovah-Rohi (je-ho'-vah ro-hi') - The Lord is our (my) shepherd.

Jehovah-Rophi (je-ho'-vah ro-fi') - The Lord is our (my) healing.

Jehovah-Sabaoth (je-ho'-vah-sab'-a-oth) - The Lord of warrior hosts.

Jehovah-Shalom (je-ho'-vah-sha'-lom) - The Lord is our (my) peace. The peace of the Lord. God is peace. Jehovah the God of peace. The peace of the Lord. God is peace. Jehovah is peace. The Lord send peace. Jehovah will send peace.

Jehovah-Shammah (je-ho'-vah-sham'-mah) - The Lord is there (ever present). Jehovah is there.

Jehovah-Tsidkenu (je-ho'-vah tsid'-ken-u)- The Lord is our (my) righteousness.

Jehozabad (je-hoz'-a-bad) - Whom the Lord gave. Jehovah gave. Jehovah has endowed. The Lord has given. The Lord's dowry. Having a dowry.

Jehozadak (je-hoz'-a-dak) - The Lord has made just. Jehovah is just. Jehovah makes just. The justice of God. Jehovah righted. The justice of the Lord.

Jehu (je-hu) - The Lord. Jehovah is He. He is. He shall be or subsist. God is. The Lord He is. Himself who exists.

Jehubbah (je-hub'-bah) - He will be hidden. Hidden. God will be hidden. Binding. Hiding. Jehovah is hidden.

Jehucal (je-hu'-kal) - He will be made able or strengthened of the Lord. Jehovah is mighty. Jehovah is able. Jehovah will prevail. He will be prevailed over. Potent. He became superior. Mighty. Perfect. Wasted. Jehovah is able.

Jehud (je'-hud) - Praise. He will be praised. Celebrated. Praised. The praise of the Lord. Honorable.

Jehudi (je-hu'-di)- Praise of the Lord. A man of Judah. A Jew. God my praise. The praise of the Lord. Judahite. Celebrated.

Jehudijah (je'-hu-di'-jah) - Jewess. A Jewish woman who is a believer. One who has crossed over. Praise of the Lord. Jah will be praised. To worship. Praising of God. The praise of the Lord.

Jehush (je'-hush) - He will gather together. To whom God hastens. Collector. A congregation. A flock. Hasty. Keeping counsel. Fastened. Bringing together.

Jeiel (je-i'-el) - Hidden of God. Treasure of God. God snatches away. Snatching away. Carried a way of God. God lives.

Jekabzeel (je-kab'-ze-el) - God will assemble together. God gathers. He collected. God will gather. The congregation of God.

Jekameam (je-kam'-e-am) - He will gather together the people. He does assemble the people. Congregation of the people. The people will rise. Rise up.

Jekamiah - (jek-a-mi'-ah) Jehovah is standing. Jehovah does gather. He will be gathered of the Lord. Let Jah arise. Let Jah establish. Flock of God. Establishing. Jehovah will rise.

Jekuthiel (je-ku'-the-el) - God is mighty. Reverence for God. The fear of God. Veneration of God. Preservation of God. God is almightiness. Reverence or piety toward God. Hope. Obedience. May God nourish.

Jemima (je-mi'-mah) - Dove. A little dove. He will spoil or mar her. The pure. Affectionate. Handsome as the day.

Jemuel (je-mu'-el) - The day of God. God is light. Desire of God. He will be made slumber of God. God circumcised. God's day. Son of God.

Jephthae (jef'-thah-e) - Whom God sets free. He opened. Greek form of Jephthah.

Jepthah (jef'-thah) - He will open. He will set free and liberate. He does open. He sets free. God opens. The breaker through. A breaker through. He opened. Inconsiderate.

Jephunneh (je-fun'-neh) - He will be beheld or cared for by God. For whom it is prepared. It will be prepared. He that beholds. Appearing. Regarding. He will be turned (prepared). He beheld. He will be prepared. Nimble. Prepared.

Jerah (je'-rah) - Moon. Son of the moon. Lunar. The moon. Month. Pleasant odor. Smelling sweet.

Jerahmeel (je-rah'-me-el) - He will obtain mercy of God. Whom God loves. God have mercy. God has compassion. God is merciful. God pities. On whom God has mercy. The mercy. God will have compassion.

Jerahmeelites (je-rah'-me-el-ites) - Descendants of Jerahmeel - He will obtain mercy of God. Whom God loves. God have mercy. God has compassion. God is merciful. God pities. On whom God has mercy. The mercy of God. God will have compassion. God is merciful.

Jered (je'-red) - Descent. Flowing. Ruling. Coming down. A descent. Going down. Low.

Jeremai (jer'-e-mahee) - He will be exalted of the Lord. Jehovah is high. Dwelling in heights. Let me have promotions. He exalted. Elevated. My height. Throwing forth waters. Jehovah is high. Dweller on heights.

Jeremiah (jer-e-mi'-ah) - Elevated of the Lord. Whom Jehovah has appointed. Jehovah is high. Exalted of God. Jah will cast forth. Jah is the exalted one. Exaltation of the Lord. Extol. Exalt. Jah will raise.

Jeremias (jer-e-mi'-as) - Whom Jehovah has appointed. Lord lifting up. Greek form of Jeremiah - Elevated of the Lord. Jehovah has appointed. Jehovah is high. Exalted of God. Jah will cast forth. Jah is the exalted one. Exaltation of the Lord. Extol. Exalt. Jah will raise.

Jeremoth (jer'-e-moth) - High places. Lifting up. Elevation. Eminences. One that fears death. Heights. Elevations.

Jeremy (jer'-e-mee)- Shortened English form of Jeremiah - Lord lifting up. Elevated of the Lord. Jehovah has appointed. Jehovah is high. Exalted of God. Jah will cast forth. Jah is the exalted one. Exaltation of the Lord. Extol. Exalt. Jah will raise.

Jeriah (je-ri'-ah) - Fear of the Lord. Jehovah has founded. Whom Jehovah regards. God looks with favor. Founded by Jah. Fear. Jah will direct. Inform. Jehovah sees.

Jeribai (jer'-ib-ahee) - Jehovah contends. He will contend. Contentious. Defended. Jehovah pleads. He contended. Fighting. Chiding. Multiplying.

Jericho (jer'-ik-o) - City of the moon. Moon city. A fragrant place. Sent a city. Let him smell it. Constant pleasant odor. Place of fragrance. His moon. His month. His sweet smell. Fragrant.

Jeriel (je-ri-el) - Founded of God. Foundation of God. Founded. God looks on. Fear. God directs. God sees.

Jerijah (je-ri'-jah) - Same as Jeriah - Fear of the Lord. Jehovah has founded. Whom Jehovah regards. God looks with favor. Founded by Jah. Fear. Jah will direct. Inform. Jehovah sees. Jah will throw. God directs.

Jerimoth (jer'-im-oth) - Heights. High places. Lifting up Elevation. Eminences. One that fears death. Elevations. There shall be elevations. He who fears. He that fears or rejects death.

Jerioth (je'-re-oth) - Curtains. Tents. Tent curtains. Breaking asunder. Kettles. Timidity.

Jeroboam (jer-o-bo'-am) - Whose people are countless. Whose people are many. The people have become numerous. Enlarged. Struggles for the people. A wrangler among the people. Let the people contend. He will multiply the people. He shall be multiplied. The people will contend. He that opposes the people. He pleads the people's cause. Enlarger.

Jeroham (je-ro'-ham) - He will obtain mercy. He finds mercy. Love. High. Merciful. Beloved. Compassionate. Loved.

Jerubbaal (je-rub'-ba-al) - Let Baal plead. Baal strives. Strives. Let Baal defend his cause. He will contend with Baal. Baal will be contended with. Baal will be taught. Baal strives or contends. He that defends Baal. Baal will contend. Let Baal show himself great.

Jerubbsheth (je-rub'-be-sheth) - Contender with idol. Let the idol of confusion defend itself. Shame i.e., the idol strives. Contender with shame. Same as Jerubbaal. Let the shameful thing contend.

Jeruel (je-ru'-el) - Same as Jeriel. Founded of God. Foundation of God. Founded. God looks on. Fear. God directs. God sees. The reverence of God. Awe.

Jerusalem (je-ru'-sa-lem) - Foundation of peace. Founded in peace. Teaching peace. Duel peace shall be taught. Lay or set ye double peace. The possession of peace. The abode of harmony. Vision of peace. Peaceful.

Jerusha (je-ru'-shah) - Possessed namely by a husband. Taken possession of or married. Hereditary possession. Possessed. Banished. Possession. Inheritance. Taken in marriage.

Jerushah (je-ru'-shah) - Same as Jerusha. Possessed namely by a husband. Taken possession of or married. Hereditary possession. Possessed. Banished. Possession. Inheritance. Taken in marriage.

Jesaiah (jes-a-i'-ah) - Jehovah is opulent. Jehovah has saved. Same as Isiah. The salvation of God. Jah has saved. Save thou Jah. Health. Jehovah saves. Jehovah is helper.

Jeshaiah (jesh-a-i'-ah)- Same as Jesaiah - Jehovah is opulent. Jehovah has saved. Same as Isaiah - The salvation of God. Jah has saved. Save thou Jah. Health. Jehovah saves. Jehovah is helper.

Jeshanah (je-sha'-nah) - Old. Ancient as if withered. Languid. To die.

Jesharelah (je-shar'-e-lah) - Upright towards God. Right before God. Just.

Jeshebeab (je-sheb'-e-ab) - Habitation of the Father. Father's seat. Seat or dwelling of father. A father's home. Seat of his father. Sitting. People will return. May the father endure.

Jesher (je'-shur) - Same as Jasher - Uprightness. Upright. Just. Ruling. Right. Singing. Rightness.

Jeshimon (jesh'-im-on) - The waste. A desolate place. The wilderness. Solitude. Desolation. Wasteland.

Jeshishai (jesh'-i-shalee) - Jehovah is ancient. Ancient of the Lord i.e., A very old good man. Ancient. Rejoicing exceedingly. Aged. Jehovah is ancient or aged. God maketh to dwell in peace.

Jeshohhaiah (je-sho-ha-i'-ah) - Depression of the Lord. Whom Jehovah humbles. He will be bowed down of Jah. The meditation of God. Jah will empty. Bowed down. The Lord pressing. Jehovah doth trouble. Humbled by Jah. Humbled by Jehovah.

Jeshua (jesh'-u-ah) - The salvation of the Lord. Same as Joshua. Jehovah is salvation. The Lord is his salvation. Lord of salvation. The Lord saves. Being saved. Jehovah is helper. A savior. Jehovah is deliverance. Jehovah helps.

Jeshuah (jesh'-u-ah) - Help. He will save. Jehovah is salvation. The salvation of the Lord. Jah will save. Jehovah is deliverance. He will save.

Jeshurun (jesh'-u-run) - Upright. Righteous. Very upright. Most righteous. Dearly beloved. Beloved.

Jesiah (je-si'-ah) - Jehovah exists. Same as Isiah. God gives as a loan. Jah will lend. Sprinkling of the Lord. To lend Lent by Jehovah.

Jesimiel (je-sim'-e-el) - Made or created by God. Jehovah sits up. God places. God sets up. Naming of God. Naming. God will place. God sets.

Jesse (jes'-se) - Jehovah exists. Firm. Wealth. Gift. My existence. My men. Gift of the Lord. To be. Who is. Existing. Substance. Oblation. One who is. Strong. Wealthy.

Jesui (jes'-u-i) - Jehovah is satisfied. Same as Ishui - Level. Equality. Even-tempered. Flat country.

Jesuites (jes'-u-ites) - Descendants of Jesui. Jehovah is satisfied. Level. Equality. Even-tempered. Flat country. Same as Ishui.

Jesurun (jes'-i-run) - Same as Jeshurum - Upright. Righteous. Very upright. Most righteous. Dearly beloved. Beloved.

Jesus (je'-zus) - Jehovah is salvation. Jehovah my salvation. Savior. Greek form of Jehoshua. Salvation of God. Deliverer.

Jether (je'-thur) - Abundance. Excellence. Pre-eminent. Same as Ithra - Excellence. Prominence. Superiority. He that excels. Surplus. Abundant.

Jetheth (je'-theth) - A tent pin. Nail. Strengthener. A remnant. A stake or post. Subjugation. Giving. Subjection.

Jethlah (jeth'-lah) - He (God) will exalt it. Lofty. He will hang. He exalts. High. Hanging. Heaping up. Hanging up. Suspended. A hanging place.

Jethro (jeth'-ro) - Same as Jether - Abundance. Excellence. Pre-eminent. Very excellent. His excellence. His posterity. Superiority.

Jetur (je'-tur) - An enclosure. Defense. He that keeps. He will arrange. He will encircle. A pillar. Inclosure. He that keeps order. Encircled. Order. Succession. Mountainous. Inclosed.

Jeuel (je-u'-el) - Same as Jeiel - Hidden of God. Treasure of God. God snatches away. Snatching away. Hid of God. God has taken away. God heaping up. Protected by God. God has healed.

Jeush (je'-ush) - Same as Jehush - He will gather together. To whom God hastens. He will succor. An assembly. Hasty. Devoured. Strong. Collector.

Jeuz (je'-uz) - Counselor. Counseling. Counsel. Same as Judah - Praised. The Lord be praised. Object of praise. Praise of the Lord.

Jew (jew) - An Israelite. Same as Judah. Praising. Celebrated. Descendant of Judah - Praised. The Lord be praised. Object of praise. Praise of the Lord.

Jewess (jew'-ess) - A Jewish woman who is a believer. A word now considered to be offensive by many. Praise. Same as Judah - Praised. The Lord be praised. Object of praise. Praise of the Lord.

Jewish (jew'-ish) - Of or belonging to Jews. Praise. Confession.

Jewry (jew'-ree) - Old English name for Judea. The land of Judea. Same as Judah - Praised. The Lord be praised. Object of praise. Praise of the Lord.

Jews (jews) - Inhabitants of Judea. Praising. Confessing. Same as Judah - Praised. The Lord be praised. Object of praise. Praise of the Lord.

Jezaniah (jez-a-ni'-ah) - Jehovah does hearken. Jehovah does determine. He will prostitute i.e., (use illicitly the name of) Jehovah. The Lord hears. Nourishment. Whom Jehovah hears. Same as Jaazaniah.

Jezebel (jez'-e'-bel) - Non-cohabitant. Unchaste. Without obligation i.e., self-righteous. Unmarried. Chaste. Free from carnal connection. Place of habitation. Father of the heavenly dwelling. Not cohabited. Unexalted. Unhusbanded.

Jezer (je'-zur) - Frame. Form i.e., of his parents. Anything made. Formation. Isle of help. Shape. Imagination. Purpose.

Jezerites (je'zur-ites) - Descendants of Jezer - Frame. Form i.e., of his parents. Anything made. Formation. Isle of help. Shape. Imagination. Purpose.

Jeziah (je-zi'-ah) - Jehovah unites. Whom Jehovah assembles. He will be sprinkled of the Lord i.e., purified or forgiven of the Lord. Jehovah exalts. He will be sprinkled of Jah. He sprinkles. Clear. White.

Jeziel (je'-ze-el) - Assembly of God. God unites. Let him be sprinkled of God. God despises. Sprinkled of God. Clear. White.

Jezliah (jez-li'-ah) - Jehovah unites. He will be drawn out or preserved of the Lord. Deliverance. He will pour out suitably. He will cause her to flow forth. He despised the toil. Jah draws out. Jah preserves. He will draw out. Jehovah delivers.

Jezoar (je-zo'-ar) - Splendid. Whiteness. He shall shine.

Jezrahiah (jez-ra-hi'-ah) - Jehovah is shining. The Lord arises. Same as Izrahiah - Jah will shine. God is risen. The Lord arises. Brightness of the Lord.

Jezreel (jez'-re-el) - God sows. He will be sown of God i.e., have a numerous progeny. God scatters. The Lord sows. God has planted. God soweth. Seed of God. Sown by God.

Jezreelites (jez'-re-el-ites) - Inhabitants of Jezreel - God sows. He will be sown of God i.e., have a numerous progeny. God scatters. The Lord sows. Seed of God. Sown by God.

Jezreelitess (jez'-re-el-i-tess) - (Feminine) Inhabitants of Jezreel. God sows. He will be sown of God i.e., have a numerous progeny. God scatters. The Lord sows. Seed of God. Sown of God. A woman of Jezreel.

Jibsam (jib'-sam) - He will smell sweetly or be pleasant. Fragrant. Lovely. Sweet. Pleasant. Their drought. Lovely scent.

Jidlaph (jid'-laf) - He will weep. Weeping. He that distills. Melting away. Shedding tears. Tearful. He that distills water.

Jimna (jim'-nah) - Same as Imna - He (God) will retain. Whom God assigns. God does restrain. Holding back.

Withdrawing. Prosperity (as betokened by the right hand). Good fortune. Numbering. Right hand. Preparing.

Jimnah (jim'-nah) - Same as Imnah - Prosperity. He allots. Success. Right-handed. He will number. Prosperity. Right hand. Numbering. Preparing. Prosperous.

Jimnites (jim'-nites) - Descendants of Jimnah. Same as Imnah - Prosperity. He allots. Success. Right-handed. He will number. Right-hand. Numbering. Preparing. Prosperous.

Jiphtah (jif'-tah) - Same as Jephthah - He will open i.e., He will set free and liberate. God opens. He opened. Opening. Breaking through.

Jiphthah-el (jif'-thah-el) - It will be opened of God. Which God opens. He opened. God will open. God opening. Opening of God. To free. God opens.

Jishui (jish'-u-i) - Man of Jehovah.

Jisshiah (jis-shi'-ah) - Jehovah exists.

Jithra (jith'-ra) - Excellent.

Jithran (jith'-ran) - Abundance.

Jizliah (jiz'-li-ah) - Jehovah delivers.

Jizri (jiz'-ri) - Creator.

Joab (jo'-ab) - Lord Father. Jehovah is Father. Jehovah is a good Father. God the Father. Whose father is the Lord. The Lord our Father. Jehovah fathered. Paternity. Voluntary. Jehovah is Father.

Joah (jo'-ah) - Jehovah is brother. God a friend. The joining of the Lord. Jehovah brothered. Fraternity. Brother of the Lord. Jehovah his brother.

Joahaz (jo'-a-haz) - Jehovah helps. Jehovah has laid hold of. God has taken. Jehovah seized. Apprehending. Possessing. Seeing. Jehovah holds.

Joanna (jo-an'-nah) - Jehovah has been gracious. Jehovah has shown favor. The Lord is grace. The Lord give graciously. The gracious gift of God. Grace or gift of the Lord. God given.

Joannas (jo-an'-nas) - God given.

Joash (jo'-ash) - Same as Jehoash - Jehovah supports. Jehovah has laid hold. Jehovah is strong. Jehovah hastens to build. The Lord gave. Whom Jehovah supports. The substance of the Lord. God's existence. Jehovah has become man. Flock of God. Jehovah fired or bestowed. Who despairs or burns. Given by Jehovah.

Joatham (jo'-a-tham) - The Lord is upright. Greek form of Jotham - Lord of integrity. God showed himself wholly.

Job (jobe) - The persecuted. Hated. One ever returning to God. He that weeps. A desert. The cry of woe. I will exclaim. Desire. One persecuted. Converted. He that weeps or cries. Returning. Persecuted. Foe or hostile one.

Jobab (jo'-bab) - Howling. Trumpet call. Crying out i.e., a desert. He will cause crying. A father's desire. Howler. Desert. Sorrowful. Shouting.

Jochebed (jok'-e-bed) - Lord of glory. Glory of the Lord. Jehovah is glorious. Jehovah is (her/our) glory. Glory of God. Jehovah glorified. Glorious. Honorable. God glorified. Jehovah is honor or glory.

Joed (jo'-ed) - Jehovah is witness. Lord of witness. Witness of the Lord. For whom Jehovah is witness.

Ornament of God. Appointer. Witness of Jehovah. Witnessing. Robbing. Passing over.

Joel (jo'-el) - Lord of God. The Lord is God. Jehovah is might. Jehovah is God. The Lord God. He that wills or commands. Jehovah God.

Joelah (jo-e'-lah) - God is snatching. Removing of oaks. He helps. Let him be profitable. He will sweep away the strong. Removing the oak. God is snatcher. Jah helps. Lifting up. Profiting. Taking away slander. Furthermore. May he avail.

Joezer (jo-e'-zer) - Lord of help. Help of the Lord. Jehovah is help. He that aids or assists. Help of God. Jehovah is his help.

Jogbehah (jog'-be-hah) - Exalted. Lofty. He will be elevated. He shall be exalted. High. An exalting. To be haughty.

Jogli (jog'-li) - Led into exile. An exile. Exiled. He will carry me captive. He shall be revealed. Passing over. Turning back. Rejoicing. May God reveal.

Joha (jo'-hah) - Jehovah is living. Haste. Lead thou Jehovah. Who enlivens. Jehovah revived. He who gives life. Jehovah lives.

Johanan (jo-ha'-nan) - The Lord graciously gave. Jehovah is gracious. Bestowed by the Lord. Merciful. Gift of God. Jehovah favored. Who is liberal or merciful. God bestowed.

John (jon) - Jehovah has been gracious. Jehovah has graciously given. Gift of God. Grace. Dove. The grace or mercy of the Lord.

Joiada (joy'-a-dah) - Jehovah set up. Jehovah has known. Same as Jehoiada

- God has known. Jehovah known. Jehovah knows.

Joiarib (joy'-a-rib) - Jehovah defends. Jehovah contends. Same as Jehoiarib - The Lord will contend. The increasing of God. Defended. Chiding.

Jokdeam (jok'-de-am) - Possessed of the people. Burning of the people. Let the people kindle. Crookedness. Anger of the people.

Jokim (jo'-kim) - Jehovah sets up. God makes to stand still. Jah will rise: That made the sun stand still.

Jokmeam (jok'-me-am) - Gathered of the people. He will establish the people. Congregation. Gathered by the people. Confirmation. People will be raised. Standing of the people.

Jokneam (jok'-ne-am) - Possessed of the people. The people will be purchased. The people will be lamented. Lamentation. Possessed by the people. Possessing. Building up of the people.

Jokshan (jok'-shan) - Sportsman. Fowler. Fowling. Insidious. Difficult. An offense. A knocking. Hardness. Snarer.

Joktan (jok'-tan) - He will be small. Little. Small. Dispute. Insignificant. He is diminished. Small dispute. Contention. Disgust.

Joktheel - Subdued of God. Absolved of God. Reward of God. Veneration. Subdued. Veneration of God. Subdued by God.

Jona (jo'-nah) - A dove. Pigeon.

Jonadab (jon'-a-dab) - Jehovah is liberal. He gave freely. Jehovah largessed. Who gives liberally. Jehovah impels. Jehovah gives. (Same as Jehonadab - Jehovah gave

spontaneously. Jehovah is bounteous. The Lord willing).

Jonah (jo'-nah) - Dove. Dove from the warmth of mating. Multiplying the people.

Jonan (jo'-nan) - God has been gracious. Dove. Pigeon. Multiplying of the people. Grace.

Jonas (jo'-nas) - A dove. Greek form of Jonah. Multiplying of the people.

Jonathan (jon'-a-than) - The Lord gave. Lord of giving. Whom Jehovah gave. The Lord gives. God's gift. Jehovah given. Given of God. God given. Jehovah has given.

Jonath-elem-recho-kim (jo'-nath-e'-lem-re-ko'-kim) - The silent dove afar off. The dove of silence. Among strangers. The dove of silence of distance. A dumb dove in distant places.

Joppa (jop'-pah) - Beautiful. Beauty. Fair to him. Comeliness. Fair. Lovely.

Jorah (jo'rah) - Autumnal rain. Watering. Let him teach. Sprinkling. To cast. Elevated.

Jorai (jo'-rahee) - He will be built up of the Lord. My early rain. My teachers. To cast. Rainy. Elevated. Jehovah teacher. Taught of God. Jehovah has seen.

Joram (jo'-ram) - Jehovah is high. (Same as Jehoram - The Lord exalts. Jehovah is high. The Lord exalted). The Lord is exalted. Height. To cast. Elevated. Exalted by Jehovah.

Jordan (jor'-dan) - Descending. Flowing down. Descending rapidly. Constant sounding. The descender. River of judgment.

Jorim (jo'-rim) - He that exalts the Lord. Jehovah extols. The height. A shortened form of Joram. (Same as Jehoram - The Lord exalts. Jehovah is high.) The Lord exalted.

Jorkoam (jor'-ko-am) - Paleness of the people. Spreading of the people. It is enlarged. Scattered people.

Josabad (jos'-a-bad) - The Lord has given. Jehovah endowed. Having a dowry. (Same as Jehozabad - whom the Lord gave. Jehovah gave. Jehovah is the one who bestows.)

Josaphat (jos'-a-fat) - The Lord judges. The Lord has judged. Jehovah judged. The Greek form of Jehoshaphat - The Lord judges i.e., pleads for him. Whom Jehovah judges.

Josech (jo'-sek) - May God increase.

Josedech (jos'-e-dek) - Jehovah is righteous. Justified by Jehovah. Same as Jehozadak - The Lord has made just. Jehovah is just. The Lord justifies.

Joseph (jo'-zef) - May God add. He shall add. Increasing. Addition. Increase. Adding. Increaser. May Jehovah increase. He adds. To perfect. To increase. To progress.

Jose (jo'-ze) - He that pardons. He gives a Savior. Raised. Who pardons. Same as Joses.

Joses (jo'-zez) - He that pardons. Increaser. Giving. A savior. Helped.

Joshah (jo'-shah) - Jehovah is a gift. Jehovah is uprightness. Aid. Jehovah presents. He will be prospered. Let him subsist. He will be made wise. Despairing. Forgetting. Dwelling. Jah a gift. Being forgetting. Owing. Jehovah established. Jehovah's gift.

Joshasphat (josh'-a-fat) - Jehovah judges. God has judged. Jehovah judged. (Shortened form of

Jehoshaphat - The Lord judges or pleads for him). Whom Jehovah judges.

Joshaviah (josh-a-vi'-ah) - Jehovah is equality. Jehovah sits upright. Set upright of the Lord. He will be prospered of Jah. Jah sustains him. God has bestowed. Jehovah set. The seat. Jehovah is sufficient.

Joshbekashah (josh-bek'-a-shah) - A seat in a hard place. A seat of hardship. Seat of hardness. Diligent seeking of a habitation. A hard seat. It is requiring or beseeching. Seat in hardness. To remain.

Joshua (josh'-u-ah) - Jehovah is salvation. The Lord is his salvation. Lord of salvation. The Lord saves. A savior. A deliverer. Jehovah saves. The deliverance of God. Jehovah saved.

Josiah (jo-si'-ah) - Jehovah supports. Given of the Lord. Whom Jehovah heals. The fire of the Lord. The spared of God. The Lord burns. Founded by Jah. The Lord gives. Jehovah heals.

Josias (jo-si'-as) - Whom Jehovah heals. The Lord gives. Founded by Jah. Greek form of Josiah - Given of the Lord. Whom Jehovah heals.

Josibiah (jos-ib-i'-ah) - Jehovah causes to dwell. He will be made to sit down of the Lord i.e., to live tranquilly or lead a peaceable life. To whom God gives a dwelling. Jah will make to dwell. The seat. Dweller with Jehovah.

Josiphiah (jos-if-i'-ah) - Added of the Lord. Whom Jehovah will increase. Jehovah will increase. Jah will add. Increase of the Lord. The Lord's finishing. Jah adds. Increases. Jah is adding. The Lord increases. Jehovah abides.

Jotbah (jot'bah) - Pleasant. She was good. Pleasantness. Goodness.

Jotbath (jot'-bath) - Goodness. Place of goodness. Pleasantness. His goodness. Turning away.

Jotbathah (jot'-ba-than) - Goodness. Pleasantness. His goodness. Turning away. Same as Jotbah.

Jotham (jo'-tham) - Jehovah is upright. The Lord is upright. Lord of integrity. The integrity of God. Jehovah is perfect. The perfection of the Lord. God is upright. The perfection of God.

Jozabad (joz'-a-bad) - Jehovah has bestowed. Jehovah has endowed. Jehovah endowed. Jehovah endows. The has given. (Same as Jehozabad - Whom the Lord gave. Jehovah gave).

Jozachar (joz'-a-kar) - Jehovah remembers. The Lord is remembered. Whom Jehovah has remembered. Remembering of the male sex. Remembered by Jehovah. He has given. Remembered.

Jozadak (joz'-a-dak) - Jehovah is great. Jehovah is just. Jah is great. God was just. (Same as Jehozadak - The Lord has made just. Jehovah is just). Jehovah is the righteous one.

Jubal (ju'-bal) - Joyful sound. Music. Jubilee. Playing. A ram's horn or trumpet. He will be carried. He that runs. A trumpet. Stream. Nomad. A constant stream.

Jubilee (ju'-bi-lee) - Productive. He will be made able.

Jucal (ju'-kal) - Able. Mighty. Perfect. Self-existent. I shall become superior. Mighty. Potent. (Same as Jehucal - He will be made able or strengthened of the Lord. Jehovah is mighty).

Juda (ju'-dah) - Praise. Confession. (Same as Judah - praised. The Lord be praised.) Object of praise. Praise of the Lord.

Judaea (ju-de'-ah) - Land of Judaea. Praise. Confession. (Same as Judea - Praised. The Lord be praised). Object of praise. Praise of the Lord.

Judah (ju'-dah) - Praised. The Lord be praised. Object of praise. Praise of the Lord. He shall be praised. Confession. The praise of the Lord. Celebrated. Praise. Praise of God.

Judas (ju'-das) - Praise of the Lord. Greek form of Judah. Praise. Confession.

Judas Iscariot (ju'-das-os-car'-e-ot) - Judas - Praise of the Lord. Iscariot - Man of Kerioth, a man of murder.

Jude (jood) - Praise of the Lord. Praise. Confession.

Judea (ju-de'-ah) - Land of Judah. Praised. The Lord be praised. Object of praise. Praise of the Lord. Praise. Confession.

Judith (ju'-dith) - Praised. The praised one. Jewess. Praise. Confession.

Julia (ju'-le-ah) - Having curly hair. Downy. Soft and tender hair. Soft haired. Curled. Frizzled. Feminine of Julius.

Julius (ju'-le-us) - Downy. Curly headed. Curled. Frizzled. Soft haired.

Junia (ju'-ne-ah) - Belonging to Juno. Youthful. Continue thou Jah. Youth. A youth.

Jupiter (ju'-pit-ur) - A father of helps. The father that helpeth. Father love. In Roman mythology he was the chief god who ruled all gods.

Jushab-hesed (ju'-shab-he'-sed) - He will return love. Whose love is returned. Loving kindness is returned. Mercy shall be restored. Dwelling place. Change of mercy. Kindness is returned.

Justus (jus'-tus) - Upright. Just. Righteous.

Juttah (jut'-tah) - It will be stretched out. Extended. Turning away. It is extended.

K

Kabzeel (kab'-se-el) - God has gathered. God will assemble together. The congregation of God. An assembly of God. God gathers.

Kadesh (ka'-desh) - Consecrated. Sanctified. Apartness or set apart for a purpose. Sacred. Holy. Sanctuary. Holiness. A place in the desert.

Kadesh-barnea (ka'-desh-bar'-ne-ah) - Sacred. Desert of wandering. A moving sanctuary. The son of wandering was set apart. Desert of a fugitive. Wilderness of wandering. A place in the desert. Holiness of an inconstant son. Consecrated. Holy.

Kadmiel (kad'-me-el) - God is of old. Eternity of God. Going before of God. Walking religiously and godly. Before or in front of God. Presence of God. God of antiquity. God of rising. God going before with benefits. Minister of God. God is first or before God.

Kadmonites (kad'-mo-nites) - Oriental. Middle Easterners. Ancients. Aboriginal. Chiefs.

Kain (ka'en) - Smith.

Kallai (kal'-la-i) - Jehovah is light. Jehovah is swift. Lightly esteemed of God. Swift. My swiftness. Frivolous. Light. Resting by fire. My voice. God was quick. Swift messenger of Jehovah.

Kanah (ka'-nah) - Place of reeds. Full of reeds. He has purchased. Readiness. Of reeds. A reed or cane.

Kareah (ka'-re-ah) - Bald. Ice. Bald head. Bare. Same as Careah.

Karkaa (kar'-ka-ah) - The floor. The ground. Pavement. Ground floor. Bottom. Dissolving coldness. Deep ground.

Karkan (kar'-kan) - Soft and level ground. A plain. Battering down. They rested. Foundation. Even or deep ground. Excavation. Collection.

Karnaim (kar-na'-am) - Ashtaroth of the two horns. The crescent moons (the new moon). Two horns. Horns. Same as Ashtaroth.

Kartah (kar'-tah) - City. Her meeting place. Calling. Meeting. Joining. Meeting together.

Kartan (kar'-tan) - Two cities. Double city. Their meeting place. City plot. A large or double city. Town.

Kattath (kat'-tath) - Very small. Diminished. Small. Littleness.

Kedar (ke'-dar) - Powerful. Dark skinned man. Black skinned. Black skin. Obscurity. Darkness. Blackness. Sorrow. Dusky. Black. Very black. Dark.

Kedemah (ked'-e-mah) - Eastward. Toward the east. Eastern. Oriental. Ancient. First. Precedence. The east.

Kedemoth (ked'-e-moth) - Beginnings. Ancients. Confrontments. Eastern parts. Antiquity. Old age. Orientals. Antiquities.

Kedesh (ke'-desh) - Sanctuary. Holy place. Holy.

Kedesh-naphtali (ke'-desh-naf'-ta-li) - (Kedesh - Sanctuary. Holy place. Holy. Naphtali - A struggle. My wrestling. My twisting. Obtained by wrestling). Consecrate. Sanctuary. Holy my wrestling.

Kehelathah (ke-hel'-a-thah) - Assembly. Convocation. A whole. A congregation.

Keilah (ki'-lah) - Fortress. Enclosed. Sling. Let the faint be alienated. She that divides or cuts. Castle fortifications. Voice of God. A citadel.

Kelaiah (kel-ah'-yah) - Congregation of the Lord. Jehovah is light. Contempt. Gathering together. Voice of the Lord. Insignificance. Swift for Jehovah.

Kelita (kel'-i-tah) - Congregation of the Lord. Dwarf. Crippled. Poverty. Lacking. Stunted. Maiming. A gathering of the people. Littleness. Same as Kelaiah.

Kemuel (kem-u'-el) - Congregation of God. God stands. Risen of God. Avenge ye God. God hath raised up. God raised. Flock of God. God is risen. Helper of God.

Kenah (ke'-nah) - Buying. Possession.

Kenan (ke'-nan) - One acquired. Begotten. Buyer. Owner. Fixed. Ample Possession. Same as Cainan - Possession. Their smith (fabricator).

Kenath (ke'-nath) - Possession. A possession.

Kenaz (ke'-naz) - Hunting. This possession. This nest. This purchase. This lamentation. A hunter. To seek. To chase. Side or hunting.

Kenezite (ken'-zite) - Descendants of Kenaz - Hunting. This possession. This nest. To hunt. Hunter. This purchase. This lamentation. To seek. To chase.

Kenite (ken'-ite) - A nest. My purchase. A smith. A fabricator. Possession. Purchase. Lamentation.

Kenites (ken'-ites) - A nest. My purchase. A smith. A fabricator.

Possession. Purchase. Lamentations. Metalsmiths.

Kenizzites (ken'-iz-zites) - Same as Kenezite. Descendants of Kenaz - Hunting. This nest. This possession. To hunt. Hunter. This purchase. This lamentation. To seek. To chase. Purchase. Possession.

Keren-happuch (ke'-ren-hap'-puk) - Beautifier or horn of paint. A horn reserved. The horn or child of beauty. Cosmetic box. Paint horn. Splendor of the carbuncle. Horn of antimony.

Kerioth (ke'-re-oth) - Cities. Readings. The cities. The callings. Buildings. A city. Citizens. Calling. Meeting.

Keros (ke'-ros) - Crook. The reed of a weaver's beam. Stooping. Crooked. Crookedness. Curved. Bent. A handle. A weaver's comb. Ankled.

Keturah (ket-u'-rah) - Incense. The smoke of incense. That makes the incense. To fume. Perfumed. To burn. Fumigation. Fragrance.

Kezia (ke-zi'-ah) - Cassia i.e., equally as precious. An excellent aromatic smell. The angle. Superficies. Peeled. To strip off. Surface. Scraped off. Cinnamon.

Keziz (ke-ziz) - Cutting off. End. Extremity. Abrupt. Clipped. The angle. Border. Cassia tree.

Kirbroth-hattaavah (kib'-roth-hat-ta'-a-vah) - Graves of lust. Graves of the longing. The graves of gluttony.

Kibzaim (kib-za'-im) - Two heaps. Double gatherings. Congregation. A double heap. Dual. Double gathering.

Kidron (kid'-ron) - Same as Cedron - Very black. Full of darkness (intense form). Turbid. Great obscurity. Wall. The mourner. The black one. Obscure.

Making black or sad. Dusky. Gloomy. Sad.

Kinah (ki'-nah) - Song of mourning. Lamentation. A dirge. Possession.

Kir (kur) - A wall. A fortress. Town. A city. Meeting. A walled place.

Kir-haraseth (kur-har'-e-seth) - Same as Kir. A wall. A fortress. Town. A city. Meeting. A walled place. Fortress of earthenware. Town of witness. City of pottery.

Kir-hareseth (kur-har'-e-seth) - Same as Kir-haraseth. The wall is earthen. Brick fortress. City of pottery.

Kir-haresh (kur-ha'-resh) - Same as Kir-haraseth. The wall is earthen. Citadel. City of pottery. Brick fortress. Town of witness.

Kir-heres (kur-he'-res) - The wall is earthen. A citadel. Brick fortress. Town of witness. Same as Kirharaseth.

Kiriathaim (kir-e-a-thay'-im) - Double city. Walled cities. Double town.

Kirioth (kir'-e-oth) - Cities. Buildings. Citizens. Calling. Meetings. Same as Kerioth.

Kirjath (kur'-jath) - City. A walled city. Vocation. Meeting. City of towns.

Kirjathaim (kur'-jath-a'-im) - Double city. Walled cities. The two cities. Callings or meetings. Double town.

Kirjath-arba (kur'-jath-ar'-bah) - City of Arba. City of four. Fourth city.

Kirjath-arim (kur'-jath-a'-rim) - Contracted from Kirjath-jearim. City of woods or full of woods or trees. City of enemies. City of cities. City of those who watch. City of forests. City of woods or of towns.

Kirjath-baal (kur'-jath-ba'-al) - City of Baal. City of the rich man.

Kirjath-huzoth (kur'-jath-hu'-zoth) - A city of streets i.e., a city that has many streets. City of broad ways. Populous city.

Kirjath-jearim (kur'-jath-je'-a-rim) - City of woods or full of woods or trees. The city of forests. City of woods. Same as Kirjatharim.

Kirjath-sannah (kur-jath-san'-nah) - City of learning. City of thorns. City of enmity. City of instruction. Palm city. City of cleanliness.

Kirjath-sepher (kur'-jath-se'-fer) - city of books. City of letters. City of separation.

Kish (kish) - Snaring. Bird catching. Power. Straw. Forage. Hard. Difficult. A bow. Fowling.

Kishi (kish'-i) - Snaring of the Lord. My snare. Also called Kushaiah - The bow of Jehovah. Hardness. His gravity. His offense. Bow of Jah. Hunting of God. Bowed. A gift.

Kishion (kish'-e-on) - Very hard. Hardness (intense form). Soreness. Hard ground.

Kishon (ki'-shon) - Tortuous. Winding about. Ensnarer. Hard. Sore. Stubbornness. Very crooked. Curved. Winding. Bending.

Kislev (kis'-lev) - Ninth Jewish month (November-December).

Kison (ki'-son) - Same as Kishan - Tortuous. Winding about. Crooked. Winding. Curved. Sanctuary. Stubborn. Bending.

Kislothtabor (kis'-lath-ta'-bor) - Loins of Tabor.

Kithlish (kith'-lish) - Wall of man. Fortified. It is a wall. The company of a lioness. Separation. A whited wall. A man's wall.

Kitron (ki'-tron) - Knotty. Burning. Incense burner. Making sweet. Binding together. Fumigation. Very small. Shortened.

Kittim (kit'-tim) - They that bruise. Beaters down. Crushers. Breaking. Bruising small. Gold. Coloring. An islander. Contusions. Knotty.

Koa (ko'-ah) - Prince. Alienation. Hope. A congregation. A line. A rule. Curtailment. Cutting off. A level country. Male camel.

Kohath (ko'-hath) - Assembly. Congregation. Obedient. Waiting. Wrinkle. Bluntness. Allied. Obedience.

Kohathites (ko'-hath-ites) - Descendants of Kohath - Assembly. Congregation. Obedient. Waiting. Wrinkle. Bluntness. Allied.

Kolaiah (ko-la-i'-ah) - The voice of the Lord. Voice of Jehovah. The voice of God. Voice of Jah.

Korah (ko'-rah) - Ice. Icy. Hail. Baldness. Bald. Frost. Frigid. Bare. Frozen.

Korohite (ko'-ra-hite) - Descendants of Korah - Ice. Icy. Hail. Baldness. Bald. Frost. Frigid. Frozen. Bare.

Korothites (ko'-ra-thites) - Descendants of Korah - Ice. Icy. Hail. Baldness. Bald. Frost. Frigid. Frozen. Bare.

Kore (ko-'re) - Partridge. A crier. Calling. Happening. One who proclaims.

Korhites (kor'-hites) - Same as Korah - Ice. Icy. Hail. Baldness. Bald. Frost. Frigid. Frozen. Bare.

Koz (coz) - The thorn.

Kushaiah (cu-shah'-yah) - Longer form of Kishi. The bow of Jehovah. Snare of Jehovah. To trap or ensnare. Hunting of God. Entrapped of Jah.

L

Laadah (la'-a-dah) - Order. Festival. For adornment. To assemble together. To testify. Passing over.

Laadan (la'-a-dan) - Put in order. Well ordered. Festival born. For their adornment. For pleasure. Devouring. Judgment. For a witness. For delight. Ordered.

Laban (la'-ban) - White. Glorious. Shining. Gentle. Brittle.

Labana (la'-ban-a) - The moon. Whiteness. Frankincense.

Lachish (la'-kish) - Obstinate i.e., hard to be captured. Impregnable. Swiftness. Walk of a man. Who walks. Invincible. For terror. Hill. Height. Who exists of himself.

Lael (la'-el) - By God. Devoted to God. To the mighty. Consecrated of God. Belonging to God.

Lahad (la'-had) - In triumph or joy. Towards exultant shout. Oppression. Oppressed. Dark colored. Praising. To confess. To be eager. For an ovation. To be earnest. Sluggish.

Lahai-roi (la-hah'-ee-roy) - To the living is sight. Who liveth and seeth me. Well of the living one. The living God looking on me. (Same as Beer Lahairoi - The well of the life of vision. The well of her that lives and of him that sees i.e., preserves me in life. The well of the living who sees me.)

Lahman (lah'-man) - Because of violence. To the violent their bread. Their war. Their bread. Food like. Provisions. Abundance of bread. Place of flight.

Lahmi (lah'-mi) - My warrior. An eater. My war. My bread. Great in a heap. Foodful. Warrior.

Laish (la'-ish) - Lion. An old lion. Crushing. Destructive blows.

Lakum (la'-kum) - Stopping up the way i.e., fortified place. Fort. The rising up. Castle. Defense. Fortification. For firmness. Way stopper i.e., a fortified place. Fortress.

Lama (la'-mah) - Why.

Lamech (la'-mek) - Powerful. Destroyer. One who overthrows. A strong young man. Who is struck. Reduced. Poor. Made low. Strong. Healthy. Overthrower. Wild man. Strong youth.

Laodicea (la-od-i-se'-ah) - Greek, Laos - People. Laity. Dicea - Opinion. Custom. Opinion or custom of the people. Justice of the people. Ruled by the people. Rule of the majority. Democratic i.e., people's rights or opinions. The people's rights. A just people. Justice.

Laodiceans (la-od-i-se'-uns) - Inhabitants of Laodicea. Greek, Laos - People. Laity. Dicea - Opinion. Custom. Opinion or custom of the people. Justice of the people. Ruled by the people. Rule of the majority. Democratic, i.e., people's rights or opinions. The people's rights. A just people. Justice.

Lapidoth (lap'-i-doth) - Torches, i.e., having eyes of fire. Enlightened. Lightning flashes. Flames. Lamps. To shine. Light.

Lasea (la-se'-ah) - Shaggy. Thick. Wise. Wine. Stony.

Lasha (la'-sha) - Fissure. Unto blindness (by covering the eyes). To call. To anoint. Bursting forth. A boiling spring. For delight. To break through. Wise.

Lasharon (lash'-ar-on) - Of the plain. For a great plain. On the plain. Of or to Sharon.

Latin (lat'-in) - The language spoken by Romans. Of Rome's strength.

Lazarus (laz'-a-rus) - God has ruled. Without helps. Greek form of Eleazar. Assistance of God. Help of God. Grace. God has helped.

Leah (le'-ah) - Wearied. Languid. Weary. Tired. Faint from sickness. Painful. Weariness.

Leannoth (le-an'-noth) - Answering. To respond.

Lebana (leb'-a-na) - Clothe.

Lebanah (leb'-a-nah) - Moon. White. A poetic designation of the moon.

Lebanon (leb'-a-on) - Very white. Mountain of snow (intense form). The white mountain. Incense.

Lebaoth (leb'-a-oth) - Lioness. Lividness. Lions.

Lebbaeus (leb-be'-us) - Man of heart. Lover. Praising. Confessing. Courageous.

Lebonah (le-bo'-nah) - Frankincense (from its whiteness). Whiteness. Sign of the heart. Incense.

Lecah (le'-cah) - Progress. Journey. Addition. Walking. A journey. Going. A promenade.

Lehabim (le'-ha- bim) - Flames. Scorching heat. Flame colored. Inflamed. Swords. Fiery. Which are inflamed. Red. Flame.

Lehi (le'-hi) - Jawbone. A cheek. Fleshiness. Soft. Cheekbone.

Lekah (le'-kah) - Walking. Going.

Lemuel (lem'-u-el) - By God. Devoted to God. God is bright. With whom God. God with them. Belonging to God. In God. One for God. Dedicated or devoted. Godward.

Leshem (le'-shem) - Precious stone. Unto desolation. A name. Putting. A precious stone. Strong. A lion. Tranquility. Fortress.

Letushim (le-tu'-shim) - Artificers. One who hammers. Those who sharpen. The hammered. Struck. Oppressed. Sharpened ones. Hammered ones. Filemen. Hammermen. Bruises.

Leummim (le-um'-mim) - Peoples. Nations. Countries. Without water. Communities. Many people.

Levi (le'-vi) - Adhesion. Joined. Associate. A companion. Associated with him. Attached. My joining. To adhere.

Leviathan (le-vi'-ath-un) - A water monster. A coiled animal. Their burrowing. Their union.

Levite(s) (le'-vite(s)) - Descendants of Levi - Adhesion. Joined. Associate. A companion. Associated with him. Attached. My joining. To adhere. My adhesion. Who is held or associated.

Levitical (le-vi'-ti-cal) - My adhesion.

Leviticus (le-vi'-ti-cus) - The book which treats the affairs of the Levitical law. Called by the Jews - Law of the priests. Law of offerings.

Libertines (lib'-ur-tines) - Freedmen. Free ones.

Libnah (lib'-nah) - Whiteness. Transparency. White. Clearness.

Libnath (lib'-nath) - A river from whose sands the Egyptians made the first glass. White.

Libni (lib'-ni) - White. Distinguished. Transparent. Whiteness. For building up.

Libnites (lib'-nites) - Descendants of Libni - White. Distinguished. Transparent. Whiteness. For building up.

Libya (lib'-e-ah) - Extension. Grazing. Afflicted. Weeping. The heart of the sea. Fat. Heat. Situated.

Libyans (lib-e-uns) - Empty hearted. Extension. Grazing. Same as Put. People of Libya.

Likhi (lik'-hi) - Jehovah is doctrine. Characterized by knowledge. Learned. Fond of learning. My doctrine. A portion learned.

Linus (li'-nus) - Flax. Nets. Linen. Like to a lion.

Lo-ammi (lo-am'-mi) - Not of my people. Not my people.

Lod (lod) - Contention. Strife. Travail. To bear. Nativity. Generation. Offspring. Birth. Fissure.

Lo-debar (lo-de'-bar) - Without pasture. Not a word i.e., nothing. No pasture. Barren. Without a guide. Pastureless.

Lois (lo'-is) - Agreeable. Desirable. No standard bearer. No flight. Better. Pleasing.

Lord (lord) - Almost uniform rendering of Jehovah in the Old Testament.

Lo-ruhamah (lo-ru-ha'-mah) - Without mercy. Not having obtained mercy. Not pitied. Not favored. Mercy is not shown by her. The uncompassionate. Receiving no compassion.

Lot (lot) - Covering. Veiled. Concealed. Covered. Myrrh. A wrapping. Heart of a man. Heart of the sea. Protection. Hidden Veil.

Lotan (lo'-tan) - Covering up. A covering. Veiling. Heart of a man. Heart of the sea. Wrapped up. Joined. Hidden.

Lubim(s) (lu'bim(s)) - Dwellers in a thirsty land. Arid country. A dry region. To thirst. Heart of a man. Heart of the sea. Inhabitants of a dry and thirsty land.

Lucas (lu'-cas) - Light giving. Luminous. Bringing light. Same as Luke.

Lucifer (lu'-sif-ur) - Light bearer. The shining one. Shining. Howling. Bringing light. Daystar. Beams of light.

Lucius (lu'-she-us) - Of the light. Luminous. A noble. Bringing light. Born in the daytime. Rising up. Light. Morning born.

Lud (lud) - Bending. Strife. To the firebrands. Travailing. To humiliate. Offspring. Tortuous. Nativity. Generation.

Ludim (lu'-dim) - Bending. Strife. To the firebrands. Travailing. To thirst. Offspring. Generation. Nativity. Same as Lud. To humiliate.

Luhith (lu'-hith) - Tables. Slabs. Abounding in boards. Pertaining to the table. Floored. Polished. A table. Elevated place. Floor. Made of boards. Tablets.

Luke (luke) - Light giving. Luminous. White.

Luz (luz) - Almond tree. A filbert. Perverse. Separation. Departure. An almond.

Lycaonia (li-ca-o'-ne-ah) - Wolf land. She-wolf. Breast of sheep.

Lycia (lish'-e-ah) - Wolfish. Inflammation. Great heat. Land of Lycus.

Lydda (lid'-dah) - Travail. That drives away sorrow. An ornament. Strife. A standing pool.

Lydia (lid'-e-ah) - Bending. Brought forth. To firebrand. Travailing. That drives away sorrow. Birth. Offspring. Lydia's land. Descendants. Native of Lydia.

Lydians (lid'-e-uns) - Same as Lud. Bending. Strife. Inhabitants of Lydia.

Lysanias (li-sa'-ne-as) - Ending sorrow. Ending sadness. That drives away sorrow. Relaxing sadness. Dissolving sadness. Grief dispelling.

Lysias (lis'-e-as) - He who has the power to set free. Releaser. Dissolving. Liberating. Relaxing.

Lysimachus (ly'-si-ma-kus) - Scattering the battle.

Lystra (lis'-trah) - Ransoming. That dissolves or disperses. Flock of sheep.

M

Maacah (ma'-a-kah) - Oppression. Compression. Depression. Squeezed. Pressure. Worn. Pressed down. Fastened. Same as Maachah.

Maachah (ma'-a-kah) - Oppression. Compression. Depression. Squeezed. Pressure. Worn. Pressed down. Fastened.

Maachathi (ma-ak'-a-thite) - Same as Maachah. Oppression. Compression. Depression. Squeezed. Worn. Pressed down. Fastened. Broken.

Maachathite(s) (ma-ak'-a-thites) - Inhabitants of Maachah. Descendants of Maachah. Oppression. Compression. Depression. Squeezed. Worn. Pressed down. Fastened.

Maadai (ma'-a-dahee) - My unclothing. My slidings. My adorning. Pleasant. Testifying. Ornament of Jehovah. The ornament of God. God promises.

Maadiah (ma-a-di'-ah) - Ornament of Jehovah. Adorned of Jah. Shaken of Jah. Pleasantness. The testimony of the Lord. The ornament of God. God promises.

Maai (ma'-ahee) - Jehovah is compassionate. Compassion. Compassionate. My bowels. Belly. Heaping up. The fountain of the Lord. Sympathetic. God is compassionate.

Maalehacrabbim (ma'a-lej-as-rab'-bim) - The going up of scorpions. Ascent of scorpions. Going up.

Maarath (ma'-a-rath) - A place naked of trees. A treeless place. Desolation. Waste. Den. Making empty. Watching. Level place.

Maaseiah (ma'-a-si'-ah) - Refuge of the Lord. Work of Jehovah. Jehovah is a refuge. Operative. The work of the Lord.

Maasiani (ma-a'-see-ahee) - Refuge of the Lord. Work of Jehovah. Jehovah is a refuge. Operative. The work of the Lord. Same as Maaseiah. The defense.

Maath (ma'-ath) - Small. Wiping away. From this time. Breaking. Fearing. Smiting. Removing.

Maaz (ma'-az) - Anger. Wrath. Counselor. Shutting. Wood. Wooden. Closure or make firm. Oppression.

Maaziah (ma-a-zi'-ah) - Consolation of the Lord. Strength of Jehovah. Rescued of God. Jehovah's consolation. Rescue of God. Jehovah is a refuge.

Macedonia (mas-e-do'-nee-ah) - Extended land. Tall. Burning. Adoration.

Machbanai (mak'-ba-na-hee) - To heap up. Poor. A smiter. Chain of God. Stout. Fat. Thick one. Thick bond of the Lord. Clothed with a cloak. He brought low my sons.

Machbenah (mak'-be-nah) - To heap up. Poor. A smiter. Chain. Cloak. Poverty of the son. Knob. Lump. Bond. Clad with a cloak. He brought low the building.

Machi (ma'-ki) - Decrease. My poverty. Pining. Poor. A smiter. Consuming of strength. Diminution.

Machir (ma'-kur) - Sold. A seller. Salesman. Acquired. Sold. Selling. Knowing. He who sells.

Machirites (ma'-kur-ites) - Descendants of Machir. Sold. A seller. Salesman. Acquired. Sold. Selling. Knowing. He who sells.

Machnadebai (mak-nad'-e-ba-hee) - What is like the liberty of the Lord i.e., how great is the liberty of the Lord. Gift of the noble one. He brought low my willing ones. A liberal man. Gift of the noble. Smiter. What is like the liberality of God.

Machpelah (mak-pe'-lah) - Double. A doubling. One above another. A fold. Spiral form. Winding.

Madai (ma'-dahee) - Extended of the Lord. Middle. My measures. My garments. What is enough. Middle land. God extends. A measure. Judging. A garment.

Madian (ma'-de-an) - Contention. Strife. Greek form of Midian. A contender. Judgment. Striving. Chiding. Covering. Great extension.

Madmannah (mad-man'-nah) - Dunghill. Heap. Madmen - A heap of dung. Garment of stimulation. Measure of a gift. Preparation of a garment. Place of manure.

Madmen (mad'-men) - Place of manure. Dung hill.

Madmenah (mad-me'-nah) - Dung hill. Heap. Place of manure. Dung heap.

Madon (ma'-don) - Contention. Strife. Place of contention. Place of judgment. Extensiveness. A chiding. A garment. His measure.

Magbish (mag'-bish) - Congregation. Crystalizing. Assembly. Fortress. Stiffening. Excelling. Height.

Magdala (mag'-da-lah) - Tower. Fortress. Castle. Greatness.

Magdalene (mag'-da-leen) - Inhabitants of Magdala. Tower. Fortress. Elevated. Grand. Magnificent. A person from Magdala. Of Magdala.

Magdiel (mag'-de-el) - Praise of God. Honor of God. Renown. My preciousness is God. Excellent or precious. Gift of God. Praise. Declaring God. Chosen fruit of God. God is precious. Renowned of God.

Magog (ma'-gog) - Expansion. Increase of family. From the top. Overtopping. Covering. Enlargement. Extension. Augmentation. A roof. Land of Gog. Enemy. Evil. Dissolving.

Magor-missabib (ma'-gor-mis'-sa-bib) - Fear round about. Fear or terror is about. Fear everywhere. Terror on every side. Fear on every side.

Magpiash (mag'-pe-ash) - Killer of moths. Moth slayer. Cluster of stars. Plague of moths. The plague is consumed. Congregation of the congregation. Moth killer. Collector. Exterminator. Collector of a cluster of stars. A body thrust hard together.

Magus (mag'-us) - Magician.

Mahalah (ma'-ha-lah) - Disease. Sickness. Praising God. Weak one.

Mahalaleel (ma-hal'-a-le-el) - Praise of God. Praiser of God. God is splendor. Praising God.

Mahalath (ma'-ha-lath) - Harp. Wind instrument. A musical instrument. Making sick. Sickness. Appeasing. Compassion. Singing. Infirm. Praising God. Mild. The spiritual malady of the sons of men.

Mahalath Leannoth (ma'-ha-lath le'-an-noth) - Title of Psalms 53 and 88.

The spiritual malady of the sons of men.

Mahali (ma'-ha-li) - Infirmity. Weak. Sick. Instability. Infirm. A harp. Pardon.

Mahanaim (ma-ha-na'-im) - Two hosts. Two camps. Marching up. Two tents. Two fields. Two armies.

Mahaneh-dan (ma'-ha-neh-dan) - Camp of Dan. Camp of judgment. Troops. Tents of judgment.

Mahanem (ma'-ha-nem) - A comforter.

Maharai (ma'-ha-ra-hee) - Impetuosity of the Lord. Impetuous. Hasty. The haste of God. Swift. Hasting. A hill. From a hill. Swift.

Mahath (ma'-hath) - Seizing. Taking hold. Instrument of seizing or dissolution. Taking or wiping away. Erasure. Grasping. Snatching. Blot out.

Mahavite (ma'-ha-vite) - Places of assembly. Declarers. Propagators. Living ones. The place of the congregation. Blotting out. Declaring a message.

Mahaz (ma'-haz) - An end. Ending. Growing hope.

Mahazioth (ma-ha'ze-oth) - Visions. Visions of significance. Seeing a sign. Seeing a letter.

Maher-shalal-hash-baz (ma'-her-sha'-lal-hash'-baz) - Haste to the spoil. Hasten the spoil. Rush on the prey. The spoil hastens. The prey speeds. Quick to the prey. To hasten the booty and hurry the spoil. Hastening to the spoil. He hasteth to the spoil. Making speed to the spoil. He hastens to the prey. The spoil hastens. The prey speeds.

Mahlah (Mah'-lah) - Disease. Sick. Ill. In pain. Mildness. Pardon. Sickness. Weak one. Same as Mahaz. An end. Ending. Growing hope.

Mahli (Mah'-li) - Infirmity. Weak. Sick. My sickness. Same as Mahali. Sickly. Pining. Mild.

Mahlites (mah'-lites) - Descendants of Mohali. Infirmity. Weak. Sick. My sickness.

Mahlon (mah'-lon) - Great infirmity. A sick person. Painful. Sick. Weak. Sickly. Mild. A heavy disease. Pining.

Mahol (ma'-hol) - Exultation. Dancing. A dance. Joy. Infirmity. Dancing in a circle. Dancer.

Mahseiah (ma-si-a) - Jehovah is a refuge. (NIV for Maaseiah)

Makaz (ma'-kaz) - End. Extremity i.e., land's end. Cutting off. Distant place. An end. Goal. A boundary.

Makheloth (mak'-he-loth) - Congregations. Assemblies. Chairs. Place where the people assemble. Assembly. Congregation.

Makkedah (mak'-ke-dah) - A place of shepherds. A staff. Branding or spotting place. Place of cattle breeders. Herdsman's place. A fold. Worshiping. Burning. Raised. Crookedness.

Maktesh (mak'-tesh) - Mortar i.e., a hollow place. Heap of the dead. A deep hollow. A mortar. Depression. A dell.

Malachi (mal'-a-ki) - Angel or messenger of the Lord. The messenger of Jehovah. My messenger. Ministrative. My angel.

Malcham (mal'-kam) - Most high king. Their king. Regnant. Rule. By their king. Exalted king. A king. God is my king.

Malchiah (mal-ki'-ah) - Jehovah's king. Jehovah is king. The Lord is king. Appointed by God. God is my king.

Malchiel (mal'-ke-el) - God's king. God is king. Appointed by God. God is my king. God is king.

Malchielites (mal'-ke-el-ites) - Descendants of Malchiel. God's king. God is a king. Appointed by God. God is my king. God is king. King of God.

Malchijah (mal-ki'-jah) - Jehovah's king. Jehovah is king. The Lord reigns. King of Jah. God is my king. Appointed by Jah.

Malchiram (mal'-ki-ram) - King of height. My king is exalted. God is exalted. Most exalted king. King of altitude. King of exaltation.

Malchi-shua (mal'-ki-shu'-ah) - King of help. King of aid. My king is salvation. King of opulence. The help of the king. King of wealth.

Malchus (mal'-kus) - King. Counselor (Greek form of Malluch - Reigning. Counselor). A king. Kingdom. My king. Ruler.

Maleleel (mal'-e-le-el) - Praise of God. Greek form of Mahalaleel.

Mallothi (mal'-lo-thi) - Jehovah is speaking. Jehovah is splendid. I speak. I have spoken. My fulness. Jah is speaking. Circumcision.

Malluch (mal'-luk) - Reigning. Counselor. Kingly. To take council. Counseling. Ruling. Possession.

Mammon (mam'-mon) - Fulness. Wealth (as trusted in). Riches.

Malta (mal'-ta) - Refuge.

Mamre (mam'-re) - From seeing. From the vision. Fatness. Vigor. Lifting

up. Strength. Bitter. Vigor. Lusty. Rebellious. Set with trees. Firmness.

Manaen (man'-a-en) - Consoler. Comforter. A leader. A comforter.

Manaheth (man'-a-hath) - Resting place. Rest. Gift. My lady. My prince of rest.

Manahethites (man'-a-heth-ites) - Resting place. Rest. Gift. My lady. My prince of rest. Inhabitants of Manaheth - Midst of the resting place.

Manasseh (ma-nas'-seh) - One who causes to forget. Forgetting. Forgetfulness. He that is forgotten. Causing to forget. He made to forget. Causing forgetfulness.

Manasses (ma-nas'-seez) - Causing forgetfulness. Greek form of Manasseh - Forgetfulness.

Manassites (ma-nas'-sites) - Descendants of Manasseh - One who causes to forget. Forgetting. Forgetfulness.

Maneh (ma'-neh) - A weight. A coin. Present.

Manoah (ma-no'-ah) - Rest. Recreation. Quiet. Consolation of parents. A resting.

Maoch (ma'-ok) - Poor. Oppression. Pressing. Squeezing. Same as Maachah - A poor one. Breastbone. Oppressed.

Maon (ma'-on) - Place of habitation. Habitation. Place of abode. Residence. Abode. House. Place of sin.

Maonites (ma'on-ites) - Inhabitants of Maon - Place of habitation. Place of abode. Residence. Abode. House. Place of sin.

Mara (ma'-rah) - Bitterness. Bitter. Sad. He was arrogant. Steep. A sacrifice of myrrh. Ascension.

Marah (ma'-rah) - Bitterness. Bitter. Sad. He rebelled. Calamity. Desert spring whose waters were sweetened. Sleep. A sacrifice of myrrh. Ascension.

Maralah (mar'-a-lah) - Place of concussions i.e., place of obnoxious or subject to earthquakes. Trembling. Causing shaking. Earthquake. Declivity.

Maranatha (mar-an-a'-thah) - Our Lord comes. Even so come. Come Lord Jesus. The Lord is coming. Our Lord has come. An exclamation of approaching divine judgment.

Marcus (mar'-cus) - A large hammer. Polite. A defense. Shining. To pine away.

Maresha (mar'-e-shah) - That which is at the head i.e., leadership. Capital. Headship. Forget to be arrogant. Summit.

Mareshah (mar'-e-shah) - At the head. Possession. Chief place at the head. Summit. Same as Maresha.

Mark (mark) - A large hammer. Polite. Same as Marcus. To whither away. Shining.

Maroth (ma'-roth) - Bitterness. Bitter fountains. Bitter springs.

Marsena (mar'-se-nah) - Lofty. Worthy. Bitter is the thorn bush. Bitterness of a bramble worn out. Sorrowful. Strong. Worthy man. Forgetful man.

Mar's Hill (marz-hill) - Martial peak. Hill of Mar's. English form of Areopagus, A rocky height of Athens.

Martha (mar'-thah) - Dominant one. Mistress. She was rebellious. Lady. Who becomes bitter. Provoking.

Mary (ma'-ry) - Bitterness. Rebellion. Obstinate. Greek form of Miriam - Their rebellion. Myrrh of the sea. Strong.

Mary Magdalene (ma'-ry-mag'-da-lene) - Mary - Bitterness. Rebellion. Obstinate. Magdalene - Tower. Castle.

Magdala (mag'-da-lah) - Tower. Castle.

Maschil (mas'-kil) - Understanding. Giving understanding. Intelligently. With understanding. A poem. Instructive.

Mash (mash) - Drawn out. He departed. He felt groped. Same as Meshech. Taken away. Extraction.

Mashal (ma'-shal) - Prayer. Entreaty. A parable. One who speaks in parables. Governing. Petition. Request.

Masrekah (mas'-re-kah) - Vineyard. Place of the choice vine. Whistling. Hissing. Place of superior vines.

Massa (mas'-sah) - Bearing patiently. Burden - A prophecy. A burden as something undertaken to carry through. Enduring. A speech. Utterance. A lifting up. Burden. Oracle.

Massah (mas'-sah) - Temptation. She fainted. Trial. Testing. Spot of temptation.

Mathusala - When he is dead it shall be sent. (Greek form of Mathuselah - When he is dead it shall be sent i.e., The flood. Messenger of death. A man of the javelin. It shall be sent (deluge)). Great extension. Man of a dart.

Matred (ma'-tred) - Thrusting forward. Pushing forward. One who expels. Constant pursuit. Continuing. Wand of government. Trouble. Propelling. Expulsion.

Matri (ma'-tri) - Jehovah is watching. Rainy. Rain. Prison. Rain of Jehovah.

Mattan (mat'-tan) - A gift. Death of them. Gift.

Mattanah (mat'-ta-nah) - Gift of the Lord. Gift of Jehovah. Gift. Present. Gift of Jah.

Mattaniah (mat-ta-ni'-ah) - Gift of the Lord. Gift of Jehovah. Gift of Jah. Gift.

Mattatha (mat-ta-thah) - A gift. He that gives. Gift of Jah. (Greek form of Mattaniah - Gift of the Lord. Gift of Jehovah). His gift.

Mattathah (mat'-te-na-hee) - Gift of Jehovah. His gift. A gift. Gift of Jah.

Mattathias (mat-ta-thi'-as) - Gift of Jehovah. The gift of the Lord. God's gift.

Mattenai (mat'-te-na-hee) - Gift of the Lord. Liberal. Bestowment. Gift of Jehovah. My gifts. Gift of God.

Matthan (mat'-than) - Gift. Present.

Matthal (mat'-thal) - Gift. He that gives.

Matthat (mat'-that) - Gift. Present.

Matthew (math'-ew) - Gift of Jehovah. Given. A reward. Gift of God.

Matthias (mat'-thias) - Gift of God. (Greek form of Mattathias - Gift of Jehovah). The twelve signs of the Zodiac. God's gift.

Mattithiah (mat-tith-i'-ah) - Gift of the Lord. The twelve signs of the Zodiac. Gift of God. Gift of Jehovah.

Mazzaroth (maz'-za-roth) - Scattered. Dispersed. The twelve signs of the Zodiac. The wain. Great bear. Gift of Jehovah. Distinction.

Meah (me'-ah) - A hundred. A hundred cubits. A hundred-fold.

Mearah (me'-a-rah) - A cave (from to strip or lay bare). Den. Making empty. A dark cavern.

Mebunnai (me-bun'-nahee) - Building of the Lord. Built. Built up. My buildings. Setup or erected by God. Built by God. Strong one. Construction. Son. Building. Understanding.

Mecherathite (me-ker'-ath-ite) - Swordite i.e., a soldier. He of the dug-out. He of the digging tool. Selling. Knowledge. Native or inhabitant of Mecherah.

Meconah (me'-co-nah) - Foundation.

Medad (me'-dad) - Love. A measurer. He that measures. Water of love. Water of the Beloved. Affection. Loving. Affectionate. Friend.

Medan (me'-dan) - Strife. Contention. A striver. Judgment. Discernment. Great enlargement. Process.

Mede(s) (meed(s)) - (Same as Medai - Extended of the Lord. My measure. My garment). Measure. Abounding.

Medeba (med'-e-bah) - Flowing water. Waters of rest or quiet. Waters of grief. Waters springing up.

Media (me'-de-ah) - (Same as Madai - Extended of the Lord. My measure. He of the measured. My garments). Measure. Habit. Covering. God extends. A garment. Middle land.

Median (me'-de-an) - (Same as Madai - Extended of the Lord. My measure). One from Media.

Medeba (med'-e-ba) - Water of rest. Water of strength. Waters of grief. Waters springing up.

Megiddo (me-ghid'-do) - Place of troops. Place of multitudes. Invading. Gathering for cutting (self). His cutting place. His precious fruit. Declaring a message. Place of the great crowd. Rendezvous.

Megiddon (me-ghid'-don) - Same as Megiddo - Place of troops. Place of multitudes. Invading. Gathering for cutting (self). His cutting place. His precious fruit. Declaring a message. Place of the great crowd. Rendezvous.

Mehetabeel (me-het'-a-be-el) - Benefitted of God. God blesses. God is doing good. How good is God? God benefits. Bettered by God.

Mehetabel (me-het'-a-bel) - (Same as Mehetabeel - Benefitted of God. God blesses. God is doing good). Whom God makes happy. God shows kindness. To whom God is good. Bettered of God.

Mehida (me-hi'-dah) - A joining together. Union. Famous. Allegorist. A riddle. Sharpness of wit. A chain. Junction. Noble one. Joining.

Mehir (me'-hur) - Price. Wages. Dexterity. A reward. Ability. A choice.

Mehola (me-ho'-lah) - A dance. Dancing.

Meholathite (me-ho'-lath-ite) - Same as Abel-meholah - Meadow for dancing. Mourning for sickness. A dance. Dancing.

Mehujael (me-hu'-ja-el) - Destroyed by God. Struck by God. God is combating. Blotted out by God. Who proclaims God. Grief of God. God is combating grief. Smitten of God.

Mehuman (me-hu'-man) - Faithful. Their discomfiture. Making an uproar. A multitude. Habitually faithful. True.

Mehunim(s) (me-hu'-nims) - Place of habitation. Abodes. Dwellings. Descendants of Maon. Residence.

Me-jarkon (me-jar'-kon) - Water of great greenness. Waters of yellowness. Waters of mildew. Waters of Verdure. The waters of Jordan. Yellow water. Yellowish water.

Mekonah (me-ko'-nah) - Base i.e., A foundation. A settlement. A fort of a pillar. Provision. Sure seat. Pedestal. Basis. A base or foundation.

Melatiah (mel-a-ti'-ah) - Delivered of the Lord. Whom Jehovah freed. Jehovah has set free. Deliverance of the Lord. Jah has delivered. Deliverance of God. Jehovah delivers.

Melchi (mel'-chi) - Jehovah is my king. My king. My counsel. The Lord is king. King appointed by Jehovah.

Melchiah (mel-ki'-ah) - Jehovah's king. God is my king. The Lord is king.

Melchisedec (mel-kis'-e-dek) - King of righteousness. King of justice. My king of righteousness. Greek form of Melchizedek.

Melchi-shua (mel'-ki-shu'-ah) - King of help. King of aid. King of health. Magnificent king. King of wealth. My king is savior.

Melchizedek (mel-kiz'-e-dek) - King of righteousness. My king of righteousness. King of justice. King of Salem.

Melea (mel'-e-ah) - Fullness. My dear friend. Object of care. Supplying. Supplied. Full. Filling.

Melech (me'-lek) - King. Counselor.

Melicu (mel'-i-cu) - Counselor. (Same as Malluch - Reigning). My royalty. They have made a king. His kingdom. His counselor. Large. Possession. Regnant. Advisor.

Melita (mel'-i-tah) - Honey. Affording honey. A refuge. Flowing with honey.

Melzar (mel'-zar) - The overseer. Steward. The circumcised. He straitened. Circumcision of a narrow place. The glory has gone. Chief butler. The overseer.

Memphis (mem'-fis) - Haven of good men. The gate of the blessed. Waving to and fro. Being made fair. Abode of the good. A place bound or enclosed.

Memucan (mem-u'-can) - Impoverished. Their poverty. To prepare. Certain. True. Abounding in honor. Dignity. Authority. Satrap. Sorcerer.

Menahem (men'-a-hem) - Consoling. Comforter. A comforter. Who conducts them. Preparation of heat. Consoler. Son of God. Who slew Shallum (Manaen).

Menan (me'-nan) - Consoling. Comforter. Soothsayer. Enchanted. Numbered. Rewarded. Prepared. Great trouble.

Mene (me'ne) - To number. Numbered. Count. He has numbered. Who reckons or is counted. Who is numbered. He is numbered.

Mene, Mene, Tekel, Upharsin (me'-ne-me'ne-te'-kel-u'-far-sin) - God has numbered thy kingdom and finished it.

Meonenim (me-on'-e-nim) - Enchanter. Observer of time. Charmers. Juggler. Sorcerer. To practice magic. Regardless of time.

Meonothai (me-on'-o-tha-hee) - Habitation of the Lord. My habitation. Dwelling of God. My dwellings. Habitative. Dwelling of the Lord.

Mephaath (mef'-a-ath) - Beauty. The shining forth. Appearance. Illuminative. A distinguished place. Splendor. Force of waters.

Mephibosheth (me-fib'-o-sheth) - Exterminating the idol. Destroying shame. Utterance of Baal. From my mouth shame. Breathing shame. Out of my mouth proceeds reproach. Dispeller of shame. Idol breaker. Exterminating the shameful idol.

Merab (me'-rab) - Multiplication. Increase. A disputer. He that fights or disputes. He who fights. Multiplying.

Meraiah (mer-a-i'ah) - Lifted up of the Lord. Revelation of Jehovah. Stubbornness. Rebellion against Jah. Provoking Jah. He is exalted. Rebellion.

Meraioth (me-rah'-yoth) - Rebellions. Revelations. Bitterness. Rebellious. Changing. Elevations.

Merari (me-ra'-ri) - Bitterness. Bitter. Unhappy. To provoke. Sorrowful. My bitterness. Excited.

Merarites (me-ra'-rites) - Bitterness. Bitter. Unhappy. Descendants of Merari - To provoke. Excited. Sorrowful. My bitterness.

Merathaim (mer-a-tha'-im) - Double rebellion. Double bitterness. Great damnation.

Mercurius (mer-cu'-re-us) - Messenger or herald of the gods. Eloquent. Learned. Shrew. Crafty. An orator. An interpreter. Speaker. Reciprocal activity.

Mered (me'-red) - Rebellion. Rebellious. Going down.

Meremoth (mer'-e-moth) - Elevations. Strong. Bitterness. Myrrh of death. Exaltation. Heights.

Meres (me'-res) - Lofty. Worthy. Moisture. Fracture. Worn out. Sorrowful. Bruised. Forgetful. Defluxion. Imposthume.

Meribah (mer'-i-bah) - Water of strife. Chiding. Contention. Strife. Dispute. Quarrel.

Meribah Kadesh (mer'-i-bah-ka'-desh) - Meribah - Water of strife. Chiding. Contention. Kadesh - Consecrated. Sanctified. Contention. Sacred.

Merib-baal (me-rib'-ba-al) - Contender against Baal. Rebellion of Baal. Baal is contentious. He that resists Baal. He who strives with Baal. Rebellion.

Merodach (mer'-o-dak) - Death. Slaughter. Your rebellion. Bitter contrition. Bruised myrrh. Death. Warlike. High. Valiant.

Merodach-baladan (mer'o-dak-bal'-a-dan) - Merodach gives a son. The son of death. Mars is a worshiper of Baal. Merodach is not lord. Your rebellion. Baal is Lord. Bitter contrition. Merodach has given a son. Merodach the mighty lord. Baal worshiper.

Merom (me'-rom) - A high place. Exalted. Eminences. Elevations. Height.

Meronothite (me-ron'o-thite) - Joyful shouter. My singing. Rejoicing. Bearing rule. An inhabitant of Meronoth.

Meroz (me'-roz) - Refuge. Of leanness. Secret. Place of refuge.

Mesech (me'-sek) - Drawing out. Durability. A possession.

Mesha (me'-shah) - Retreat. Deliverance. Freedom. Burden. Salvation. A refuge. Departure. Safety.

Meshach (me'-shak) - Agile. Expeditious. Biting. Waters of quiet. Who is what thou art? That drives with force. Guest of Ram, the sun god. Quick. Who is God? Who is this? The shadow of the prince.

Meshech (me'-shek) - Drawing out. Durability. Same as Mesech - Who is drawn by force. Extraction. Long. Tall.

Meshelemiah (me-shel-e-mi'-ah) - Whom the Lord repays or rewards graciously. Jehovah repays. Peace. Jehovah recompenses. The retribution of the Lord. Ally of Jah. The Lord my felicity. Friendship of Jehovah.

Meshezabeel (me-shez'-a-be-el) - God sets free. Liberated of God. God delivers. God taking away. The salvation of God. Delivered by God. God is deliverer.

Meshillemith (me-shil'-le-mith) - Recompense. Reconciliation. Peaceable. Perfect. Giving again. Parables of death. Retribution.

Meshillemoth (me-shil'-le-moth) - Those who repay. Retribution. Those who requite. Reconciliation.

Meshobab (me-sho'-bab) - Returning. Brought back. Restored. Delivered. Rewarded. Returned.

Meshullam (me-shul'-le-meth) - Repaying. Those who repay. Associate. Friend. Reconciled. Perfect. Peaceable. Their parables. Allied. Reworded. Friend of God.

Meshullemeth (me-shul'-le-meth) - Repaying. Those who repay. Retribution. Reconciliation. Same as Meshullam - Peaceable. Perfect. Their parables. Friendly. Restitution. Rewarded. Friend of God.

Mesobaite (me-so'-ba-ite) - Congregation of the Lord. The one set up of Jah. The Lord's standing place. Little doe. Found of Jah. Congregation of Jehovah.

Mesopotamia (mes-o-po-ta'-me-ah) - (Same as Aram - High. Elevated. Lifted up. Magnified. Amidst the rivers. Aram of the rivers). Between two rivers. To be elevated.

Messiah (mes-si'-ah) - Anointed. Consecrated. One anointed with holy oil.

Messias (mes-si'-as) - Anointed. Greek form of Messiah, the anointed Christ.

Metheg-ammah (me'-theg-am'-mah) - The bridle of the metropolis. A bridle. A cubit length. Bridle of bondage. Bridle of the arm. To curb.

Methusael (me-thu'-sa-el) - Man who is of God. Asking for death. They died enquiring. They died who are of God. Who demands his death. Infirmity. Death from God. Man of God.

Methuselah (me-thu'-se-lah) - When he is dead it shall be sent i.e., the flood. Messenger of death. A man of the javelin. It shall be sent (deluge). Man of the dart. He has sent his death. Sending forth of death. Man of the offspring or the dart.

Meunim (me-u'-nim) - Place of habitation. Same as Maon - Dwelling places. Afflicted. Habitations. A residence.

Mezahab (mez'-a-hab) - Offspring. The shining one. Waters of gold. Gilded. Water of gold. Luster of gold. Seed or shoot of the sun.

Miamin (mi'-a-min) - From the right hand. On the right hand. Fortunate. The right hand.

Mibhar (mib'-har) - Most choice i.e., best. Choicest. Youth. Choice. Chosen. Most select. Best. Elite.

Mibsam (mib'-sam) - Sweet odor. Sweet smell. Fragrant. Delight. Smelling sweet.

Mibzar (mib'-zar) - Defense. A fortress. A stronghold. Fortified. Defending. Taking away. Forbidding. Defended or fortified place.

Micah (mi'-cah) - Who is like unto Jehovah? Who is like this? Poor. Humble. Diminishing. Godlike.

Micaiah (mi-ka-i'-ah) - Who is like unto Jehovah? Who is like unto God? Poor. Who is like Jehovah?

Micha (mi'-cah) - Who is like Jehovah? Like Jehovah. Diminishing. Poor. Humble. Same as Micaiah.

Michael (mi'-ka-el) - Who is like unto God? Who is perfect? Spiritual power. Like Jehovah. Godlike. As God.

Michah (mi'-cah) - Who is like unto Jehovah? Who is perfect? Like Jehovah. Who is like God?

Michaiah (mi'ka-I'-ah) - Who is like unto Jehovah? Same as Micha. Who is perfect? Who is like to God? Like Jehovah.

Michal (mi'-kal) - A little stream of water. Brook. Who is all? Who is like Jehovah? Who is perfect? Rivulet. Prevailing. Who is like God?

Michmas (mik'-mas) - Treasure. Treasury. Poverty was melted.

Poverty of servile work. Something hidden. Place of hiding.

Michmash (mik'-mash) - Treasure. Treasury. He that is removed. Poverty was felt. Poverty has departed. He that strikes. Something hidden. Hidden place. Place of hiding.

Michmethah (mik'-me-thah) - A hiding place. The poverty of the dead. The poverty of the reward. The gift or death of a striker. Place of hiding. Concealment. Hiding place.

Michri (mik'-ri) - Bought of the Lord. Precious. Jehovah possesses. Valuable. My price. Selling. Grief. Knowledge. Prize of Jehovah. Purchase price.

Michtam (mik'-tam) - Writing. The poverty of the perfect. Blood staining or deep dyeing. Golden psalm. A song graven upon stone. A monumental inscription. Engraving. A psalm.

Middin (mid'-din) - Measures. Extensions. From judgment. Judging. Judgment. Striving. Extension. Brawling.

Midian (mid'-e-an) - Strife. Contention. Contender. Judgment. Covering. Habit. Great extension.

Midianites (mid'-e-an-ites) - Inhabitants of Midian - Strife. Contention. Contender. Judgment. Covering. Habit. Great extension.

Midianitish (mid'-e-an-i-tish) - Referring to Midian. Belonging to Midian - Strife. Contention. Contender. Judgment. Covering. Habit. Great extension.

Migdal-el (mig'-dal-el) - Tower of God i.e., a very high tower. Tower of God.

Migdal-gad (mig'-da-gad) - Tower of fortune. Tower compassed about. Tower of God.

Migdol (mig'-dol) - Tower. Greatness.

Migron (mig'-ron) - Place of great conflict. A precipice. A threshing floor. Hurling down. Fear. Farm. Throat. Place of great fear. Landslip.

Mijamin (mij'-a-min) - Fortunate (Same as Miamin - from the right hand. On the right side). Right hand. Preparing waters. Rectitude.

Mikloth (mik'-loth) - Staves. Rods. Sticks. To punish with a rod. Sprouts. Triflings. Little wants. Little voices. Looking downward. Scorn. Branches. Twigs. Sticks as lots. To germinate.

Mikneiah (mik-ne-i'-ah) - Possession of Jehovah. Jehovah is jealous. Possession of the Lord. Acquisition.

Milalai (mil'-a-la-hee) - Eloquent. The promise of the Lord. Jehovah is elevated. Jehovah is eloquent. My utterances. Circumcision. My talk. Talkative.

Milcah (mil'-cah) - Queen. Counsel. A woman of counsel.

Milcom (mil'-com) - High king (intensive form). Their king. Reigning. Exalted king. The ruler. King. Royal.

Miletum (mi-le'-tum) - Pure white fine wool. Cared for. Red. Scarlet. Purest wool. Refuge.

Miletus (mil-le'-tus) - Pure white fine wool. Cared for. Refuge. Purest wool. Red. Scarlet.

Millo (mil'-lo) - Rampart. A mound filled with stones and earth. Filled. Fullness. A bastion. Entrenchment. Fortification. A citadel. Mound.

Miniamin (min'-e-a-min) - On the right hand. Fortunate. Right hand. At the right hand. Reason.

Minni (min'-ni) - Part. From me. Reckoned. Prepared. Provision. Gift disposed. Division.

Minnith (mi'-nith) - Small. Allotment. From her. Division. Enumeration. Distribution.

Miphkad (mif'-kad) - Place of meeting. Muster. Apportionment. Appointed. Assignment. Review. Census.

Miriam (mir'-e-am) - Bitterness. Their rebellion. Rebellion. Star of the sea. Celebrated. Bitter. Rebelliously. Exalted.

Mirma (mur'-mah) - Deceit. Fraud. Height. Speech of guile.

Misgab (mis'-gab) - Refuge. Height. Inaccessible place. Safety. A high place. Defense. Stronghold.

Mishael (mish'-a-el) - Who is what God is? High place. Who asks? Who is asked for or lent? Who is God? Steadfast. Who is like God?

Mishal (mis'-shal) - Enquiry. Parables. Governing. Request. Entreaty. Prayer request. Requiring.

Misham (mi'-sham) - Their cleansing. Swiftness. Impetuous. Their regarding. Their savior. Taking away. Hearing. Inspection. Swift going. Fame.

Misheal (mish'-e-al) - Prayer. Entreaty. Asking. Request. Requiring. Lent. Pit. Same as Mashal.

Mishma (mish'-mah) - Hearing. Fame. Report. Obeying.

Mishmannah (mish-man'-nah) - Fatness. Vigor. Strength. Taking away. Fat land. Provision.

Mishraites (mish'-ra-ites) - A slippery place. Touching evil as removing or drawing out. Spread abroad. Extension. A shepherd.

Mispar (mis'-par) - Number i.e., a few. Hot waters.

Mispereth (mis'-pe'reth) - Writing. A narrative. Hot waters. Enumeration. Of numbers.

Misrephoth maim (mis'-re-foth-mah'-yim) - The burning of waters. The burning upon the waters. Warm water. Hot waters. Purifying.

Mithcah (mith'-cah) - Sweetness. Sweet fountain. Pleasantness.

Mithnite (mith'-nite) - Strength. An athlete. Literally. He of loins. A giver. Loin. Gift. Hope. Appellation. Slenderness. Looking for.

Mithredath (mith'-re-dath) - Given by the genius of the sun. Given by Mithro god of the sun. Animating spirit of fire. Remainder of law. Searching out of law. Breaking the law. Beholding.

Mitylene (mit-i-le'-ne) - Mutilated. Purity. Cleansing. Press. The last. Curtailed.

Mizar (mi'-zar) - Smallness. Small. Diminutive. Young. Little. Petty. A small place.

Mizpah (miz'-pah) - A watch tower. Tribulations. Lofty place. Inquiry.

Mizpar (miz'-par) - Fear. Writing. A number large or small. Number.

Mizpeh (miz'-peh) - A watch tower. Observatory. Tribulations. Lofty place. Inquiry.

Mizraim (miz'-ra-im) - Two distresses. Fortresses. Two-fold Egypt i.e., upper and lower Egypt. Black. Oppressors.

Tribulations. Double straitness. Limits. A hemming in. Double pressure.

Mizzah (miz'-zah) - Terror. Joy. From sprinkling. Fear. Defluxion from the head. Trembling. Dropping.

Mnason (na'-son) - A diligent seeker. Solicitor. The number is safe. An exhorter. About to call to remembrance. Remembering.

Moab (mo'-ab) - Water of a father i.e., seed or progeny. Desire. Progeny of a father. Of the father. Waste. Nothingness. From father. Of his father. Entering of the father. Longed for one.

Moabite (mo'-ab-ite) - Inhabitants of Moab. Descendant of Moab - One from Moab. Water of a father i.e., seed or progeny. Desire. Progeny of a father. Of the father. Waste. Nothingness. From father. Of his father. Entering of the father. Longed for one.

Moabitess (mo'-ab-i-tess) - Female descendant of Moab. A woman from Moab - Water of a father i.e., seed or progeny. Desire. Progeny of a father. Of the father. Waste. Nothingness. From father. Of his father. Longed for one.

Moabitish (mo'-ab-i-tish) - Same as Moab. Belonging to Moab - Water of a father i.e., seed of progeny. Desire. Progeny of a father. Of the father. Waste. Nothingness. From father. Of his father. Entering of the father. Longed for one.

Moadiah (mo-ad-i'-ah) - Festival of Jehovah. Festival of Jah. Ornament of God.

Moladah (mo-la'-dah) - Birthplace. Generation. Birth. Origin. Place of nativity. Lineage.

Molech (mo'-lek) - King. Governing. The ruler. Nativity. Generation. Dominion. Rule.

Molid (mo'-lid) - Begetting. Begetter. Causing to bring forth. Nativity. Generation. He makes to generate.

Moloch (mo'och) - King. Governing. Nativity. Generation. Rule. The king or ruler. Dominion.

Morasthite (mo'-ras-thite) - Inhabitant of Moresheth - Gath. Possession of Gath.

Mordecai (mor'-de-cahee) - Little man. Bitter. Bruising. Bitterly reduces. Bitterness of my oppression. Contrition. Taught of God. Worshiper of Mars. Related to Marduk.

Moreh (mo'-reh) - Teacher. Illustrious. Archer. Stretching. One who throws a dart. Refreshing. Rain. Diviner.

Moresheth-gath (mor'-e-sheth-gath) - The possession of Gath.

Moriah (mo-ri'-ah) - Visible of the Lord. Chosen of the Lord. Provided by Jehovah. Instruction of God. Bitterness of the Lord. High. Seen by Jah. Chosen. Known. Chosen of Jehovah. Jehovah provides.

Mosera (mo-se'rah) - Bonds. Taken out. Drawn forth. Chain. Binding. Discipline. Chastisement. Correction.

Moseroth (mo-se'-roth) - Same as Mosera - Bonds. Taken out. Drawn forth. Corrections. Chains. Chastisement.

Moses (mo'-zez) - Taken out of the water. Saved out of the water. Saved from the water. Drawn out. Drawn forth. A son. Taken out. Rescued. Drawn out of water. Experience. Extracted.

Moza (mo'-zah) - Fountain. Offspring. Going forth. Bubbling waters. The springhead. Drained. Origin.

Mozah - Fountain. Offspring. Going forth. Wringing out. Same as Moza - Unleavened. Origin. Bubbling waters. The springhead. Drained. An issuing of water. To drain.

Muppim (mup'-pim) - Anxieties. Obscurities. Shakings. Wavings. Out of the mouth. Waverings. Covering. Darkness.

Mushi (Mu'-shi) - Proved of the Lord. Drawn out. Withdrawn. My yielding. My departure. Depart thou. He that touches. Refuge. Sensitive. He who touches. Deserted.

Mushites (mu'-shites) - Inhabitants of Mushi - Proved of the Lord. Drawn out. Withdrawn. My yielding. My departure. Depart thou. He that touches. Sensitive. Refuge. He who touches. Deserted.

Muthlabben (muth-lab'-ben) - Psalms 9 title. Death to the son. Death. On the death of the son. To die for the son.

Myra (mi'-rah) - A balsam. Myrtle juice. Burnt up. Flowing. Pouring. I flow. Pour out. Weep. Weeping.

Mysia (miz'ye-ah) - Land of beech trees. Closure. Abomination. Abominable. Criminal. Beech tree country.

N

Naam (na'-am) - Pleasantness. Sweetness. Fair. Pleasant. Beautiful. Pleasure.

Naamah (na'-a-mah) - Pleasant. Sweetness. That foretells. That conjectures. Pleasing. Agreeable. Lovely. Beautiful.

Naaman (na'-a'man) - Pleasantness. Pleasant. Delight. Agreeable. That foretells. That conjectures. Very pleasant. Very agreeable.

Naamathite (na'-a-math-ite) - Same as Naaman - Pleasantness. Pleasant. Delight. Agreeable. That foretells. That conjectures. Very pleasant. Very agreeable. Dweller in Naaman.

Naamites (na'-a-mites) - Descendants of Naaman. Pleasantness. Pleasant. Delight. Agreeable.

Naarah (na'-a-rah) - Handmaid. A girl. Girl or child of the Lord. Maiden. That foretells. That conjectures. Wandering. Watching. Youth. A damsel. A mill.

Naarai (na'-a-ra-hee) - Pleasantness of Jehovah. Child of the Lord. Youthful. My boys. My shaking. My roarings. That foretells. That conjectures. My young children. Born of God. Boyish.

Naaran (na'-a-ran) - Handmaid. A girl. Same as Naarah. Wandering. Juvenile. Youthful.

Naarath (na'-a-rath) - Handmaid. A girl. To maidenhood. To maiden place. Wandering. A girl. Youthful. Same as Naarah.

Naashon (na'-a-shon) - An enchanter. Oracle. One that foretells. A diviner. That foretells. That conjectures. Lucky omen.

Naasson (na'-as-son) - Enchanter. (Greek form of Naashon - An enchanter. Oracle. One that foretells. Prosperous.) Lucky prediction. Serpent.

Nabal (na'-bal) - A fool i.e., impious, foolish, prominence. Fool. Senseless. Lean. Wicked. Mad. Stupid. Foolish. Empty person.

Naboth (na'-both) - Fruits. Prominence. Productive i.e., Abundance. Words. Prophecies. Increase. Words. Distinction. Fruit. A sprout.

Nachon (na'-kon) - Smitten. Stroke. Prepared. Established. Reedy. Sure. Violent stroke. Firm.

Nachor (na'-kor) - Noble. Burning. Snorting. White. Snorer. Greek form of Nahor. Bright.

Nadab (na'-dab) - Volunteer or willing. Of one's own free will. Liberal. Free and voluntary gift. Prince. Spontaneous. Liberally.

Nagge (nag'-e) - Splendor of the sun. My shining. Brightness. Clearness. Splendor.

Nahalal (na'-ha-lal) - Pasture i.e., where sheep were led. Often led. Strength. Pasture.

Nahaliel (na-ha-le'-ed) - Torrents of God. Valley or river of God. Inheritance. Valley of God. Valley of the oak. Brook of God.

Nahallal (na'-hal-el) - Pasture i.e., where sheep were led. Often led. Strength. Same as Nahalal. Praised. Bright.

Nahalol (na'-ha-lol) - Same as Nahalal - Pasture i.e., where sheep were led. Often led. Strength. Praised. Bright.

Naham (na'-ham) - Consolation of his parents. Solace. My nostrils. Hot Anger. Consolation. Repentant. Comfort.

Nahamani (na-ham'-a-ni) - Repenting. Comforter. Compassionate. My comfort. Consolatory. My nostrils. Hot. Anger.

Naharai (na'-ha-ra-hee) - Snorter. One who snores. Snorting one. My nostrils. Hot. Anger. Chosen of God. Snorer. Intelligent.

Nahari (na'-ha-ri) - Same as Naharai - Snorter. One who snores. Snorting one. Chosen of God. Snorer.

Nahash (na'-hash) - Serpent. Oracle. Foretelling. Forewarning. Snake.

Nahath (na'-hath) - Letting down. Descent. Lowness. Quiet. Rest. A leader. Quietness.

Nahbi (nah'-bi) - Hidden of the Lord. Jehovah's protection. Concealed. My hiding. Hid by God. Occult. Very secret. Hidden. Faint hearted.

Nahor (na'-hor) - Snorting. Breathing hard. Slayer. Inflamed. Heated. Hoarse. Dry. Hot. White. Angry. Snorer. Piercer.

Nahshon (nah'-shon) - Enchanting. Ominous. Good omen. Enchanter. Oracle.

Nahum (na'-hum) - Comforter. Comforted. Full of comfort. Consolation. Compassionate. Penitent. Comfort. Comfortable.

Nain (nane) - Pasture. Afflicted. Beautiful. Pleasantness. Beauty. Pasture ground.

Naioth (nah'-yoth) - Habitations. Dwellings. Beauties. Residence.

Naomi (na'-o-mee) - Pleasant. Pleasantness. Agreeable. Attractive. My joy. My bliss. Pleasantness of Jehovah. Beautiful. Delight.

Naphish (na'-fish) - Refreshment. Numerous. Respiration. Cheerful. The soul. He that rests. Increased. Refreshed. Pleasure the senses.

Naphtali (naf'-ta-li) - A struggle. My wrestling. My twisting. Obtained by wrestling. That struggles or fights. Wrestling of Jah.

Naphtuhim (naf'-too-him) - Openings. The nine bows. Border people. An opening.

Narcissus (nar'-sis'-sus) - Benumbing. Flower causing lethargy or astonishment. Narcotic. Stupidity. Astonishment. Daffodil. Surprise. Stupefaction.

Nashon (na'-shon) - An enchanter. Oracle. One that foretells. Helper. Entryway.

Nathan (na'-than) - Given of God. Gift. Given. He has given. Giving. Rewarded. He gave. Conscience. Recompense.

Nathanael (na-than'-a-el) - Gift of God. Conscience. God has given.

Nathan-melech (na'-than-me'-lek) - Gift of the king. Placed of the king i.e., constituted. The king is giver. The king gave. Ruled by conscience. Given by the king. King's gift.

Naum (na'-um) - Comfort. Ease. Comforter. Same as Nahum.

Nazarene (naz-a-reen') - Branch. Preservation. Girded. Kept. Guarded. A native of Nazareth.

Nazareth (naz'-a-reth) - Branch. Preservation. Separated. Crowned. Sanctified. Watchtower.

Nazarite(s) (naz'-a-rite(s)) - One separated. To separate. To consecrate. One chosen or set apart. One consecrated to God by a vow.

Neah (ne'-ah) - Wondering. Of a slope. A shaking. Moved. Moving. Motion. Shaking down. The settlement.

Neapolis (ne-ap'-o-lis) - New city. Regenerate.

Neariah (ne-a-ri'-ah) - Servant of Jehovah. Jehovah has shaken. Jehovah drives away. Child of the Lord. The Lord cast off. Servant of Jah. Attendant of Jehovah.

Nebai (ne'-ba-hee) - Fruit of the Lord. Fruitful. Narrowing. Projecting. Budding. Speaking. Prophesying. Budding forth.

Nebaioth (ne-bah'-yoth) - High places. Productive. Prophecies. Husbandry. Increasing. Words. Buds. Removals. Fruitfulness.

Nebajoth (ne-ba'-joth) - High places. Productive. Husbandry. Prophetesses. Removals. Words. Fruits. Heights. Fruitfulness.

Neballat (ne-bal'-lat) - Folly in secret. Prophecy. Budding. Concealed habitation. Foolish secrecy. Secret wickedness. Blessed with life.

Nebat (ne'-bat) - Aspect. An investigator. Cultivation. Behold. We speak idly. That beholds. View. Look. Regard. Favor. God has regarded.

Nebo (ne'-bo) - Mercury. Interpreter. Foreteller. A lofty place. Height. Fertile. His prophecy. That speaks or prophesies. Height. An idol. High.

Nebuchadnezzar (neb-u-kad-nez'-zar) - Nebo is the god of fire. Nebo protect the landmark. Nebo defend the boundary. An entangled adversary. Confusing the lord of treasure. Prophesy the earthen vessel is preserved. Speech. Prophecy. Springing. Flowing. Nebo the lord of brightness. Protection. The prince of gods. May Nebo protect the crown. May Nebo protect my son.

Nebuchadrezzar (neb-u-kad-rez'-zar) - Another way of spelling Nebuchadnezzar. Confusion of the abode of treasure. Prophesy, the seer's vessel is preserved. Speech. Prophecy. Springing. Flowing. Nebo, the fire of brightness. The prince of gods. May Nebo protect the crown. May Nebo protect my son.

Nebushasban (neb-u-shas'-ban) - Nebo will save me. Nebo save me. Worshiper of Mercury. Prophesy their deliverance. The deliverance of Nebo. Speech. Prophecy. Springing. Flowing. Nebo deliver me.

Nebuzaradan (neb-u-zar'-a-dan) - Nebo gives posterity. Nebo hath an offspring. Mercury's leader lord i.e., the leader whom Mercury favors. Winnowing over the threshold. Prophesy the lord is estranged. Fruits or prophecies of judgment. Whom Nebo favors. Nebo has given seed. Nebo sends prosperity.

Necho (ne'-ko) - The lame beaten. Who was beaten. Conqueror. His smiting. Lame. Beaten. Injured in the foot.

Nechoh (ne'-ko) - Same as Necho - The lame beaten. Who was beaten.

Conqueror. His smiting. Lame. Injured in the foot.

Nedabiah (ned-a-bi'-ah) - Spontaneous gift of the Lord. Jehovah is bountiful. Jehovah is willing. Prince or vow of the Lord. The Lord gave willingly. Jah impels. To offer freely. Largess of Jah. Moved of Jehovah.

Neger (neg'-er) - Dry. Parched.

Neginah (neg'-i-nah) - A stringed instrument. Harp songs. To be accompanied by a stringed instrument.

Neginoth (neg'-i'-noth) - Stringed instruments. (Title of Psalms 4, 6, 54, 55, 67,76). Harp songs. To be accompanied by a stringed instrument. Stringed instruments.

Nego (ne'-go) - Same as Nebo. Mercury. Interpreter. Foreteller. A lofty place. Height. Fertile.

Nehelamite (ne-hel'-am-ite) - Made fat. Dreamer. Vale. Brook. A strong one. Dreamed. Dweller of Nehelam

Nehemiah (ne-he-mi'-ah) - Jehovah comforts. Jehovah has consoled. The comforter is aid of the Lord. Consolation. Repentance of the Lord. Consolation of Jehovah. Jah comforts. Comforted of Jehovah. God is consolation.

Nehiloth (ne'-hi-loth) - Flutes. We will cause profanation. We shall divide the inheritance. Perforated. The flute and similar wind instruments.

Nehum (ne'-hum) - Merciful. Consolation. Comfort. Penitent. Compassion. Consoled. Comforted.

Nehushta (ne-hush'-tah) - Brass. Bronze. A piece of brass. Made of Brass. Brazen fetter. Copper. Metal. Serpent.

Nehushtan (ne-hush'-tan) - A little brazen serpent i.e., a contemptible piece of brass. Brazen. Enchanted. Piece of brass or copper. Brass image. Serpent of the desert. A trifling thing of brass. Serpent. Made of copper.

Neiel (ne'-i-el) - Shaken of God. Moved by God. Commotion. The moving of God. Moved of God. Dwelling place of God.

Nekeb (ne'-keb) - Cavern. A hole. Dell. Which penetrates. Hollow. Cave.

Nekeda (ne-ko'-dah) - Distinguished. A herdsman. Spotted. Painted. Inconstant. Famous. Shepherd. Speckled.

Nemuel (ne-mu'-el) - Circumcision of God. God is spreading. They were made to slumber of God. The sleeping of God. Day of God. God is speaking.

Nemuelites (ne-mu'-el-ites) - Descendants of Nemuel - Circumcision of God. God is spreading. They were made to slumber of God. The sleeping of God. Day of God. God is speaking.

Nepheg (ne'-feg) - Sprout. Bud. Shoot. An offshoot. We will cease or grow numb. Weak. Slacked. Faint. To spring forth. Boaster.

Nephilim (ne'-fi-lem) - Giants.

Nephish (ne'-fish) - Refreshment. Numerous. Respiration. Cheerful. Increased. He that rests. Pleasure. Refreshed. Expansions.

Nephishesim (ne-fish'-e-sim) - Expansions. Diminished. Torn in pieces. Scatter.

Nephthalim (nef'-tha-lim) - Wrestling. Greek form of Naphtali. Strugglings. My wrestlings. A struggle. Twisting.

Obtained by wrestling. We will take the spoilers. Refreshed of spices.
Nephtoah (nef-to'-ah) - Opening. Opened. Open. A spring.
Nephusim (ne-fu'-sim) - Expansions. Scatter spices. Enlargement. Torn in pieces. Same as Nephishesim.
Ner (nur) - Lamp. Light. Brightness. New tilled land. Land newly tilled.
Nereus (ne'-re-us) - A water nymph (ancient sea god). Light. Roose.
Nergal (nur'-gal) - Mars (the planet). Lion. A slanderer. The lamp rolled. The great man. The hero. Fountain of light. A great hero.
Nerhal-Sharezer (nur'-gal-sha-re'-zur) - Nergal, protect the king. Mars is the brightest of lights. Nergal is the prince of fire. The rolling lamp observed the treasure. Treasurer of Nergal. Nergal, the splendor of brightness. Nergal save the king. A prince of fire. May the god Nergal defend the prince.
Neri (ne'-ri) - Light of the Lord. My light. Light. Light of God. Lamp is Jehovah.
Neriah (ne-ri'ah) - Lamp of Jehovah. Light. Lamp of the Lord. The light of the Lord. Jah is light. Jehovah is a lamp.
Nero (ne'-ro) - Brave.
Netaim (ni-ta'-im) - Plants.
Nethaneel (ne-than'-e-el) - God gave. Given of God. God has given. Gift of God. Conscience. God gives.
Nethaniah (neth-a-ni'-ah) - Whom Jehovah gave. Jehovah has given. The gift of God. Given of the Lord. Jehovah gives. Given of God.
Nethinims (neth'-in-ims) - The appointed. Appointed. Given ones.

Given or offered. Rewarded. Dedicated. Temple server.
Netophah (ne-to'-fah) - A dropping. Distillation. Flowing.
Netophathi (ne-to'-fa-thi) - Inhabitants of Netophah - A dropping. Distillation. Flowing. One distilled.
Netophathite (ne-to'-fa-thite) - Dwellers of Netophah - A dropping. Distillation. Flowing.
Neziah (ne-zi'-ah) - Overseer. Preeminent. Pure. Illustrious. Conqueror. Strong. Victory. Conspicuous. Faithful.
Nezib (ne'-zib) - Garrison. Standing place. Military station. Strength. An idol. Statue.
Nibhaz (nib'-haz) - Lord of darkness i.e., the evil demon. We shall utter what is seen. Budding. Prophesying. High. Conspicuous. To speak. Barker. An idol.
Nibshan (nib'-shan) - Level. Level and soft soil. We shall prophesy quiet. Growing of a tooth. Prophecy. Equal. To change. Light soil. Plain.
Nicanor (ni-ca'-nor) - Conqueror. Victorious. I conquer. Untimely victory. Conqueror of Men.
Nicodemus (nic-o-de'-mus) - Innocent blood. Victor of the people. Conqueror over the populace. Victory over the people. Victories among his people.
Nicolaitanes (nic-o-la'-i-tans) - Destroyer of the people. Named after Nicolas - Conqueror of the people. Submission of the people. Followers of Nicolas.
Nicolas (nic'-o-las) - Conqueror of the people as a whole. Submission.

Nicopolis (ni-cop'-o-lis) - City of victory. Victorious city.

Niger (ni'-jur) - Black. Dark. Purple.

Nile (nile) - Dark blue.

Nimrah (nim'-rah) - Same as Bethnimrah. House of pure water. Limpid water. He was rebellious. Leopardess. Rebellion. Water abounding. Limpid and sweet waters. Clear water.

Nimrim (nim'-rim) - Same as Bethnimrah. House of pure water. Clear waters. He was rebellious. Leopardess. Rebellion. Change. Clear. A leopard. Limpid. Pure. Basins of clear water.

Nimrod (nim'-rod) - Rebel. To be rebellious. Valiant. Strong. He that rules. We will rebel. Rebellion. Increase. Rebellions. Apostate. Valiant one. Impious.

Nimshi (nim'-shi) - Jehovah reveals. Selected. Drawn out (of the Lord). Disclosure. Woven. Rescued from danger. Chosen. Extricated. Jah is revealer. Saved. Weasel.

Nineveh (nin'-e-veh) - Offspring's habitation. Habitation of Ninus. A place of habitation. Dwelling. Offsprings at ease. Handsome. Agreeable. The dwelling of Ninus.

Ninevites (nin'-e-vites) - Inhabitants of Nineveh. Offspring's habitation. Habitation of Ninus. Place of habitation. Dwelling. Offsprings at ease. Handsome. Agreeable.

Nisan (ni'-san) - First Jewish month (March-April). Their flight. Standard. Miracle. Flight. Banner. Proof. Tender. The first month of greenness.

Nisroch (nis'-rok) - Eagle. Great eagle. Superintendent. Ensign of delicateness. Flight. Proof. Temptation. Delicate. Bright. Shining.

Nissi (nis-se') - Banner.

No (no) - Temple. Portion. Habitation or temple. Handsome. Disrupting. Frustrating. Stirring up. Forbidding.

Noadiah (no-a-di'-ah) - Jehovah has met. Met with of the Lord i.e., to whom the Lord manifested Himself. Whom Jehovah meets. One to whom the Lord revealed Himself. Assembled or ornament of the Lord. Witness. Convened of Jah. The Lord manifested Himself. Jehovah convenes.

Noah #1 (no'-ah) - Rest. Comfort. Comforter. Repose. Consolation. Quiet.

Noah #2 (no'-ah) - Motion. Wandering. The second daughter of Zelophedad, born during the wandering of Israel. That quavers or totters. Commotion. Agitation.

No-amon (no-a'-mon) - Place of Amon.

Nob (nob) - High place. Noble. Fertile. Fruit. Empty. Discourse. Prophecy. Height. Sublimity. Fruitful. Increase.

Nobah (no'-bah) - A barking. A loud voice. A bark as a dog. Howling. That barks or yelps. Vehement in voice. Prominent one.

Nod (nod) - Wandering. Vagabond. Flight. Fugitive. Exile.

Nodab (no'-dab) - Nobility. Liberal. Vowing of his own accord. Wandering of a father.

Noe (no'-e) - Greek form of Noah. Repose. Consolation. Rest. Comfort. A comforter.

Nogah (no'-gah) - Shining. Splendor. Brightness. Brilliance. Clearness. A shining. Brilliancy.

Nohah (no'-hah) - Rest. A guide. Quietude.

Non (non) - A fish. Continuation. Posterity. Eternal. Increase. Perpetuity.

Noph (nof) - To wave. Presentability. Honeycomb. Anything that distills or drops. Distilling from the top. To drop.

Nophah (no'-fah) - A blast. Windy. Breathing. Blowing. Fearful. Binding. A gust. Which is blown upon by the winds. Inflate.

Nun (nun) - A fish. Continuation. Perpetuity. Increase. Posterity. Eternal.

Nymphas (nim'-fas) - Spouse. Bridegroom. Sacred to the muses. Bridal. Gift of the nymphs or bridegroom.

O

Obadiah (o-ba-di'-ah) - A servant of the Lord. Worshiper of Jehovah. Servant of the Lord. Worshiper of God.

Obal (o'-bal) - Stripped. Bare of leaves. Bare. Inconvenience of old age. Heaping confusion. Very fat. Bare district. Old age. Flowing. Fat.

Obed (o'-bed) - Serving. A servant who worships. Worshiping God. A servant. Workman. Worshiper.

Obed-edom (o'bed-e'-dom) - Serving Edom. Servant of Edom. A laborer of the earth. Servant of the god Edom.

Obil (o'-bil) - Overseer of camels. Camel keeper. Driver. Leader. One who weeps. Causing mourning. Who deserves to be bewailed. That weeps. Shepherd of camels. Mournful. Chief of camels. Tender.

Oboth (o'-both) - Pythons. Oracular serpents. Familiar spirits. Necromancers. Dragons. Fathers. Desires. Place of leather bottles. Water skins. Hollow passes. A mumble. A necromancer.

Ocran (o'-cran) - Troubled. Troublesome. Troubler. To disturb. One that creates disorder. A disturber. Muddler. Afflicted. To disturb or afflict.

Oded (o'-ded) - Setting up. Established. Aiding. He has restored. A sustainer. To sustain. He propped up. Erecting. Reiteration. Canter.

Og (og) - Long necked. A furrow i.e., as long as a furrow. A circle. A hearth-cake. Bread baked in ashes. A cake. Spirally. Giant.

Ohad (o'-had) - Joined together. Might. Powerful. Power. He shouted. Praising. Confessing. Union. A part. Unity. Strength.

Ohel (o'-hel) - Tabernacle. Tent. Brightness of a tent. Brightness. House. Pavilion. Home.

Oholibah (o-hol'-i-ba) - My tent is in her.

Olivet (ol'-i-vet) - Place of olives. A place planted with olives. An olive yielding illuminating oil.

Olympas (o-lim'-pas) - Bright. Heavenly. Gift of Juniper Olympius.

Omar (o'-mar) - Uppermost. Mountaineer. He that speaks. Eloquent. Talkative. I will say. He that speaks. Bitter. Very elevated. Speaking Commander.

Omega (o'-me-gah) - Last letter in the Greek alphabet. Finality. The last.

Omri (om'-ri) - Servant of the Lord. Jehovah apportions. Like a sheaf. A bundle of corn. Impetuous. Sheaf of corn. Handful. My pupil. Pupil of Jehovah. God taught. To chastise. Pilgrim of God.

On (on) - The sun. Strength. Vigor. Iniquity. Pain. Force. Sorrows. Stirring up. A forbidding sun. Inquiry.

Onam (o'-nam) - Weariness. Iniquity. Wealthy. Strength. Profitable. Useful. Their vigor. Their iniquity. Strong. Stout. Ability. Powerful. Vigorous.

Onan (o'-nan) - Iniquity. Pain. Strong. Their vigor. Their iniquity. Profitable. Useful. Stout. Ability. Powerful. Vigorous.

Onesimus (o-nes'-i-mus) - Profitable. Useful.

Onesiphorus (o-ne-sif'-o-rus) - Bringing advantage. Profit bringing. Who brings profit. Bringing usefulness.

Ono (o'-no) - Strength. Strong. His vigor. His iniquity. Grief or strength. Iniquity of him. Safe abode. Rich. Gain bringing. Grief.

Onycha (o-ny'-cha) - Whose travail. Roaring as a lion. A spice.

Onyx (o'-nyx) - Setting them equal. Justifying them.

Ophel (o'-fel) - A hill. Impregnable. A tower. Darkness. A small white cloud. Elevated place. A tumor. A mound. Knoll.

Ophir (o'-fur) - Abundance. Rich. Fat. Reduced to ashes. Fruitful region. Ashes. Fatness. Fruitful.

Ophni (of'-ni) - Man of the hill. My flying. Wearisome. Folding together. Soreness. Moldy. The high place.

Ophrah (of'-rah) - Fawn. Hind. Hamlet. Dustiness. Fawnlike (from its color). Dust. Lead. A young hind. Female fawn. Dust.

Oreb (o'-reb) - Raven. Crow. Cautious. Evening. Caution. A swarm. Swarming.

Oren (o'-ren) - Pine tree i.e., tall and strong. Strength. Wild ash. Pine. Strength. Power. Cedar.

Orion (o-ri'-on) - A fool. Streams of light. Stupid. Silly.

Ornan (or'-nan) - Large pine i.e., as tall as a great pine. Strong. That rejoices. Light was perpetuated. Their fir tree. Great wild ash. Strong one. Active. Prince.

Orpah (or'-pah) - Mane or the neck of an animal. A fawn. A young doe. Hind. Hardened. Double minded. The neck or skull. Young stag. Mane. The neck. Stiff necked.

Osee (o'-see) - Salvation. Same as Hosea - Jehovah is help or salvation. Salvation. Causing to save. He saved. The prophet Hosea. Greek form of Hosea.

Oshea (o-she'-ah) - God saves. Same as Hosea - Jehovah is help or salvation. Salvation. Causing to save. He has saved. Deliverer.

Othni (oth'-ni) - Lion of the Lord i.e., most powerful. Jehovah is force. Powerful. My seasonable speaking. My time. My hour. Lion of God. Most brave. Forcible. Jehovah is power.

Othniel (oth'-ne-el) - Powerful one i.e., lion of God i.e., most powerful. Powerful man of God. My season of God. The hour of God. Lion of God. Force of God. God is power.

Ozem (o'zem) - Strong. Strength. One that fasts. I will hasten them. Their eagerness. Strengthening. To be strong. Eagerness. Irritable.

Ozias (o-zi'-as) - Strength from the Lord. Strength of Jehovah. Strength of God. Greek from of Uzziah.

Ozni (oz'-ni) - Hearing. Attentive. Jehovah hears. An ear. My hearkening. Having ears. Hearing by Jah. Having quick ears.

Oznites (oz'-nites) - Descendants of Ozni - Hearing. Attentive. Jehovah hears. An ear. My hearkening. Having ears. Hearing by Jah. Having quick ears.

P

Paarai (pa'-ar-a-hee) - Revelation. Jehovah is opening. Opening. Yawning. Stripped by God. To open wide. Revelation of Jehovah. Devotee of Peor.

Pacatiana (pa-ca-she-a'-nah) - Dry. Barren.

Padan (pa'-dan) - The plain of Aram. Their ransom. Wide lying plain. Table land. Plain. Field. To extend.

Padan-aram (pa'-dan-a'-ram) - The plain of Aram. The ransom of Syria. Their ransom is high. Table land. Cultivated field. Plain of Syria. Table land or Aram. Fields of Aram. Plain table land of Aram.

Padon (pa'-don) - Redemption. Deliverances. Ransom. His redemption. Ox yoke. Wished for liberty. Deliverance.

Pagiel (pa'-ghe-el) - Prayer of God i.e., answer from God. Praying to God. God meets. Prevention of God. Intervention of God. Prevention. The asking of God. Event of God. Chance. God's intervention.

Pahath-moab (pa'-hath-mo'-ab) - Governor of Moab. Pit of Moab. Ruler of Moab. Prince of Moab. To dig a pit. A snare.

Pai (pa'-i) - Bleating. Crying out. My groaning. Great noise. Screaming. Howling. Sighing. To cry. Thinking.

Palal (pa'-lal) - Judge. He has judged. Mediator. Judge as intervening. Thinking. God judges.

Palestina (pal-es-ti'-nah) - The land of wanderers. Land of strangers. Rolled in dust. Wallowing. Which is covered. Watered or brings and causes ruin. Removing. Migratory. Land of emigrants. Rolling.

Palestine (pal'-es-tine) - Same as Palestina. The land of wanderers. Land of strangers. Rolled in dust. Which is covered. Wallowing. Watered or brings and causes ruin. Removing. Migratory. Rolling land of emigrants.

Palet (pa'-let) - Flight.

Pallu (pal'-lu) - Separated. Distinguished. Wonderful. Marvelous. Hidden.

Palluites (pal'-lu-ites) - Descendants of Pallu. Separated. Distinguished. Wonderful. Marvelous. Hidden.

Palti (pal'-ti) - Deliverance of Jehovah. My escape. Deliverance. Flight. To escape. Deliver. Delivered.

Paltiel (pal'-te-el) - Deliverance of God. Deliverance of the Lord. Deliverance or banishment. God delivers. Delivered.

Paltite (pal'-tite) - Descendants Palti. Deliverance of Jehovah. My escape. Flight. To escape. Delivered.

Pamphylia (pam-fil'-e-ah) - Of every tribe. A coastal region in the south of Asia Minor. A nation made up of every tribe. Mixed nation. Heterogeneous.

Pannag (pan'-nag) - Preparation of affliction. A place where fine grain grew. Sweet meats or produce. A confection or spice.

Paphos (pa'-fos) - Boiling hot. Suffering. Which boils. Gates. Which is very hot. That which boils.

Paradise - Pleasure ground. Park.

Parah (pa'-rah) - Village of heifers. Heifer. He increased. A cow. Increasing. Fruitful. Kine. Young cow.

Paran (pa'-ran) - Abounding in foliage. Fruitful. Cavernous. Their beautifying. Beauty. Glory. Ornament. Much digging. Region with caverns. Ornamental.

Parbar (par'-bar) - Fertile in corn. Open apartment. He annulled the corn. A suburb. The outside place. The gate or building belonging to the Temple.

Parmashta (par-mash'-tah) - Strong fisted. Superior. Spoiled is the banquet. A yearling bull. Strong in flight.

Parmenas (par'-me-nas) - Standing firm. I abide. Faithful. That abides. To abide. Permanent. Constant. Steadfast.

Parnach (par'-nak) - Very nimble. The bullock we smote. A bull striking. Very agile and swift. Nimble. Delicate. Gifted.

Parosh (pa'-rosh) - A flea i.e., a cowardly man. A fugitive. Fruit of the north. The fruit of a moth. Insect. Fleeing.

Parshandatha (par-shan'-da-thah) - Of noble birth. Given to Persia. Dung of impurity. Given by prayer. Interpreter of the law. Revelation of corporeal impurities. Son of Haman. Inquisitive.

Parthians (par-the'-uns) - A pledge (Parthia was a rival power to Rome). Exiled. An exile. Horseman.

Paruah (par'-u-ah) - Flourishing. Increase. That flies away. Flowery. Blossomed. Adorned. Blooming

Parvaim (par-va'-im) - Oriental regions. Eastern. He broke their hooks. Fruitful places.

Pas (pas) - The border.

Pasach (pa'-sak) - Torn asunder. A divider. Limping. Your vanishing. Your spreading out. Thy broken piece. He cut off. To divide.

Pas-dammim (pas-dam'-mim) - The border of blood. Extremity of Dammim. Borders of Dammim. Vanishing of bloods. He spread our bloods. Portion or diminishing of blood. Dell of bloodshed.

Paseah (pa-se'-ah) - Lame. Vacillating. Halting. Passing over. Limping.

Pashur (pash'-ur) - Most noble. Free. Multiplies liberty. Prosperity round about. Spreading over a hole. Increasing of white linen. That extends or multiplies the hole. Whiteness. Liberation. Splitter. Cleaver.

Patara (pat'-a-rah) - Railing. Reviling. Suffering it seems. Scattered cursing. Trodden under foot. Interpretation. Oracle. Trodden.

Pathros (path'-ros) - Southern region i.e., Egypt. A sprinkled variegated piece. A morsel moistened. Mortal. He cut. Extension, the southern land of ruin. Region of the south.

Pathrusim (path-ru'-sim) - The southland. Inhabitants of Pathros. Southern region i.e., Egypt. A sprinkled variegated piece. A morsel moistened. Mortal. Southerner. He cut. Extension of ruin. Region of the south. The southern land.

Patmos (pat'-mos) - My killing. Mortal. Belonging to turpentine.

Patrobas (pat'-ro-bas) - One who pursues the steps of his father. Paternal. Life of a father. One who lives like his father.

Pau (pa'-u) - Bleating. Crying out. Same as Pai. Bawling. Screaming. Sighing.

Paul (pawl) - Little. Small. To restrain. To pause or check. To lessen or make small.

Paulus (pawl-us) - Same as Paul. Little. To repress. Desist. Refrain. To lessen.

Pedahel (ped'-a-hel) - Redeemed of God. God redeemed. God delivers. God has saved. Saved of God.

Pedahzur (pe-dah'-zur) - Redemption of strength i.e., God. The Rock redeemed. The Rock delivers. Powerful. Strong or powerful savior. Stone of redemption. God delivers. The rock has redeemed. God has ransomed.

Pedaiah (pe-dah'-yah) - Redemption of the Lord. Whom Jehovah redeemed. Jehovah delivers. God redeemed. Jah has ransomed.

Pekah (pe'-kah) - Open eyed. Watchfulness. A keen observer. Opening. He that opens. That is at liberty. An opening. That opens the eye. Alert.

Pekahiah (pe-ka-hi'-ah) - Opening of the Lord i.e., deliverance. Whose eyes Jehovah opened. Jehovah has given sight. It is the Lord that opens. Jah has observed. Jehovah has opened his wick.

Pekod (pe'-kod) - Visitation i.e., punishment. Noble. Rulers. Surveying. Reviewing. To avenge or punish.

Punishment. Become licentious. Visited by judgment.

Pelaiah (pel-a-i'-ah) - Distinguished of the Lord. Whom Jehovah made distinguished. Jehovah has made illustrious. The Lord's secret or miracle. He was wonderful. Jah has distinguished. Jehovah is wonderful. Distinguished of Jehovah.

Pelaliah (pel-li'-ah) - Judge of the Lord. Whom Jehovah judged. Jehovah judges. Intervention of Jah. Entreating the Lord. Thinking on God. Jah has judged. Jehovah intervenes. Jah judges.

Pelatiah (pel-a-ti'-ah) - Deliverance of the Lord. Whom Jehovah delivered. Jehovah delivers. Jehovah and free. Let the Lord deliver. Deliverance of God. Jah delivers.

Peleg (pe-leg') - Division. A channel (as a cleft, dividing). Separation. To cut. Earthquake.

Pelet (pe'-let) - Deliverance. Liberation. Escape.

Peleth (pe'-leth) - Swiftness. Flight. Separation. Banishment. Haste.

Pelethites (pel'-e-thites) - Runners. Judges. Destroyers. Couriers.

Pelonite (pel'-o-nite) - Such a one. A certain unnamed one. Falling. Secret. Hidden. Separate. Separated.

Pelusium (pe-lu'-se-um) - In the KJV, it is the Egyptian city of Sin. City of mud.

Peniel (pe-ni'-el) - The face of God. God's face. Turn ye to God. Face or vision of God. That sees God. Divine presence.

Peninnah (pe-nin'-nah) - Coral. A ruby. A pearl. Precious stone. Jewel. The face.

Pentapolis - Five cities.
Pentateuch - The five books of Moses.
Pentecost (pen'-te-cost) - Fifty. Fiftieth. The fiftieth day.
Penuel (pe-nu'-el) - Same as Peniel. The face of God. God's face. Turn ye to God. Face or vision of God. That sees God.
Peor (pe'-or) - Opening. Point. A gaper. Hole. A gap. Cleft.
Perazim (per'-a-zim) - Breaches. Divisions. Defeats, Instruction. Observation.
Perea (pe-re'-a) - The land beyond.
Peres (pe'-res) - Divided. Breach. Crush. Break. Divide.
Peresh (pe'-resh) - Excrement i.e., That which is sifted out. Distinction. Horseman. Dung. Separate. Eliminated.
Perez (pe'-rez) - Breach. Bursting through. Divided. A break. Divisions. Breaking forth.
Perez-uzza (pe'-rez-uz'-zah) - Breach of Uzza. The breach was strengthened. Division of Uzza.
Perez-uzzah (pe'-rez-uz'zah) - Breach of Uzza. The breach was strengthened. Division of Uzzah. Breaking of Uzzah.
Perga (pur'-gah) - Earthy. Much earth. Very earthy. All earthy. Tower.
Pergamos (pur'-ga-mos) - Citadel. Fortified. High power. Height. Elevation. (A root word from which we get our words bigamy and polygamy). Much marriage, idea of a marriage i.e., mixture of the church and the world. Elevated.

Perida (per-i'-dah) - Distinguished. Separation. A recluse. Division. Dispersion. Kernel. Unique.
Perizzite(s) (per'-iz-zite(s)) - Villagers. Belonging to a village. Open. Without walls. Rustic. Squatter. Dwelling in villages. Inhabitant of the open country.
Persepolis (per-sep'-o-lis) - City of Persia.
Persia (per'-she-ah) - A horseman. Divided. That cuts or divides. A nail. A gryphon. Cutting. Dividing. A horse.
Persians (per'-she-uns) - Same as Persia. A horseman. Be divided. Belonging to Persia. Inhabitants of Persia.
Persis (pur'-sis) - One who takes by storm. That which divides. Overturning. Fighting. Persian.
Peruda (per'-u-dah) - Distinguished. A recluse. Same as Perida. Separation. Dividing. Dispersion. Kernel.
Peter (pe'-tur) - A stone. A rock. A piece of rock.
Pethahiah (peth-a-hi'-ah) - Loosed of the Lord. Whom Jehovah looses. Jehovah has set free. Opened of Jah. The Lord opening. The gate of the Lord. The Lord opens. Jah sets free. Freed by Jehovah. Jehovah opens up.
Pethor (pe'-thor) - Interpretation of dreams. To interpret. Extension. Soothsayer.
Pethuel (pe-thu'-el) - Ingenuousness of God i.e., great simplicity of mind. God delivers. The noble mindedness of God. God's opening. Persuaded by God. Mouth of God. Persuasion of God. Enlargement of God. Man of God. Enlarged of God.
Petra (pet'-ra) - Rock.

Peulthai (pe-ul'-thahee) - Wages of the Lord. Deed of Jehovah. Jehovah works. Full of work. My works. My wages. Work of God. Laborious. Wages.

Phalec (fa'-lek) - Division. Greek form of Peleg. Separation. To cut.

Phallu (fal'-lu) - Admirable. Wonderful. Deliverance. Separated. Hidden. Distinguished.

Phalti (fal'-ti) - Deliverance of Jehovah. Deliverance. My escape. Flight. Delivered.

Phaltiel (fal'-te-el) - Deliverance of God.

Phanuel (fan-u'-el) - Vision of God. Greek form of Penuel - The face of God. God's face. Turn ye to God. Face or vision of God. Sight of God.

Pharaoh (fa'-ra-o) - Son of the sun. Mouth of the sun. Sun. Great house. Voice of God. The king. The destroyer. A curtailer. (Title ruler of Egypt). His nakedness. That disperses. That spoils. To be free. Sun king. The sun. Inhabitant of the palace.

Pharaoh-hophra (fa'-ra-o-hof'-rah) - Pharaoh, the priest of the sun. Priest of the sun. His nakedness. Covering evil.

Pharaoh-necho (fa'-ra-o-ne'-ko) - Pharaoh, the lame. His nakedness. He is smitten. Prince Crocodile.

Pharaoh-nechoh (fa'-ra-o-ne'-ko) - Pharaoh, the lame. His nakedness. He is smitten. Prince Crocodile. Sun king.

Phares (fa'-rez) - Breach. Rupture. Tearing asunder. Divisions. Greek form of Perez.

Pharez (fa'-rez) - Break forth violently. Division. Rupture. Breach. Divisions.

Pharisee(s) (far'-i-see(s)) - The separated. One who expounds. Set apart. A separatist. Self-righteousness. Separated ones.

Pharosh (fa'-rosh) - Same as Parosh. A flea i.e., a cowardly man. A fugitive. Fruit of the north. The flea as the isolated insect. Expose.

Pharpar (far'-par) - Most swift. Swift. Breaking asunder. That produces fruit. Very quick. Producing fruit. Rapid.

Pharzites (far'-zites) - Descendants of Pharez. Breaking forth violently.

Phaseah (fa'-se'-ah) - Same as Paseah. Lame. Limping. Halt.

Phebe (fe'-be) - Moon. Pure or radiant as the moon. Shining. Pure. Chaste. Shining as the moon.

Phenice (fe-ni'-se) - Palm tree. Palm land. The mouth of all. A red tree. Palm country. Date palm.

Phenicia (fe-nish'-e-ah) - Land of palms. The mouth of all. Palm land. Date land. The palm tree.

Phichol (fi'-kol) - Mouth of all. Attentive. Great. Strong. Mouth of the whole or all. Perfection of the mouth. All commanding. Dark water.

Philadelphia (fil-a-del'-fe-ah) - Brotherly love. Love of a brother.

Philemon (fi-le'-mon) - Affectionate. Friendly. One who kisses. An affectionate man. Friendship.

Philetus (fe-le'-tus) - Beloved. Worthy of love. Amiable. Who is amiable.

Philip (fil'-ip) - Lover of horses. Warrior. Warlike.

Philipi (fil-ip'-pi) - Lover of horses. A town named after Phillip of Macedonia. Warlike. Warrior.

Philipians (fil-ip'-pe-uns) - The people of Phillipi. Lover of horses. Warlike. Warrior.

Philistia (fil-is'-te-ah) - The land of the Philistines. Same as Palestine. The land of wanderers. The land of strangers. Rolled in dust. Wallowing. Removal. Migratory. Covered. Watered. Those who dwell in villages. Migration. Land of sojourners.

Philistim (fil-is'-tim) - Same as Palestine. The land of wanderers. Land of strangers. Wanderers. Removal. Migratory. Covered. Watered. Rolling.

Philistine(s) (fil-is'-tin(s)) - Same as Palestine. The land of wanderers. Land of strangers. Wanderers. Those who dwell in villages. Removal. Migratory. Covered. Watered. Rolling.

Philologus (fil-ol'-o-gus) - Talkative. A lover of words. A lover of wandering. Lover of the word. A lover of letters. Lover of learning or the word.

Phinehas (fin'-e-has) - Mouth of brass. Face of trust. Serpent's mouth. Mouth of pity. Bold mouth. Aspect. Face of protection. Look of compassion. Mouth of a serpent or brass. Brazen mouth. The nubian.

Phlegon (fle'-gon) - Zealous. Burning. Blazing.

Phoenicia (phoe-ni'-ci-a) - Land of palm trees.

Phrygia (frij'-e-ah) - Dry. Barren. Parched. Torrid.

Phurah (fu'-rah) - Branch. Bough. Beauty. Bears fruit. He was fruitful. That bears fruit. Foliage.

Phut (fut) - A bow. Extension. Brow. Enlargement. To pour.

Phuvah (fu'-vah) - Mouth. Utterance. A blast. Scattered. Splendor. Madder of the dyer. Mouth blast.

Phygellus (fi-jel'-lus) - Little fugitive. Fugitive.

Phylacteries (fi-lak-tuh-ree)- Things to be especially observed. Either of two small, black, leather cubes containing a piece of parchment inscribed with Scriptures, one is attached with straps to the left arm and the other to the forehead.

Pibeseth (pi-be'-zeth) - Portion of the spouse. Mouth of loathing. Abode of the goddess Bahest or Bast. An Egyptian goddess represented with the head of a cat. House of Bast.

Pi-hahiroth (pi-ha-hi'-roth) - Mouth of caverns. The mouth of wrath. Kindlings. The mouth. The pass of Hiroth. Mouth of caves. Place where grass grows. Place of reservoirs. Mouth of the gorges.

Pilate (pi'-lut) - Armed with javelin. One armed with a dart. Close pressed (as a piece of felt). Close pressed i.e., firm.

Pildash (pil'dash) - Lamp of fire. Flame of fire. Steel. Flame. Ruinous.

Pileha (pil'-e-hah) - Servitude. Ploughman. Worship of plowing. Breaking out. To divide. A slice. Slicing. Worship.

Piltai (pil'-ta-hee) - Jehovah causes to escape. (Same as Palti - Deliverance of Jehovah. Whom Jehovah delivers. My escapes). Deliverance. Flight. Jah causes to escape. My deliverance.

Pinon (pi'-non) - Ore. Pearl. (Same as Punon - Distraction). Darkness. Gem. That beholds. Great anxiety. Mouth of eternity. Perplexity. Ore pit.

Piram (pi'-ram) - Like a wild ass. Swift. A wild ass of them. Great fruitfulness. Wild ass like i.e., indomitable. Wild. Roving.

Pirathon (pir'-a-thon) - Just revenge. Leader. His dissipation or deprivation. His rupture. Righteous vengeance. Chieftaincy. Princely. Leadership. Peak.

Pirathonite (pir'-a-thon-ite) - Inhabitation of Pirathon. Just revenge. Leader. His dissipation or deprivation. His rupture. Righteous very cause. Chieftaincy. Princely. Leadership. Peak.

Pisgah (piz'-gah) - Divided rock. A part. Boundary. Conspicuous. Survey. Hill. Eminence. Fortress. High hill. Provision. Cleft. Part.

Pisidia (pi-sid'-e-ah) - Pitchy. Persuasion of right. Pitch. A channel of water.

Pison (pi'-son) - Great diffusion of waters. Flowing stream. Freely flowing. Great pouring forth. Overflowing. Diffusion. To spread. Spread abroad. Increase. Changing. Extension of the mouth.

Pispah (piz'-pah) - Dispersion. Expansion. Disappearance. Spreading. Swelling. Scattering.

Pithom (pi'-thom) - An enclosed space. Mouth of integrity. Their mouthful. A dilation of the mouth. Very great space. Temple of Tem. Narrow pass. Secret part.

Pithon (pi'-thon) - Great enlargement. Simple. Harmless. Gift of mouth. Mouth of a monster. Mouthful. Persuasion. Expansive. Mouth. Hinge. Secret part. Harmless.

Pleiades (ple'-ya-dez) - A group of stars named from the Hebrew word meaning heap. Coming at the sailing season. The seven stars. To sail. Heap. Cluster of stars.

Pochereth (po-ke'-reth) - Binding. Here the cutting off. Cutting of the mouth of warfare. To entrap. Beguiling. Cutting off the mouth of man. Ensnaring.

Pochereth of Zebaim (po-ke'-reth of ze-ba'-im) - Retarding the gazelles, i.e., ensnaring them. Offspring of gazelles. Binder or hunter of gazelles.

Pollux (pol'-lux) - Meaning uncertain. Castor and Pollux the twin sons of Zeus (Jupiter) and Leda. Great power.

Pontius (pon'-she-us) - Belonging to the sun. Of the sea. Marine. Bridged.

Pontius Pilate (pon'-she-us-pi'-lat) - Marine. Dart. Carrier.

Pontus (pon'tus) - Sea. The open sea.

Poratha (por'-a-than) - Ornament. Having many chariots. Fruitful. Frustration. A gift. Given by lot. Faithful. Favored. Bounteous.

Porcius Festus (por'-ci-us fes'-tus)- Porcius - Swinish. Festus - Festival. Swinish festival. A hog.

Potiphar (pot-i'-far) - Priest of the bull. A fat bull. Belonging to the sun. Who is of the sun. My affliction was broken. Bull of Africa. Dedicated. Belonging to the sun god. Fruit of fatness.

Poti-pherah (pot-if'-e-rah) – (spelled Potiphera in other translations) Priest of the sun i.e., one who belongs to the sun. Belonging to the sun. Affliction of the locks of hair. That scatters abroad. Priest or prince of On. Dedicated. Given of the sun god.

Praetorium (prae-to-ri'-um) - The chief magistrate's court.

Prisca (pris'-cah) - Ancient. Primitive. (hence worthy, venerable).

Priscilla (pris-sil'-lah) - Diminutive of Prisca. Ancient. Little old woman. Old. Ancient one.

Prochorus (prok'-o-rus) - He that presides over the choir. Leading in a chorus or dance. Leader of singers. Choir leader.

Ptolemais (tol-e-ma'-is) - War like.

Pua (pu'-ah) - (Same as Phuvah - Mouth. Utterance. A blast. Scattered). Madder of the dyer. Mouth.

Puah #1 (pu'-ah) - (Same as Phuvah - Mouth. Utterance. A blast. Scattered). Mouth. Corner. Bush of hair.

Puah #2 (pu'-ah) - Exodus 1:15. Splendor. Splendid. Light. Child bearing i.e., joy of the parents. Brightness.

Publius (pub'-le-us) - Common. Popular. Who is of the people. First.

Pudens (pu'-denz) - Shamefaced. Bashful. Modest.

Puhites (pu'-hites) - Simple. Openness. To seduce. Deceive. A hinge.

Pul (pul) - Elephantine. Strong. Distinguishing. Bean. Destruction. Fat. Thick. Elephant. Lord. King.

Punites (pu'-nites) - Scattered. Distracted. Beholding. My face. Descendants of Pua or Phuvah.

Punon (pu'-non) - (Same as Pinon - Distraction). Darkness. Precious stone. That beholds. Great anxiety. Perplexity. To be perplexed. Ore pit.

Pur (pur) - Poor. A superstition. The casting of lots. God is my fatness.

Purah (pu'-rah) - Beauty.

Purim (pu'-rim) - Lots. Piece. God is my fatness. An annual Jewish festival (Esther 9:26).

Put (put) - (Same as Phut - A bow. Extension. Brow. Afflicted). To pour.

Puteoli (pu-te'-o-li) - Wells. To stink. Sulfurous springs. Little wells. Sulfurous wells.

Putiel (pu'-te-el) - Afflicted of God. Contemned by God. God enlightens. God is my fatness. Enlargement of God.

Pyrrhus (pir'-es) - Fiery red. Red haired. Flame colored.

Q

Quartus (quar'-tus) - The fourth. Fourth.

R

Raamah (ra'-a-mah) - Thundering. Trembling. Greatness. Striking. Smiting. Terror. Thunder. Some sort of evil.

Raamiah (ra-a-mi'-ah) - Thunder of the Lord. Jehovah causes trembling. Thunder of Jah. Thunder of God. Jah has shaken. Thunder. Trembling.

Raamses (ra-am'-seze) - Son of the sun. Thunder of the standard. Field of the sun. Destroying evil. Grandson.

Rabbah (rab'-bah) - Great city i.e., metropolis. Capital city. Great. Populous. Powerful. Contentious. Plenteous.

Rabbath (rab'-bath) - (Same as Rabbah - Great city i.e., metropolis). Capital city. Great. Populous. Multitude.

Rabbi (rab'-bi) - Master. My master. Who overthrows or destroys a multitude.

Rabbith (rab'-bith) - Great. Multitude. Populous. Abundant.

Rabboni (rab'-bo-'ni) - Master. My chief master. My great master. Who overthrows or destroys a multitude.

Rabmag (rab'-mag) - Most exalted. Head of the magi. Chief of the magicians. Chief soothsayer. Much melting. Who overthrows or destroys a multitude. Chief magician or priest.

Rabsaris (rab'-sa-ris) - Grand master of the eunuchs. Chief eunuch. The head chamberlain. Chief of the eunuchs. Chief cupbearer.

Rabshakeh (rab'-sha-keh) - Chief cupbearers. Chief butler. Cupbearer of the prince.

Raca (ra'-cah) - Worthless. Empty i.e., a senseless empty-headed man. A vain fellow. Good for nothing.

Rachab (ra'-kab) - Wide. Spacious. Broad. A wide place. Extending. Large. Greek form of Rahab.

Rachal (ra'-kal) - Traffic. Trafficking. Merchant. To whisper. An embalmer. Trade.

Rachel (ra'-chel) - An ewe. A sheep. Sheep. To journey. Root - to cherish. Serene. Meek.

Raddai (rad'-da-hee)- Jehovah subdues. Subduing. To subdue. To rule over. Cutting under. My subduing. The Lord extended. Domineering. Trodden down. Ruling. Coming down. Treading down.

Ragau (ra'-gaw) - A friend. Fellowship. Shepherd. Friend of God. Greek form of Reu.

Raguel (ra-gu'el) - Friend of God. Jehovah is a friend. Shepherd. Associate with God. Tend ye God. Shepherd or friend of God.

Rahab #1 (ra'-hab) - Insolence. Fierceness. Arrogance. Job 9:13; Is. 3:5; Pr. 6:3; Ps. 138:3. A poetic name applied to Egypt. Ps. 87:4; Ps. 89:10; Is. 30:7; Is. 51:19. Extending. Pride. A sea-monster. Proud. Quarrelsome. This word is applied to Egypt as a whole.

Rahab #2 (ra'-hab) - This refers to the woman of Jericho. Spacious. Broad. A wide place. Breadth. Josh. 2:1; Josh. 3:6; Josh. 6:17, 23, 25. Enlarging. A pear. Proud. Large. Extended.

Raham (ra'-ham) - Merciful. Love. Affection. Pity. Compassion. Womb. Belly. A friend. Mercy.

Rahel (ra'-hel) - (Same as Rachel - An ewe. A sheep). Serene. Meek. To journey.

Rakem (ra'-kem) - Variegated. Friendship. Embroidered. Empty. Vain. Versicolor. To embroider. Needlework.

Rakkath (rah'-kath) - A shore. The bank of a river. Leanness. Her spitting. Bank. Shore. Vain. Empty. Temple of the head. A beach.

Rakkon (rak'-kon) - Extreme shore. An intense form of Rakkath. Emaciation. Spitting out. Thinness. Void. Vain. Mountain of enjoyment. Emaciated. Narrow place.

Ram (ram) - High. Exalted. Elevated. Lifted up. Sublime. Exalt. Haughty.

Rama (ra'-mah) - A hill. (Greek form of Ramah - The height. Lofty place. High place i.e., a place consecrated to idols. Cast down).

Ramah (ra'-mah) - The height. Lofty place. High place. i.e., a place especially consecrated to idols. Cast down. Highness. Same as Ram. Elevated.

Ramath (ra'-math) - The high place of the watchtower. The height. High places. Seeing death. The two watchtowers. Heights. Elevation.

Ramathaim (ram-a-tha'-im) - Double high place. The double height of the watchers. The two watchtowers.

Ramathaim-zophim (ram-a-tha'-im-zo'-fim) - (Ramathaim - the double eminence. Double high place. Zophim - Watchmen. Watchers). The two places of Zophim. The double height of the watchers. The two watchtowers. Twin heights.

Ramathite (ra'-math-ite) - Inhabitants of Ramah - The height. Lofty place. High place i.e., a place especially consecrated to idols. Cast down.

Ramath-lehi (ra'-math-le'-hi) – (Ramath - The high place of the watchtower. Lehi - Jawbone). Delight of Lehi. Jawbone height. Height of the jawbone. Elevation of the jawbone. Lifting up of the cheek.

Ramath-mizpeh (ra'-math-miz'-peh) - Height of the watchtower. Height of Mizpeh. High places. Watchtower. Elevation of watchtower. Height of the watchtower. Place of the watchtower.

Rameses (ram'e-seze) - Son of the sun. Dissolving evil. Evil is the standard bearer. Field of the gun. Grandson. Child of the sun.

Ramiah (ra-mi'-ah) - Placed of the Lord. Jehovah is high. Exalted of Jehovah. The Lord is exalted. Jah has raised. Exaltation of the Lord. Exalted by Jehovah.

Ramoth (ra'-moth) - Heights. Eminences. High places. Coral.

Ramoth-gilead (ra'-moth-ghil'-e-ad) - Heights of Gilead. (Ramoth - Heights. Eminences. High places. Gilead - Perpetual fountain. A heap of testimony. A witness. Mass of testimony. Strong). Heights. Spring. Perpetual.

Rapha (ra'-fah) - He has healed. Fearful. Relaxation. Giant. Tall. He healed. Medicine. God has healed. Vision of the Lord.

Raphu (ra'-fu) - Healed. Feared. Released. Comforted. Vision of the Lord. Cured.

Reaia (re-ah'-yah) - Vision of the Lord. Jehovah has seen. Seen of Jah. The Lord looked. Jehovah has provided for. Jehovah sees.

Reaiah (re-ah'-yah) - Jehovah has seen. Jehovah has provided for. Jehovah sees. The Lord looked. Whom Jehovah cares for. Vision of the Lord.

Reba (Re'-bah) - Offspring. Fourth i.e., a fourth son or a fourth part. One who stoops. The fourth. A square. That lies or stoops down. Sprout.

Rebecca (re-bek'-kah) - Ensnarer. (Greek form of Rebekah - A rope with a noose i.e., to tie firmly). A noose. Captivating. Fattened. To ensnare by beauty. Fattened animal.

Rebekah (re-bek'-kah) - A rope with a noose (to tie firmly). A tie rope for animals. A noose. Captivating. Fattened. Fettering by beauty. A quarrel appeased. Fat. A noosed cord. Cow.

Rechab (re'-kab) - Horseman. A rider. Companionship. Square. Charioteer. Acquisition of a father. Chariot with a team of four horses. Rider.

Rechabites (rek'-ab-ites) - Descendants of Rechab - Horseman. Companionship. Square. Charioteer. Acquisition of a father. Chariot with a team of four horses. Rider.

Rechah (ray-kaw') - Spacious. Side. Uttermost part. Tenderness. Border. Softness. Hind part.

Red Sea - The weed. The weedy sea i.e., the sea of weed. To come to an end. A whirlwind.

Red - As applied to blood.

Reelaiah (re-el-ah'-yah) - Trembling caused by Jehovah. Shaken of Jah. The shaking of the Lord. Whom Jah makes tremble. Shepherd or companion to the Lord.

Regem (re'-ghem) - Friend. Friendship. Stoning. A throng. Stone heap. He that stones. Purple. That stones or is stoned.

Regem-melech (re'-ghem-me'-lek) - Friend of the king. Stoning of the king. A throng or troop. King's heap. Royal friend. Purple of the king. He that stones the king. Friend of the kings.

Rehabiah (re-hab-i'-ah) - Enlarging of the Lord. Jehovah enlarged. Jehovah is comprehensive. God is my extent. The extension of the Lord. Jah has enlarged. Breadth. Whom Jehovah enlarges. Jehovah is a widener.

Rehob (re'-hob) - Open space. Width. Street. A wide street. Market place. Room. Breadth. Space. Extent.

Rehoboam (re-ho-bo'-am) - Freer of the people. The people are enlarged. Who enlarges the people. Extension of the people. Who sets the people at liberty. Jah enlarges the people.

Rehoboth (re'-ho-both) - Streets. Wide. Wide streets. Wide spaces. Roominess. Breadth. Enlargement. Spaces. Places. Broad land.

Rehum (re'-hum) - Pitied. Beloved. Merciful. Compassionate. Friendly. Pity.

Rei (re'i) - Jehovah is a friend. Friend of God. Friendly. Sociable. My friend. My shepherd. My companion.

Rekem (re'-kem) - (Same as Rakem - Variegated. Friendship. Embroidered). Needlework. Versicolor. Vain. Vain pictures. Divers pictures. Colorful. Variegation.

Remaliah (rem-a-li'-ah) - Adorned of the Lord. Whom Jehovah adorned. Jehovah increases. Exaltation of the Lord. The Lord is exalted. Jah has bedecked. Jehovah adorns.

Remeth (re'-meth) - A high place. Elevation. Height. Rejected.

Remmon (rem'-mon) - (Same as Rimmon - Pomegranate. Very high). Greatness. Elevation. Pomegranate tree.

Remmon-methoar (rem'-mon-meth'-o-ar) - Stretching. The marked-out pomegranate. Rimmon defined in a circle.

Remphan (rem'-fan) - The drunken as lifeless. (An Egyptian idol worshiped by Israel). Prepared. Set in array. Arrayed.

Rephael (re'-fa-el) - Healed of God. Whom God healed. God is a healer. Medicine of God. Enfeebling of the breath. Healing of the breath. God healed. The physic or medicine of God. Whom God heals. God heals. God has healed.

Rephah (re'-fah) - Riches. Healing. Healed of Jah. Enfeebled of Jah. Rich. Recreating. To sustain. Agreeable.

Rephaiah (ref-a-i'-ah) - Jehovah heals. Healed of the Lord. Whom Jehovah healed. The Lord healed. Medicine or refreshment of the Lord. Healed of Jehovah. Jehovah is healing.

Rephan (re'-phan) - The shrunken. (An idol worshiped by the Israelites in the wilderness).

Rephaim(s) (re-fa'-ims) - (Same as Rapha - He has healed. Fearful. Relaxation. Giant. Healing. The dead. Giants). Of the giants. Physicians. Relaxed. Strong. Lofty men.

Rephidim (ref'-i-dim) - Props. Supports. Joiners. Solderers. Shrinking of hands. Beds. Places of rest. Balusters. Rests or stays. Refreshments.

Resen (re'-zen) - Bridle. To curb. To restrain. Bit. A halter. Restraining.

Resheph (re'-shef) - Lightening. Flame. Haste. Burning coal. Fever.

Reu (re'-u) - Associate i.e., of God. A friend. Friendship. Feed ye. Fellowship. His friend. His shepherd.

Reuben (ru'-ben) - Behold a son. Vision of the son. Son seen. Son of a vision. Provided in my affliction. Who sees the son.

Reubenite(s) (ru'-ben-ites) - Descendants of Reuben - Behold a son. Vision of the son. Son seen. Son of a vision. Provided in my affliction. Who sees the son.

Reuel (re'u'-el) - Friend of God. God is a friend. Associate ye with God. Tend ye God. Fellowship of God. The shepherd or friend of God. God is his friend.

Reumah (re-u'-mah) - Exalted. Behold what. Raised up. See you aught. Concubine. Elevated. Lofty. Sublime. Raised high. Coral.

Rezeph (re'-zef) - Baking stone i.e., cake baked on the coals or stones. A stone. Burning. Glowing. Wide smooth pavement. Heated stone. Burning coal. Hearthstone. A hot stone. Glowing coal.

Rezia (re-zi'ah) - Jehovah is pleasing. Delight. Haste. Desire.

Rezin (re'-zin) - Firm. Stable. Dominion. Goodwill. A fugitive. Delightsomeness. Sure. Affection. Messenger. Pleasure.

Rezon (re'-zon) - Prince. Noble. Princeliness. To wax lean. Grave in manners. Small. Lean. Secret. Important.

Rhegium (re'-je-um) - Breach. A passage as broken through. Rupture. Fracture. To break through.

Rhesa (re'-sah) - Chieftain. Will. Course. The head. The first. Prince.

Rhoda (ro'-dah) - A rose. Rosebush.

Rhodes (ro'-dah) - A rose. Rosebush (Same as Rhoda).

Ribai (rib'-ahee) - Jehovah contends. Judgment of the Lord. Contentious. Whom Jehovah defends. Contention of the Lord. Strife.

Riblah (rib'-lah) - Multitude of people. Fertility. The strife ended. Fruitful. Fertile. Quarrel. Greatness to him.

Rimmon (rim'-mon) - A pomegranate. (Same as Remmon - Pomegranate. Very high). Exalted. Very high.

Rimmon-parez (rim'-mon-pa'rez) - Pomegranate of the breach or rent. Breaches of the pomegranates. Pomegranate of the cleft.

Rinnah (rin'-nah) - A joyful cry i.e., joy of parents. Shout. A wild cry. Strength. Song. Rejoicing. Shouting for joy. Outcry. A cry of joy or wailing. A loud cry. A shout.

Riphath (ri'-fath) - A crusher of enemies. A stable. Bruising. Shriveling. Healing. Fault. Slander. Fraction of a fraction. Remedy. Medicine. Release. Pardon. Spoken.

Rissah (ris'-sah) - Dew. Ruin. Rupture. Watering as the dew. Distillation. Heap of ruins.

Rithmah (rith'-mah) - Broom. Juniper. Binding. Juniper tree. Bush. Noise. Place of the broom. Wild broom bush. Health.

Rizia (ri'-zi-a) - Delight.

Rizpah (riz'-pah) - A baking stone. Hot coal. A hot stone. Pavement. Burning coal. Heat. Beat. Bed. Extension. Glowing stone. A coal.

Roboam (ro-bo'-am) - Enlarger of the people. (Greek form of Rehoboam - Freer of the people). Extending of the people.

Rogelim (ro'-ghel-im) - (Same as Enrogel - Fountain of the fuller. Fullers fountain. Footmen. They who tread upon). Fullers. Fullered cloths. Fuller's place. A foot or footmen. Place of fullers.

Rohgah (ro'-gah) - Outcry. Clamor. Alarm. Copious rain. Fear cured. Agitation. Filled for discourse. Filled or drunk with talk.

Romamti-ezer (romam'-ti- e'-zur) - I have lifted up help. I have exalted help. Highest place. I have exalted the helper. Exaltation of help. I will draw forth help. I have raised help.

Roman(s) (ro'-muns) - Men of Rome. Strength. Strong. Powerful. Height.

Rome (rome) - Strength. Strong. Power. Height. Might. City of Romulus.

Rosh (rosh) - Head. Chief. Prince. The beginning. Top.

Rufus (ru'-fus) - Red. Reddish.

Ruhamah (ru-ha-mah) - Compassionate. Having obtained mercy. Having mercy. Mercy is shown.

Rumah (ru'-mah) - High. Height. Exaltation. Exalted. Sublime. Rejected. Lofty. High place.

Ruth (rooth) - Beauty. Something worth seeing. Friendship. Female friend. Trembling. Satisfied. Looking on with delight. Friend. Drunk. Companion.

S

Sabachthani (sa-bak'-tha-ni) - You have forsaken me. Have you forsaken me? Thou hast forsaken me.

Sabaoth (sab-'a-oth) - The Lord of hosts. Lord of hosts or armies.

Sabbath (sab'-a-oth) - Rest.

Sabeans #1 (sab-e'-uns) - Inhabitants of Sheba. Eminent. Drunkards. Captivity. Conversion. Old age. Leading into captivity.

Sabeans #2 (sab-e'-uns) - Joel 3:8 - They who come. Go about. Busybodies.

Sabeans #3 (sab-e'-uns) - Job 1:15 - He who is coming.

Sabta (sab'-tah) - Breaking through i.e., terror to foes. He compassed the chamber. A stroke. Striking. To surround.

Sabtah (sab'-tah) - Breaking through i.e., terror to foes. He compassed the mark. A stroke. Terror. Breaking. A going about or circuiting. Old age. Striking.

Sabtecha (sab'-te-kah) - Surrender. Greatest stroke. Extreme. Terror. That surrounds. Striking.

Sabtechah (sab'-te-kah) - Beating i.e., terror. He compassed the seat. He compassed the smiting. Greatest stroke. Extreme. Terror. That surrounds. That causes the wounding. Striking.

Sacar (sa'-kar) - Wages. Hire. Reward. Recompense. Hire of labor. Wares. A price.

Sachia (sa-ki'-a) - Captive of the Lord.

Sadducees (sad'-du-sees) - Just. Righteous. (Named after Zadok founder of the sect). The righteous. He cut. Righteousness.

Sadoc (sa'-dok) - Righteous. Just (Greek form of Zadok - Just. Righteous. Upright. Justified).

Sala (sa'-lah) - Sprout. Offspring. A race. Branch. Petition. (Greek.

Salah (sa'-lah) - Sprout. A missile. A weapon. Mission. Sending. Branch. Sending away. Javelin. Petition. (Hebrew)

Salamis (sal'-a-mis) - A surging. Salt. Shaken. Test. Beaten. Bitten by serpents. Tossed.

Salathiel (sa-la'-the-el) - I have asked for from God. I have asked God. Ask or loan of God. A loan. The loan of God. Petition of God. Asked or lent of God. Requested of God.

Salcah (sal'-kah) - He lifted up the blind. Straitened basket. Firm binding together. Lifting up. Moving about. Extension. Thy basket. Thy lifting up. Wandering. Migrating. Migration.

Salchah (sal'-kah) - He lifted up the blind. Straitened basket. Firm. Binding together. Same as Salcah. Wandering. Migration. Lifting up. Moving along. Firmly bound.

Salem (sa'-lem) - At peace. Perfect. Complete. Peace. Complete or perfect peace. Peaceful.

Salim (sa'-lim) - Peace. Tossing. Crafty fox. Completed. Foxes. Fists. Path. Peaceful.

Sallai (sal'-lahee) - Lifted up of the Lord. Exaltation. Weighed. My basket. My castings up. Treading under foot. My rising. A basket maker. Peace. Perfection. Rejecter.

Sallu (sal'-lu) - Elevated. Weighed. They have raised up. Very high. Measured. Perfection. Peace. Contempt.

Salma (sal'-mah) - Garment. Strength. Firmness. Raiment. Clothing. Peace. Perfection.

Salmai (sal'-mi) - My thanks.

Salmon #1 (sal'-mon) - Shady. His peace. Peaceable. Clothing. Distinguished garment. Perfect. He that rewards. Clothed. Raiment.

Salmon #2 (sal'-mon) - Image. Resemblance. Ps. 68:14. Distinguished robe. Peaceable. He that rewards. Very shadowy. Darkness. A shady place.

Salmon #3 (sal'-mon) - Raiment. A garment. Ruth 4:20. Distinguished garment. He that rewards. Perfect.

Salmone (sal-mo'-ne) - Clothed. From the surging. Very shady. Commotion. Flowing. Peace.

Salome (sa-lo'-me) - Peace. Peaceful. Perfect. Very shady i.e., shady character. Reward.

Salu (sa'-lu) - Weighed. Elevated i.e., highly esteemed. Unfortunate. Very high. Miserable.

Samaria (sa-ma'-re-ah) - A watch mountain. A place of watching. Lookout. Guardianship. Guard. Watch station. An adamant stone. Sure keeping. His lees. Prison. Watch height.

Samaritan(s) (sa-mar'-i-tuns) - (Inhabitants of Samaria - A watch mountain. A place of watching). Sure keeping. His lees. Prison. Guardianship.

Samgarnebo (sam'-gar-ne'-bo) - Sword of Nebo. Be gracious. Nebo.

Spice dragged away in his prophecy. Keeping of Nebo. Cupbearer. Warrior. Servant of the king. Grace of Nebo.

Samlah (sam'-lah) - Garment. Enwrapping. Distinguished robe. Raiment. His name. His left hand. His astonishment. His raiment.

Samos (sa'-mos) - A token. A sandy bluff. A height. High place. Sandy. Full of gravel. Lofty place.

Samothracia (sam-o-thra'-she-ah) - A sign of rags. Height of Thrace. An island in the Aegean Sea possessed by the Samians and Thracians.

Samson (sam'-sun) - A little sun. Splendid sun i.e., great joy and felicity. Like the sun. Distinguished. Strong. A perfect servant. Sun-man. Sunlight. His service. Distinguished sun. Excellent sun. Hero. His sun. There the second time. Sun-like. Sunny.

Samuel (sam'-u-el) - Heard of God i.e., asked of God. Offering of God. Appointed by God. Heard. His name by God. His name is of God. Name of God. Placed by God. God hath heard.

Sanballat (san-bal'-lat) - Hate in disguise. The enemy is secret. A hidden branch. Hatred or throne in secret. Lauded by the army. Enemy in secret. Bramble bush. Obstruct. Deter. Strength. The god sin has given life.

Sanhedrin (san'-he-drin) - Sitting together. A council or assembly.

Sansannah (san-san'-nah) - Palm branch. Thorniness. Frequent purifying. Bough. Bough or bramble of the enemy. Thorn bush. Palm leaf.

Saph (saf) - Tall. Threshold. Preserver. Consummation. Extended. Basin.

Vestibule. Rushes. Sea moss. A threshold or dish.

Saphir (sa'-fur) - Beautiful. Fair. Delightful.

Sapphira (saf-fi'-rah) - Beautiful. Pleasant. Delightful. Handsome. One who composes books. That relates or tells. Sapphire.

Sapphire (saf'-fire) - Telling out. Recounting.

Sara (sa'-rah) - Princess (Greek form of Sarah - Princess. Chieftainship. Noblewoman). A ruler. To prevail.

Sarah (sa'-rah) - Princess. Chieftainship. Noblewoman. A ruler. The prince breathed. Lady. Princess of the multitude. Noble lady. To get dominion.

Sarai (sa'-rahee) - Contentious. Quarrelsome. My ruler. My princess. Dominative. My lady. Princess. Noble lady.

Saraph (sa'-raf) - Serpent. Burning. Fiery. Fiery serpent. A venomous serpent. Poisonous.

Sardis (sar'-dis) - Remnant. Builders rule. Escaping ones. Those who come out (Idea of restoration). Red ones. The remainder. Prince of joy. The sun.

Sardites (sar'-dites) - Descendants of Sered - Fear. Taking away. Dissension. Removing a dissension.

Sardius (sar'-di-us) - Ruddiness.

Sardonyz (sar'-do-nyx) - Ruddy.

Sarepta (sa-rep'-tah) - Smelting. (Greek form of Zarepath - Workshop for melting and refining metals. Refined. Smelting house. She has refined). Pouring forth. Refine. Smelting to fuse. A goldsmith shop. Smelting house.

Sargon (sar'-gon) - God appoints the king. The constituted king. Prince of the sun. Sun prince. Stubborn rebel. Righteous prince. Who takes away protection. A cloak. Coat. The king is legitimate.

Sarid (sa'-rid) - Survivor. Escaped. Remainder. Residue. Hand of a prince. Remaining. Refugee.

Saron (sa'-ron) - Full of darkness. (Greek form of Sharon - A great plain. A place for singing. Rightness). His field. His song.

Sarsechim (sar'-se'-kim) - Chief of the eunuchs. Prince of the eunuchs. Prince of the coverts. Master of the wardrobe.

Saruch (sa'-ruk) - Branch. (Greek form of Serug - Branch. Shoot). Interwoven. Connection. Binding. Layer. Lining.

Satan (sa'-tun) - Adversary. Accuser. Enemy. Contrary. An opponent. Chief of evil spirits.

Satyr (sa'-tyr) - A demon (in he-goat form or as bristling with horror).

Saul (sawl) - Asked for. Demanded. Required. Desire. Prayed for. Persuaded. Unrestrained. Lent. Ditch. Death. Asked. Asked of God.

Sceva (see'-vah) - Left-handed. I dispose. Mind reader. Expectation. Hope. Prepared. Disposed. Fitted.

Scythian (sith'-e-un) - Rude. Rough. A hut. Ignorant. Degraded.

Seba (se'-bah) - Eminent. Old man. Drink thou. A gate. Amethyst. A drunkard. That turns. Sheba.

Sebat (se'-bat) - Rest. Smite thou. A twig. Sceptre. Red. Eleventh month of Jewish Sacred year. Tribe.

Secacah (se-ca'-cah) - Enclosure. A hedge. Shadow. Covering. Defense. Thicket. Inclosure.

Sechu (se'-ku) - They hedged up. Watchtower. An observatory. A bough. Defense. A hill. A watch place.

Secundas (se-cun'-dus) - Second. Secondary. Favorable. The second.

Segub (se'-gub) - Elevated. Protected. Fortified. Exalted (inaccessible). Raised. Highness. Made strong. Aloft. Might. Protection.

Seir (se'-ur) - Rough. Hairy. Bristly. Wooded. Shaggy. Goat-like. A rock.

Seirath (se'-ur-ath) - The hairy she goat. Well wooded. Roughness. A rock. Tempest. Shaggy.

Sela (se'-lah) - Rock. Crag. To be lofty. Fortress. Cliff.

Selah (se'-lah) - Forte. A musical direction. Pause. Pause and consider. Lift up. Exalt. Make prominent. Elevation. To rest. The end. A musical term.

Sela-hammahlekoth (se'-lah-ham-mah'-le-koth) - Rock of division. Rock of escapings. Cliff of escapes.

Seled (se'-led) - Exultation. Burning. Recoil. Of supplication. Affliction. Exaltation. Warning.

Seleucia (sel-u-si'-ah) - White light. Called after Selecus. White with brightness. Troubled. Tossed. Shaken or beaten by the waves.

Sem (sem) - Strengthen. (Greek form of Shem - A name celebrated. Distinguished). Celebrated name. Fame.

Semachiah (sem-a-ki'-ah) - Sustained of the Lord. Whom Jehovah sustains. Jehovah supports. Joined to God. Cleaving. Jah sustains. Joined to the Lord. Heard of Jah. Sustained by Jehovah.

Semei (sem'-e-i) - Hear. Obey. My fame. That hears. Obeys. Hearing. Obeying.

Senaah (sen'-a-ah) - (Same as Hassenaah - Elevated i.e., the idea of lifting up. Thorny. The thorn hedge. Hated). Distinguished. Thorny. To prick. An enemy. Bramble.

Seneh (se'-neh) - High. Crag. Thorny. Height. Bush. Bramble. Thorn bush. Pointed rock.

Senir (se'-ner) - Coat of mail. Bear the lamp. A sleeping candle. Cataract. Pointed. Bed candle. Changing. A peak. Snow mountain.

Sennacherib (sen-nak'-er-ib) - The thorn laid waste. San (the moon god) has multiplied brethren. The moon god. Destruction of the sword. A destructive branch. Devastation by an enemy. Bush of destruction. Bramble of destruction. Assyrian king. Sin has compensated me with brothers. Sin multiplied brothers.

Senuah (sen'-u-ah) - Light. Bristling. The violated. The hatred. Pointed. Thorny. Hated one.

Seorim (se-o'-rim) - Fear. Distress. Barley. Bearded ones. Bearded. Gates. Tempests. Hairs. Barley grains.

Sephar (se'-far) - Numbering. Enumeration. Census. Conspicuous. Book. Scribe. Number. Border country.

Sepharad (sef'-a-rad) - End of wandering. End of spreading out. Separated. Boundary. Limit. Separated tract. A book descending. Descending.

Sepharvaim (sef-ar-va'-im) - Enumeration. Scribes. II Kings 17:31 - Census of the sea. City of the sun. Sephor of the Parvaims. The two books. The two scribes.

Sepharvites (sef'-ar-vites) - Enumeration. Two-fold. Inhabitants of Sepharvaim. Who burnt their children in the fire of Adrammelech and Anammelech.

Serah (se'-rah) - Abundance. The prince breathed. Redundant. To govern. Lady of scent. Song. The morning star. Extension.

Seraiah (se-ra-i'-ah) - Prince or soldier of the Lord. Soldier of Jehovah. Ruling with God. The Lord is my prince. Jehovah is prince. Prevailing of Jehovah. God my prince. Jah has prevailed. Jehovah has prevailed. Warrior of Jehovah.

Seraphims (ser'-a-fims) - Burning ones. Burning. Fiery.

Sered (se'-red) - Stubbornness subdued. Fear. Deliverance. Surviving. Trembling. A dyer's vat. Escape.

Sergius (sur'-je-us) - Earthborn. Born a wonder. (The proconsul of Cyprus). Net. Born to wander. Who acts late.

Serug (se'-rug) - Branch. Shoot. Firmness. Interwoven. Binding. A bow. Plant. Tendril. Layer. Twining. Branch or shoot. Strength.

Seth (seth) - Appointed. Compensation. Substitute. To replace. Replacing. Who puts. Substituted. Fixed. Puts. Appoint or compensate.

Sethur (se'-thur) - Hidden. Mysterious. Secreted. A hiding place. Hid. Destroying.

Shaalabbin (sha-al-ab'-bin) - Place of foxes. Earths of foxes. Hand of skill. Jackal of discernment. Cunning foxes. Fox holes. Understanding. Foxes.

Shaalbim (sha-al'-bim) - He regarded the heights. He regarded the lions. (Same as Shaalabim - Place of foxes. Earths of foxes. Hand of skill. Jackal of discernment). Cunning foxes. Fox holes. That beholds the heart.

Shaalbonite (sha-al'-bo-nite) - He regarded the heights. He regarded the lions. (Inhabitants of Shaalbim - Place of foxes. Earths of foxes. Hand of skill. Jackel of discernment). The way of understanding. A fox's building.

Shaalim (sha-lim) - Foxes.

Shaaph (sha'-af) - Who flew. Anger. Union. Friendship. Balsam. Division. Fleeing. Thinking.

Shaaraim (sha-a-ra'-im) - Two gates. Doors. Goats. Tempest. Demons. Gates. Valuation. Hairs. Double gates.

Shaashgaz (sha-ash'-gaz) - Who succored the cutoff. Servant of the beautiful. Beauty's servant. Keeper of the treasure. He that presses the fleece. He that shears the sheep. Lover of beauty.

Shabbethai (shab'-be-tha-hee) - Rest of the Lord i.e., born on the Sabbath. Sabbath born. My Sabbath. Sabbath of the Lord. My rest. Restful. Servant of the beautiful. Sabbatical.

Shachia (sha-ki'-ah) - Captive of the Lord. The return of Jah. Taken captive of Jah. Refuge. Protection of God. Captivation. Protection of the Lord. Fame of Jah. Announcement. Fame of Jehovah.

Shaddai (shad-di) - Name for God translated "Almighty" in KJV. See El Shaddai under the Names of God.

Shadrach (sha'-drak) - Rejoicing in the way. A tender breast. Soft. Tender. Decree of the moon god. The breast was tender. Zealous. Royal. Command of the god, Aku.

Shage (sha'-ghe) - Wandering. Erring. I wander. Touching softly. Multiplying much.

Shageh (sha'-geh) - Erring.

Shaharaim (sha-ha-ra'-im) - Two dawns. Double dawns. It dawns. Double dawn.

Shahazimah (sha-haz'-i-mah) - To the proud ones. Place of the proud. Lofty places. Abundance of lions. Heights. To strut proudly. Height.

Shalem (sha'-lem) - At peace. Complete. Safe. Perfect. Whole. Peace. Peaceful. Secure. Peace or safety.

Shalim (sha'-lim) - Handfuls. Foxes. Cunning foxes. Foxes pathways. Foxes region.

Shalisha (shal'-i-shah) - Triangular. A third part. Third place. Treble. Three. Triad. Prince. Captain. The third.

Shallecheth (shal'-le-keth) - Casting down. Felling. To be cast down. Thrown down. A gate. Casting out.

Shallum (shal'-lum) - Retribution. Recompense. Spoilation. Rewarder. Requital. Restitution. Reward. Peaceable. Perfect. Agreeable. Recompenser.

Shallun (shal-lun) - They spoiled them. He spoiled the lodging. Retribution. Spoilation. Reward. Revenge. Recompenser.

Shalmai (shal'-ma-hee) - Jehovah is recompense. Peace offering of the Lord. Peaceful. My garments. My peace offerings. Reward of God. My

thanks. Jehovah is recompenser. My garment.

Shalman (shal'-man) - He spoiled them. Their peace offering. Peaceable. A rewarder. Great perfection. Perfect. That rewards. Fire worshipers. Fire worshiper.

Shalmaneser (shal-man-e'-zer) - He spoiled them of the bond. Their peace offering of bondage. Fire worshiper. Peace taken away. A withholder of rewards. The god Shalmana is chief. Shalmana be propitious. Perfection of a prince. Reverential. Retribution. Peace. Tied. Chained. Perfection. Gracious.

Shama (sha'-mah) - Hearing. Obedient. He has heard. He heard. Hearer.

Shamariah (sham-a-ri'-ah) - Guarded of Jah. The Lord kept. Jah has guarded. Throne or keeping of the Lord. Whom Jehovah protects.

Shamed (sha'-med) - Destroyer. Watcher. Guardian. Exterminator. Destroying. Wearing out. Persecution. Of keeping. Extinction. Keeper.

Shamer (sha'-mur) - Keeper. Preserver. Guardian. Who is kept. Preserved. A thorn. Lees. Prison. Dregs.

Shamgar (sham'-gar) - Destroyer. Here a stranger. Cupbearer, of a surprised stranger. The desolate dragged away. Most careful keeping. Named a stranger. He is here a stranger. Cup bearer. Fleer. Sword.

Shamhuth (sham'-huth) - Notoriety. Fame. Renown. Desolation of iniquity. Exaltation. Desolation. Astonishment. Destruction. Waste.

Shamir (sha'-mur) - Keeping. Guarding. A thorn. A prison. Oppression. Kept. Hardness. Loss. Desolation. Astonishment. A precious stone. A sharp point. Hardstone.

Shamma (sham'-mah) - Desert. Desolation. Fame. Renown. Amazement. Destruction. Loss. Astonishment. Ruin.

Shammah (sham'-mah) - Astonishment. Desolation. Loss. Amazement. Destruction. Fame. Renown.

Shammai (sham'-ma-hee) - Astonishment of the Lord. Celebrated. Waste. My desolations. The astonishment of God. My name. Destructive. Desolated.

Shammoth (sham'-moth) - Renown. (Same as Shammah - Astonishment. Desolation. Loss. Desert. Desolations). Astonishments. Names. Desolations.

Shammua (sham-mu'-ah) - Hearing of the Lord. Famous. A hearkener (One who listens or hearkens to God). Hearing. He that is obeyed. Renowned. He that is heard. Heard by God. Fame.

Shammuah (sham-mu'-ah) - (Same as Shammua - Hearing of the Lord. Famous. A hearkener (One who listens or harkens to God). Hearing. He that is obeyed. Rumor. He that is heard. Renown. Heard by God. Fame.

Shamsherai (sham'-she-ra-hee) - Heroic. He desolated my observers. Safe watchfulness of God. Sun-like. There a singer or conqueror.

Shapham (sha'-fam) - He bruised them. He swept them bare. Youthful. Vigorous. Bare i.e., naked of trees.

Bald. Universal contrition. Shaven. Judge.

Shaphan (sha'-fan) - Prudent. Shy rock. Badger (Coney). A rabbit. Their lip. Judge. To conceal. Hide. Rock badger. Coney.

Shaphat (sha'-fat) - Judge. Judges. He has judged. He judged. Hath judged.

Shapher (sha'-fur) - Beauty. Pleasantness. Goodliness. Fair. Lovely. Agreeable. Brightness. Beautiful.

Shaphir (sha'-phir) - Beautiful.

Sharai (sha'-ra-hee) - Jehovah is deliverer. Liberated of the Lord. Free. My son. My observers. My settings free. My prince. Hostile. Dominative. My Lord. My song. Releaser.

Sharaim (sha-ra'-im) - (Same as Shaaraim - Two gates. Double gates). Doors. Goats. Tempests. Demons.

Sharar (sha'-rar) - Unyielding. An observer. Hard. Firm. Strong. Stay of family. Thought. Settlement. Twist. Cord. Hostile. Navel. Singing. Enemy.

Sharezer (sha-re'-zur) - He beheld treasure. Protect or preserve the king. God protect the king. Prince of fire. Splendor of brightness. Splendor of the shining. Overseer of the treasury. He has protected the king.

Sharon (sha'-run) - Rectitude. Observation. A great plain. A place for singing. His song. His plain.

Sharonite (sha'-run-ite) - Inhabitants of Sharon. Rectitude. Observation. A great plain. A place for singing. His song. His plain.

Sharuhen (sha-ru'-hen) - They beheld grace. A pleasant dwelling place. Free. Gracious house. Munificent gift. Abode of pleasure. Refuge of grace.

Shashai (sha'-shahee) - Habitation of the Lord i.e., a servant of God. Noble. Free. White. Pale. Whitish. My white ones. My linens. Habitation of God. Rejoicing. Mercy. Linen. Clean.

Shashak (sha'-shak) - Vehement desire. Activity. Runner. Assaulter. The rusher. The longed for. Longing. The kiss. Eagerness. A bag of linen. The sixth bag. Pedestrian.

Shaul (sha'-ul) - (Same as Saul - Asked for. Demanded. Required). Desire. Longing. Eagerness. The plain. That makes equality. Interrogated. Asked of God. Asked.

Shaulites (sha'-ul-ites) - Descendants of Shaul. (Same as Saul - Asked for. Demanded. Required). Desire. Longing. Eagerness. The plain. That makes equality. Interrogated. Asked of God. Asked.

Shaveh (sha'-veh) - Plain. Equality. To level. Equalize. That makes equality. Valley of the plain.

Shaveh Kiriathaim (sha'-veh-kir-e-a-thay'-im) - Plain of the double city. (Shaveh – Plain. Kiriathaim - Same as Kirjathaim - Walled cities). Plain of the walled city. Plain of Kiriathaim.

Shavsha (shav-shah) - The plain was vain. Habitation of the Lord. Nobility. Splendor. Habitation. Joyful. God's warrior.

Sheal (she'-al) - Petition. Prayer. Requesting. Asking. Demand. Request. Ask.

Shealtiel (she-al'-te-el) - I have asked of God. (Same as Salathiel - I have asked for from God. I have asked God. Ark or loan of God). Asked of God. I have asked of God.

Sheariah (she-a-ri'-ah) - Gate of Jehovah. Jehovah is decider. Jehovah has esteemed. Gate of Jah. God opened. Tempest of the Lord. Jah estimates. Gate. Gate of the Lord. Whom Jehovah estimates. Esteemed of Jehovah. Valued of Jehovah.

Shear-jashub (she'-ar-ja'-shub) - A remnant shall return from captivity. The remnant shall return. The residue shall return. A remnant returns.

Sheba (she'-bah) - Main. He who is coming. An oath. Captive. Amethyst. Violet color. Seven. Oath. Captivity. Old man. Repose. Seven or an oath. Covenant. Fulness.

Shebah (she'-bah) - The place of an oath. To the oath. Captive. Seven. An oath. Well of seven.

Shebam (she'-bam) - Their hoar head. Sweet smell. Fragrance. Sweetness. Kindness. Gentleness. Coolness. Compassing about. Old men. Spice.

Shebaniah (sheb-a-ni'-ah) - Jehovah is powerful. Jehovah has dealt tenderly. The Lord converts. Caused to grow up of the Lord. Whom Jehovah hides. Who is built of Jehovah. Who is discerned of Jehovah. God has drawn near. Jah has grown i.e., prospered. The Lord that converts. Whom Jehovah built up. Reared by Jehovah.

Shebarim (sheb'-a-rim) - Fractures. Terrors. Breaches. Ruins. Hoping. Looking for. Breaking. Hope. Broken places.

Shebat (she'-bat) - Eleventh Jewish month (January - February). A rod.

Sheber (she'-bur) - Breach. Breaking. Fracture. Fraction. Hope. Ruin.

Shebna (sheb'-nah) - Who built. Tarry, I pray. Grown up. Youth.

Youthfulness. Tenderness. Who rest himself. Dwell here. An approach. Growth. Who is now captive. A youth. Vigor.

Shebuel (she-bu'-el) - Captive of God. God is renown. Return O God. Abide ye with God. Led captive of God. The returning of God. Turning.

Shecaniah (shek-a-ni'-ah) - Inhabited of the Lord. Habitation of the Lord i.e., one of the Lord's people with whom He is pleased to dwell. Jehovah has dwelt. The abode of God. Jah has dwelt. Jehovah is a neighbor.

Shechaniah (shek-a-ni'-ah) - Same as Shecaniah - Inhabited of the Lord. Habitation of the Lord i.e., one of the Lord's people with whom the Lord is pleased to dwell. Jehovah is a neighbor. Jehovah has dwelt. Jehovah dwells. Habitation of God. Familiar with Jah.

Shechem (she'-kem) - Back. Shoulder. Literally early rising. Diligence. A portion. Ridge. Early in the morning. Part. Back early in the morning. A shoulder or ridge.

Shechemites (she'-kem-ites) - (Same as Shechem - Back. Shoulder. Literally early rising. Diligence. A portion. Ridge). Early in the morning. Part. Back early in the morning. A shoulder or ridge. Family and descendants of Shechem.

Shedeur (shed'-e-ur) - Breasts of light. Breasts of fire. The Almighty is fire. Casting forth of fire i.e., lightning, thunderbolt. Giving forth of light. Shedding of light. Almighty. Casting of fire. Spreading of light. Field of light. Light of the Almighty. Sender of revelation. Spreader of light. Shedder of light.

Sheerah (she'-e-rah) - Blood relationship. Kinswoman.

Shehariah (she-ha-ri'-ah) - Sought of the Lord. Jehovah seeks. Jehovah is the dawn. The Lord has enquired. Jah has sought. Mourning or blackness of the Lord. Drawing of Jehovah.

Shelah #1 (she'-lah) - Prayer. Petition. Peace. That unites.

Shelah #2 (she'-lah) - Sent. Shooting forth of waters. Sending. Spoiling. That breaks. That unties. A son of Arphaxed of the line of Shem. A descendant.

Shelanites (she'-lan-ites) - Descendants of Shelah #1 - Prayer. Petition. Peace. The third son of Judah. (Numbers 26:20)

Shelemiah (shel-e-mi'-ah) - Repaid of the Lord. Whom Jehovah repays. Jehovah is recompense. Recompenses of God is my perfection. Reward of God. God my peace. My peace. My happiness. God is my perfection. Whom Jehovah rewards. Jehovah has recompensed. Jehovah rewards.

Sheleph (she-lef) - Drawn out or selected. Drawing out. Peace offering of Jehovah. To draw out. Extract. A drawing forth. Plucking. Draws out. Who draws out.

Shelesh (she'-lesh) - Triad. Third. Might. Tried. Triplicates. Triplet. Captain. Prince. Strength.

Shelomi (shel'-o-mi) - Jehovah is peace. My peace. Peaceful. Peaceable. Reward. Perfect. Pacific. God is my peace.

Shelomith (shel'-o-mith) - Retribution. Love of peace.

Peacefulness. (In I Chronicles 23:9, 25-26 - Pacifications). Rewards. Peaceful.

Shelomoth (shel'-o-moth) - Retributions. Rewards. Peacemaking. Pacifications. Love of peace. Peacefulness. Peaceful.

Shelumiel (she-lu'-me-el) - Friend of God. God's peace. God my reward. Reward of God. Peace of God. God is peace.

Shem (shem) - A name celebrated. Distinguished. Renown. Name. Eminency. To honor.

Shema (she'-mah) - Hearing. Fame. Echo. Repute. Rumor. Sound. Obeying.

Shemaah (she'-mah) - One who harkens. The fame. Hearing. Annunciation. Obeying. Rumor. Fame.

Shemaiah (shem-a-i'-ah) - Heard of the Lord. Jehovah has heard. Jehovah is fame. Obeys the Lord. The hearkener of Jah. Jah has heard. Obeying Jah. Hearing. That hears or obeys the Lord. Heard of Jehovah. Jehovah hears. Jehovah heard.

Shemariah (shem-a-ri'-ah) - Guarded of the Lord. Jehovah guards. God has kept. Whom Jehovah keeps. Safe keeping of the Lord. God is my guard. Whom Jehovah guards. Jehovah hath kept.

Shemeber (shem'-a-bur) - Splendor. Heroism. Name of wing i.e., a winged name of great celebrity. Soaring on high. Lofty flight. Illustrious. Name of force. Name of the strong. Lofty. Flight.

Shemer (she'-mur) - One kept by the Lord. Custody i.e., the object of

watchfulness. Guardian. Kept. Preserved. A thorn. Lees. Watch.

Shemida (shem-i'dah) - Fame of knowledge. Fame of wisdom. Science of the heavens. Name of knowledge. My name he knows. Invocation of the name. That puts knowledge. Fame of knowing.

Shemidah (Shem-i'-dah) - (Same as Shemida - Fame of knowledge. Fame of wisdom. Science of the heavens). Invocation of the name. Name of knowing. Name of knowledge. That puts knowledge.

Shemidaites (shem-i'dah-ites) - Descendants of Shemida - Fame of knowledge. Fame of wisdom. Science of the heavens.

Sheminith (shem'-i-nith) - Eighth. A musical instrument with eight notes. An eight stringed instrument. An eight stringed lyre.

Shemiramoth (she-mir'-a-moth) - Most exalted name. Most high name. Fame of the highest. Height of the heavens. Exaltation of the names. Heights of heaven. The height of the heavens. Name most high. An exalted name.

Shemuel (shem-u'-el) - Same as Samuel - Heard or asked of God. His name by God. Hearing of God. Appointed by God. Name of God. Heard of God.

Shen (shen) - Tooth. A sharp rock. Crag. Change. Ivory. The tooth.

Shenazar (she-na'-zar) - Repetition of treasure. Light. Splendor. Light of brightness. Fiery tooth. Tribulation. Treasure of a tooth. Vicious. May the god Sin protect.

Shenazzar (she-na'-zar) - Splendid leader. (I Chronicles 3:18)

Shenir (she'-nur) - (Same as Senir - Coat of mail. The fallow ground. Bear the lamp). Peak. Light. Reveals. Lantern. Light that sleeps. Pointed peak.

Shepham (she'-fam) - Their bareness. (Same as Shapham - Youthful. Vigorous. Bare or naked of trees. Bald). Nakedness. Greatest declivity. Bareness. Cold. Bare spot. Wild.

Shephathiah (shef-a-ti'-ah) - (Same as Shephatiah - Judge of the Lord. Jehovah is judge. Whom Jehovah defends). The Lord judged. Whom Jah defends. The Lord that judges. Whom Jehovah judges. Jehovah judges. (I Chronicles 9:8)

Shephatiah (shef-a-ti'-ah) - Judge of the Lord. Jehovah is judge. Whom Jehovah defends. The Lord judged. Jah judges. Whom Jehovah judges.

Shepher (she'-pher) - Beauty.

Shephi (she'-fi) - My barrenness. My prominence. High or eminent. Illustrious. Baldness. Excellent. A beholder. Wearing away. Naked. Honeycomb. Garment. Beholder. A naked hill. Bare. Bald.

Shepho (she'-fo) - His bareness. His prominence. Unconcern. Smoothness. Desert. Excellent. Breaking in sunder. Bald.

Shephuphan (shef'-u-fan) - Their sinuosity. Their bareness. Serpent. An adder. Great trouble. Serpent like.

Sherah (she'-rah) - Consanguinity i.e., a female relation by blood. Near kinship. Kinswoman. Flesh. Relationship.

Sherebiah (sher-e-bi'-ah) - Jehovah has made to tremble. Jehovah is originator. Deliverance of the Lord from captivity. Heat of Jehovah. Delivered or set free by God. Heat of God. Singing with the Lord. Flame of Jehovah. Jehovah has scorched.

Sheresh (she'-resh) - Root of the family. Union. A root. Bottom.

Sherezer (she-re'-zur) - He beheld treasure. (Same as Sharezer - Protect or preserve the King (God). Protect the king. Prince of fire. Splendor or brightness). Splendor of the shining.

Sheshach (she'-shak) - Your fine linen. Confusion. A stopper of the way. Secure habitation. Bag of linen. Bag or flax of linen. A symbol. Humiliation. Thy fine linen.

Sheshai (she'-a-shahee) - My fine linen (garments). Whitish. Clothed in white. Free. Noble. Six. Mercy. Rejoicing. Flax.

Sheshan (she'-shan) - Their fine linen. Lily. Free. Noble. Princely. Rose. Joy. Flax.

Sheshbazzar (shesh-baz'zur) - Fine linen in the tribulation. Worshiper of fire. Rejoicing in the distress. O sun god, protect the son. Setting free of splendor. Joy in tribulation. Joy of the vintage. Protect the son. O god Shamash protect the father.

Sheth (sheth) - (Same as Seth - Appointed. Compensation. Substitute. To replace. Tumult). Replacing. Substituted. Confusion. Compassion.

Shethar (she'-thar) - Who searches. Appointed searcher. Star. Commander. Searching out. A remnant. Putrefied. Searching.

Shethar-boznai (she'-thar-boz'-nahee) - Who searched my despisers. Star of splendor i.e., brilliant star. Splendor. Bright star. A star of brightness. One that despiseth. That makes to rot. That seeks those who despise me. Starry splendor.

Sheva (she'-vah) - Habitation of the Lord. Vanity. Self-satisfying. A habitation. False. Guile. Fame. Elevation. Tumult. Jehovah contends.

Shibboleth (shib'-bo-leth) - An ear of corn. A flowing stream or flood. A branch. Ears of corn. Stream. Fall of water. Burden. Over much captivity. A stream or flood.

Shibmah (shib'-mah) - Sweetness. Fragrant. Spice (Same as Shebam and Sibmah - Sweet smell. Fragrant. Why hoary?) Over much captivity. Coolness. Fragrance.

Shicron (shi'-cron) - Drunkenness. Great drunkenness. His gift. His wages.

Shiggaion (shig-gah'-yon) - Erratic. Irregular. Inadvertency. Wanderings. A dithy-ramb ode. Varieties in song. A song of trouble or comfort. To wander.

Shigionoth (shig-i'-o-noth) - Irregular. Inadvertency. Wanderings. A dithy-rambic ode. Wanderers.

Shihon (shi'-hon) - Desolation. Overturning. Ruin. Great size. Wall of strength. Sound. Destruction.

Shihor (shi'-hor) - Very black. Turbid. Blackness. Dark. Black.

Shihor-libnath (shi'-hor-lib'nath) - Blackness of whiteness. River of glass. Blackness of Libnath. Darkish whiteness. Dark. Turbid stream of Libnath. Turbid.

Shilhi (shil'-hi) - Armed of the Lord. Dart of the Lord. Darter. One armed with darts. Planted by deity. Missive. Armed. Peace. Perfection. Retribution. Dart thrower.

Shilhim (shil'-him) - Missiles. Sent one. Armed men i.e., a fortress. Aqueducts. Gifts. Fountains. Armed men. Javelins. Sprouts. Peace. Perfection. Retribution. Armed.

Shillem (shil'-lem) - Recompense. Retribution. Reward. Requital. Peace. Perfection.

Shillemites (shil'-lem-ites) - The descendants of Shillem. (Same as Shallum - Retribution. Requital. Rewarder).

Shiloah (shi-lo'-ah) - Sent. Sending forth. Sent forth. Outlet of water. Pouring forth. To put off.

Shiloh (shi'-loh) - Peace bringer. Bringer of prosperity. Pacification. Tranquility. Rest. His descendant. Great tranquility. Peace. A Saviour. Sent. The desired. The longed for one. Prince of Peace. Place of rest. Quiet. Abundance.

Shilom (shi'-lom) - Tarrying. Peacemaker.

Shiloni (shi-lo'-ni) - Sent one. Tranquil. Peace bringer.

Shilonites (shi'-lon-ites) - (Same as Shiloh - Peace bringer. Bringer of prosperity. Pacificator. Tranquility. Rest. His descendant). Name or resident of Shiloh.

Shilshah (shil'-shah) - Might. Heroism. Triad. The third son. Triplication. The third. Three. Chief. Captain. Trial.

Shimea (shim'-e-ah) - Splendor. Something heard. Hearing. Rumor. A report. Amazement. Fame. God has heard a prayer.

Shimeah (shim'-e-ah) - (Same as Shimea - Splendor. Something heard. Hearing. Rumor. My reports. Appalment. Desolation. Harkening. Amazement. Annunciation. Rumor or fame). God has heard a prayer. Fame.

Shimeam (shim'-e-am) - Their desolation. Astonishment. Rumor. Fame. Great admiration. Hearing. Their fame.

Shimeath (shim'-e-ath) - Hearing. Fame. Famous. A report. Obeying. Annunciation. Rumor.

Shimeathites (shim'-e-ath-ites) - Responders. A report. Descendants of Shimeath.

Shimei (shim'-e-i) - One who hearkens. My report. Jehovah is fame or famous. Famous of the Lord. My fame. My listener. That hears or obeys. Famous. Renowned. Jehovah is fame.

Shimeon (shim'-e-on) - A hearkening. Hearing. An answer of prayer. Gracious hearing. A famous one. A hearing.

Shimhi (shi'-mi) - (Same as Shimei - Jehovah is fame or famous. Famous of the Lord. My fame. My listener). The hearing of God. Renowned. Fame. Rumor.

Shimi (shi'-mi) - (Same as Shimei - Jehovah is fame or famous. Famous of the Lord. My fame. My listener). That hears or obeys. Renowned.

Shimites (she'-mites) - Descendants of Shimei - Jehovah is fame or famous. Famous of the Lord. My fame. My listener.

Shimma (shim'-mah) - A report. Fame. Rumor. Hearing. Amazement. Annunciation.

Shimon (shi'-mon) - A waste. Tried. Valuer. Great desert. Astonishment. Desert. Waste Providing well. Fatness. Oil. Trier.

Shimrath (shim'-rath) - Guardianship. Watch. Watchfulness. Guarding. Ward i.e., one in the hands of the guardian of men. Watchings. Hearing. Obedient. Guard.

Shimri (shim'-ri) - Jehovah is watching. Word of the Lord. Watchful. My keeper. Keeping of God. Vigilant. Thorn. Dregs.

Shimrith (shim'-rith) - Guarded of the Lord. Vigilant. A guardian. Keepings. Watchings. Female guard. Father of changing. God preserves.

Shimrom (shim'-rom) - Vigilant guardian. A guard or watch. Watch post. Watchful. Watch height.

Shimron (shim'-ron) - (Same as Shimrom - vigilant guardian. A guard or watch. Watch post. Watchful). Careful. Keeping. Watch place. Father of changing. Watch height.

Shimronites (shim'-ron-ites) - Descendants of Shimron - Vigilant guardian. A guard or watch. Watch post. Watch.

Shimron-meron (shim'-ron-me'-ron) - Guardian of arrogance. Most careful watching. Guard of lashing. Watch height of Meron.

Shimshai (shim'-shahee) - My minister. My sons. Jehovah is splendor or sunny. Sun of the Lord. Sunny. My sun. Shining one.

Shinab (shi'-nab) - Tooth of the father. Father's tooth. Hostile. Light of the father. Father has turned. Sin is my father. Splendor of the father. A father has turned.

Shinar (shi'-nar) - Tooth of the city. Change of city. Casting out. Scattering all manner of ways. Wholly cast off. Country of the two rivers. Watch of him that sleeps. Confusion.

Shion (shi'-on) - Ruin.

Shiphi (shi'-fi) - Jehovah is fullness or abounding. Eminent. Nakedness. Abundant. My abundance. Troop of God. A multitude. Copious. Jehovah is fullness.

Shiphmite (shif'-mite) - (Inhabitants of Shapham - Bare i.e., naked of trees. Bald). Fruitful.

Shiphrah (shif'-rah) - He garnished. Fairness. Beauty. Prolific. To procreate. Fair. Trumpet. That does good. Handsome. Brightness. Splendor.

Shiphtan (shif'-tan) - Their judgment. Judge. Most just judge (intense form). Judicial. Most judge judgment.

Shisha (shi'-shah) - Whiteness. Brightness. Distinction. Nobility. An habitation. Pleasant. Of marble.

Shishak (shi'-shak) - Greedy of fine linen. He who will give drink. Illustrious. A waterer. Like to a river. Present of the bag or the pot. Of the thigh. Of the pot.

Shitrai (shit'-ra-i) - My officers. Jehovah is deciding. Scribe of the Lord. Official. The Lord reigns. Jah is arbitrator. Gatherer of money. Magistrate. Scribe.

Shittim (shit'-tim) - Same as Abel-shittim - Plains. Meadows of acacias. Promoters of error. Turning away from rods. Thorns. To flog. Acacia.

Shiza (shi'-zah) - Splendor. Vehement love. Rising up i.e., increase of family. Cheerful. Lifting up. Loved. Brightness. This gift.

Shoa (sho'-zah) - Opulent. Noble. Free. Cry. Rich. Fruitful. Kings. Tyrants.

Shobab (sho'-bab) - Returning. Restored. Backsliding. Apostate. Repaid. Turned back. Rebellious. Returned. A spark. Erring.

Shobach (sho'-bak) - Your turning back. Poured out. Pouring. One who pours out. Expansion. Captivity. Copious extension. Enlarging. Your bonds. Your chains. Pouring out.

Shobai (sho'-bahee) - My captive. My backslidings. Jehovah is glorious. Recompense of the Lord. One who leads captive. Returning of God. Taking captive. Sitting. A returned family. Turning captivity.

Shobal (sho'-bal) - Flowing. Shooting forth. Waving. Stream. Wandering. Travel. Continually. Overflowing. Increasing. Path. Ear of corn.

Shobek (sho'-bek) - Forsaker. One who forsakes. Free. He keeps. Forsaking. Made void. Forsaken.

Shobi - (sho'-bi) - Same as Shobai - My captive. My backslidings. Jehovah is glorious. Recompense of the Lord. One who leads captive. Returning of the Lord. Captor. One who captures. Glorious.

Shocho (sho'-ko) - A hedge. Fence i.e., A strong fortification. His hedge. His branch. Branches. To entwine. Thorn hedge.

Shochoh (sho'-ko) - (Same as Shocho - A hedge. Fence i.e., a strong fortification. His hedge. His branch).

Branches. To entwine. Defense. A bough. Thorns. Thorn hedge.

Shoco (sho'-ko) - (Same as Sochoh - A hedge. Fence i.e., A strong fortification. His hedge. His branch). Branches. To entwine. Thorns. Thorn hedge.

Shoham (sho'-ham) - Their equalizing. Justifying them. Onyx. Beryl. Precious as the onyx. Keeping back. A precious stone.

Shomer (sho'-mur) - Keeper or guarded of the Lord. Watchman. Guarded. He keeps. An adamant stone. Keeper. Dregs.

Shophach (sho'-fak) - Extension. Expansion. Effusion. Pouring out. Poured forth. (Same as Shobach - Poured out. Pouring. One who pours out. Captivity.

Shophan (sho'-fan) - Their bruising. Baldness. Great sorrow. Nakedness. Hidden. Rabbit. Hid. Hollow. Burrow.

Shoshannim (sho-shan'-nim) - Upon the lilies. Title of Psalms 45 and 69. Lilies. Tubular. Trumpets. Those that shall be changed. Lily.

Shoshannin-Eduth (sho'-shan'-nim-e'-duth) - Lilies of testimony. Title of Psalm 80. Lilies. A testimony. Denotes the manner after which the Psalm was to be sung.

Shua (shu'-ah) - Opulence. Salvation. wealth. Rich. Prosperity. Noble. Crying. Pit. Saving. Riches. Cry.

Shuah (shu'-ah) - Prostration. Affluence. Depression. I Chronicles 4:11 - A pit. Dell. Melancholy. Wealth. Ditch. Swimming. Humiliation. Bow down.

Shual (shu'-al) - A jackal. A fox. A small pet. Wolf. A burrower. Path. First.

Shubael (shu'-ba-el) - (Same as Shebuel - Captive of God. God is renown. Return, O God). Return of God. Captive. Returning captivity. Seat of God. God's captive.

Shuhah (shu'-ha) - Pit.

Shuham (shu-ham) - Pit digger. Pitman. Depression. Their pit. Great astonishment. Sink humbly. Talking. Thinking. Humiliation. Budding. Humility.

Shuhamites (shu'-ham-ites) - Descendants of Shuham - Pit digger. Pitman. Depression.

Shuhite (shu'hite) - Descendants of Shua - Wealth. Rich. Prosperity. Noble.

Shulamite (shu'-lam-ite) - The perfect. The peaceful. Complete. Rewarded. Peaceful. Perfect. That recompenses. Peaceable.

Shumathites (shu'-math-ites) - The exalted. Garlic. Distinguished. Astonished.

Shunammite (shu'-nam-mite) - (Inhabitants of Shunem - Two resting places. Their sleep). Perfect. Peaceful. Double resting place.

Shunem (shu'-nem) - Two resting places. Their sleep. The tranquility of rest. Their change. Quietly. Resting places.

Shuni (shu'-ni) - Tranquility. Quiet. Fortunate. Calm. My rest. My sleep. Changed. Sleeping.

Shunites (shu'-nites) - Descendants of Shuni - Tranquility. Quiet. Fortunate. Calm. My rest.

Shupham (shu'-fam) - Their bareness. Serpent. Complete sorrow. Serpent like.

Shuphamites (shu'-fam-ites) - Descendants of Shupham - Their bareness. Serpent.

Shuppim (shup'-pim) - Bared ones. Serpent. Attritions. Serpents. Wall. Ox. That beholds.

Shur (shur) - Rampart, as a point of observations. Beheld. A fort i.e., a fortified city. A watcher. A wall. Ox. That beholds.

Shushan (shu'-shan) - Lily. A Rose. Joyfulness. Joy.

Shushan-Eduth (shu'-shan-e'-duth) - Lily of the testimony. Title of Psalm 60. A musical direction. The lily of testimony. Lily.

Shuthalhites (shu'-thal-hites) - (Descendants of Shuthelah - Crashing. Rending). Plantation.

Shuthelah (shu'-he-lah) - Freshly appointed. Resembling. Rejuvenation. Crashing. Rending. Plantation. A plant. Planting of offspring. Noise of breaking. Verdure. Moist. Pot. Setting of Telah.

Sia (si'-ah) - Departing. Council. Assembly. Congregation. A troop. Multitude. Moving. Help.

Siaha (si'-a-hah) - Departing. Council. Assembly. Congregation. Troops. Multitude.

Sibbecai (sib'-be-cahee) - My thickets. Jehovah is intervening. Entangling. Thicket of the Lord. The troubling of God. Thicket of Jah. Bough. Cottage. Of spring. Thicket like.

Sibbechai -(sib'-be-kahee) (Same as Sibbecai - My thicket. Jehovah is intervening. Entangling. Thicket of the Lord). The troubling of God. Crowd of God's people. Bough. Cottage. Of springs. Weaver. Thicket like.

Sibboleth (sib'-bo-leth) - A burden. (Same as Shibboleth - An ear of corn. A flowing stream or flood). Great captivity. Old age. A stream.

Sibmah (sib'-mah) - (Same as Shebam - Sweet smell. Fragrance). Ears of corn. Spice. Fragrant. River of water. Conversion. Captivity. Splendor. Conspicuous. To be cold. Coolness.

Sibraim (sib'-ra-im) - Double purpose. Two-fold hope. Two hills. Hope. Double hope.

Sichem (si'-kem) - The shoulder blade. The shoulder as a place for burdens. A portion. Back. Shoulder. Early in the morning. Ridge.

Siddim (sid'-dim) - Cultivators. Furrows. Plains. The plains. Uprightness. Flats. Open fields. The tilled field. The valley of the fields. Tilled fields. Field or plain.

Sidon (si'-don) - Hunting. Fishing. Plenty of fish. A place for hunting. Fortified. Abundant prey. Fishery. Venison. Catching fish. Fortress.

Sidonians (si-do'-ne-uns) - (Inhabitants of Sidon - Hunting. Fishing. Plenty of fish. A place for hunting. Fortified). Abundant prey. Fishery.

Sihon (si'-hon) - Sweeping away i.e., a general who drives everything before him. Brash. Great. Self-possession. Pleasure greatly desired. Tempestuous. Rooting out. Conclusion. Conquering. Bold. Warrior.

Sihor (si'-hor) - (Same as Shihor - Very black. Turbid. Dark). Black. Trouble. The river Nile.

Silas (si'-las) - Woody. (Shortened from of Silvanus - Lover of woods. Of the forest). Considering. Third. Marking. Three. Forest.

Silla (sil'-lah) - He weighed. Compared. Weighing place. Heap of earth. Highway. A way heaped up. Embankment. Branch. Exalting. Basket. Twig.

Siloah (si-lo'-ah) - A missile as sent. Sent. Pouring forth. Dart. Branch. Who loves the forest.

Siloam (si-lo'-am) - (Same as Shiloah - Sent. Sending forth. Sent forth. Outlet of water). One sent. Dart. Branch. Who loves the forest. Sent or conducted.

Silvanus (sil-va'-nus) - Lover of woods. Of the forest. Born, in a wood. Woody. Who loves the forest.

Simeon (sim'-e-un) - Hearkening. Hearing with acceptance. Hears and obeys. An obeyer. Hearing. Gracious hearing. That hears or obeys. That is heard. Favorable hearing. God hears.

Simeonites (sim'-e-un-ites) - The descendants of Simeon - Hearkening. Hearing with acceptance. Hears and obeys. An obeyer. Hearing.

Simon (si'-mun) - (Same as Simeon - Hearkening. Hearing with acceptance. Hears and obeys. An obeyer. Hearing). Hearing graciously. Obeying. That hears. That obeys. Hearing. God hears.

Simri (sim'-ri) - Same as Shimri - Jehovah is watching. Ward of the Lord. Watchful. Alert. Renown.

Sin (sin) - Clay. Thorn. Mire. Mud. Bush. Muddy. Clayey. Sin the man god.

Sina (si'-nah) - Thorny. (Greek form of Sinai - Bush of the Lord. Pointed. My bushes). The bush of the Lord. Enmity. Cliffs. A bush.

Sinai (si'-nahee) - My thorns. Bush of the Lord. Pointed. My bushes. Bramble of the Lord. Rock fissures. A bush. Enmity. Cleft with ravines. Thorny.

Sinim (si'-nim) - Thorns. South country. A remote region.

Sinite (si'-nite) - Dwellers in a marshy land. Thorn or clay.

Sion #1 (si'-on) - Parched place. (Another name for Mt. Zion). Lifted up. Tumult. Noise. Very high. Elevated. High peak. Greek form of Zion - Rev. 14:1. The holy hill.

Sion #2 (si'-on) - Deut. 4:28 - Elevation. A bearing. Carrying. (Another name for Mt. Hermon). The holy hill. Elevated.

Siphmoth (sif'-moth) - Lips i.e., languages. Bare places. Declivities. Fertile. Fruitful places.

Sippai (sip'-pahee) - My basins. My thresholds. Jehovah is preserver. Belonging to the doorstep. Long. Basin like. Threshold. Silver cup. Bowl.

Sirah (si'-rah) - Withdrawing. Turning aside. Going back. Retreat. Departure. Retired. Turning.

Sirion (sir'-e-on) Breastplate. A coat of mail. Little prince. Large and splendid coat of mail. Sheeted with snow. The holy hill. A breastplate. Deliverance.

Sisamai (sis'-a-mahee) - Water crane. Swallow. Jehovah is distinguished.

The sun. Fragrant. Dissolution of the Lord. Distinguished one. House. Blindness. Distinguished.

Sisera (sis'-e-rah) - A crane of seeing. Swallow of seeing. A field of battle. Battle array. Sea of horses. Meditation. Binding in chains. Found on a horse. Crane. Crow. That sees a horse or a swallow. Army.

Sithri (sith'-ri) - A hiding place.

Sitnah (sit'-nah) - Accusation. Hatred. Contention. Hostility. Opposition. Strife. Enmity.

Sivan (si'-van) - Bright. Their covering. (Third Jewish month, May-June). A bush or thorn.

Smyrna (smir'-na) - Bitterness. Suffering. Myrrh. Cold habitation. Tribulation.

So (so) - Concealed. Conspicuous. Lifted up. A measure for grain. Veil. Vizier. The god, Saturn.

Socho (so'-ko) - (Same as Shocho - A hedge. Fence i.e., A strong fortification. His hedge. His branch). A hedge. To entwine. Inclosure. Branches. Brambly. Hedge.

Sochoh (so'-ko) - (Same as Shocho - A hedge. Fencing i.e., A strong fortification. His hedge. His branch). A hedge. Branches. To entwine. Brambly.

Socoh (so'-ko) - (Same as Shocho - A hedge. Fence i.e., A strong fortification. His hedge. His branch). A hedge. Branches. To entwine. Tents. Tabernacles. Brambly.

Sodi (so'-di) - My confident. Jehovah determines. Acquaintance of God. An acquaintance. My secret. Counsel. Confidant. Assembly of God. Favorite. God is my secret counsel. Intimate.

Sodom (sod'-om) - Flaming. Burning. Mystery. Their secret. Fettered. Abundance of dew. To scorch. Their cement.

Sodoma (sod'-o-mah) - Burning. (Greek form of Sodom - Flaming. Burning. Mystery. Their secret. Fettered). Abundance of dew. Their secret.

Sodomite(s) (sod'-om-ite(s)) - Set apart one for unholy purposes. Temple prostitutes. Persons who were as wicked as the men of Sodom. (The term identifies one of the sins of homosexuality). One who has the character of the people of Sodom.

Solomon (sol'-o-mun) - Peaceable (intense form). Peace. His peace. Peaceableness. Great peace. Perfect. Peace much desired. Peaceful. Obedient. One who recompenses.

Son of God - The divinity of Christ. One of the titles of the Messiah.

Son of Man - The humanity of Christ. This title was applied by Christ to Himself.

Sons of God - A designation for certain god like beings or angels. It also can refer to the company of Christians who in the last days have allowed the Holy Spirit, The Word and the dealings of God to perfect them, or who are conformed to Christ's image.

Sopater (so'-pa-tur) - Saving father. Of good parentage. Defends the father. Saviour of his father. Scribe.

Sophereth (so-fe'-reth) - Registrar. Learning writer. Scribe. Female scribe. His children were returned captive. Writer.

Sorek (so'-rek) - Choice vine. Noble vine. Generous vine. Vine. Hissing. A color inclining to yellow.

Sosipater (so-sip'-a-tur) - Saviour of his father. Saving father. Saving or health of his father. One who defends the father.

Sosthenes (sos'-the-neze) - Preserver of strength. Of sound strength. Saving strength. Strong savior. Secure in strength. Saviour. Strong. Powerful. Of full strength.

Sotai (so'-tahee) - My swervings. Jehovah is turning back. Drawn back of the Lord. Deviator. One who turns aside. The Lord has departed. Roving. Conclusion in pleading. Binding. One of deviates.

Spain (spane) - Scarceness. Rabbit. Race. Precious. Land of rabbits. Rain.

Stachys (sta'-kis) - An ear of corn. Spike or ear of corn.

Stacte (stac'-te) - A drop.

Stephanas (stef'-a-nas) - Crowned. A crown. Crown bearer.

Stephen (ste'-ven) - Wreath. Crown. Crowned. Crown bearer.

Stoicks (sto'-ics) - Of the portico. (Followers of the Stoic philosopher). In the gate.

Suah (su'-ah) - Riches. Distinction. Sweepings. Offal (the entrails of a butchered animal). Speaking. Entreating. Filth. Refuse.

Succoth (suc'-coth) - Booths. Tabernacles. Hats. Tents.

Succoth-benoth (suc'-coth-be'-noth) - Tabernacles of daughters. The tabernacles built. The daughters' booths. Tents of daughters. Booth of daughters.

Suchathites (soo'-kath-ites) - Bush men. Hedgers. Dwellers in booths or tents. Descendants of Sucha.

Sud (sud) - My secret.

Sukkims (suk'-ke-ims) - Dwellers in tents. Thicket men. Anointing. Covered. Dwellers in booths. Hut dwellers. Booth dwellers.

Suph (suff) - Reeds.

Suphah (suf'-ah) - Honeycomb.

Sur (sur) - Turning aside. Go back. Recession. Departure. Deteriorated. That withdraws or departs. Rebellion. Gate of the temple.

Susanchites (su'-san-kites) - (Same as Susanna - Lily. A white lily. They of the lily. They of the place (Sushan)). Inhabitants of Susa or Susi.

Susanna (su-zan'-nah) - Lily. A white lily. Rose. Joy.

Susi (su'-si) - Jehovah is swift. Rejoicing. Horseman. My horse. Joy. My house. Moth. Swallow. Horse like.

Sychar (si'-kar) - Drunken. Hired. End. A conclusion. Finishing. Falsehood. Drunkard.

Sychem (si'-kem) - Shoulder. Diligence (literally, early rising). (Greek form of Shechem - Back. Shoulder). A gift. Portion.

Syene (si'-e-ne) - Opening. Key i.e., of Egypt. Her veiling. Remotest dwelling. Bush. Opening. Key. Enmity.

Syntyche (sin'-ti'-ke) - Fortunate. Well met. That speaks or discourses. An accident. A chance. Fate. With fate.

Syracuse (sir'-a-cuse) - A Syrian hearing. Tyre hidden. Secret. That draws violently.

Syria (sir'-e-ah) - The highland. A citadel. Exalted. Sublime. That deceives. High. Descending. Slander of them. Highlands.

Syriack (sir'-e-ak) - Language. The Syrian language. Ancient language of Syria.

Syria-damascus (sir'e-ah-ma'a-kah) - Syria - The highland. A citadel. Damascus - Activity. Moist with blood.

Syria-maachah (sir'-e-ah-da-mas'-cus) - (Syria - The highland. A citadel. Maachah - Oppression. Compression. Depression). To be elevated. A citadel. A castle. Palace.

Syrophenician (sy'-ro-fe-ne'-she-un) - Exalted palm. Redness. Purple.

Syrtis (sur'-tis) - Sands. Shallows. Quicksands.

T

Taanach (ta'-a-nak) - She will afflict thee. Wandering. Through. Castle. Breaking asunder. Humbling thee. Sandy. Who humbles thee. Who answers thee.

Taanath-shiloh (ta'-a'nath-shi'-lo) - Shilo's opportunity. Shilo's fig tree. Entrance to Shiloh. Who produces figs. Approach to Shiloh. Breaking down a fig tree.

Tabbaoth (tab'-ba-oth) - Rings. Spots. Good time. Good hour.

Tabbath (tab'-bath) - Renowned. Celebrated. Pleasantness. You were good. Fame. Good. Famous.

Tabeal (tab'-e-al) - God is good. The goodness of God. Not scornful. Good for nothing. Burning. God showed Himself good.

Tabeel (tab'e-el) - (Same as Tabeal - God is good. The goodness of God. Not scornful. Good for nothing. Burning). God showed Himself gracious. Burning. God is good.

Taberah (tab'-e-rah) - Consuming. Burning. You may burn. It's burning.

Tabitha (tab'-ith-ah) - (Same as Dorcas - Gazelle). A roe. Gazelle. Clear sighted. A roe deer.

Tabor (ta'-bor) - You will purge. Stone quarry. Separated. Height. Purity. Broken. Mound. Rising. Choice. Bruising. To break. Broken hearted. Broken region.

Tabrimon (tab'-rim-on) - The pomegranate is good. Rimmon is god. Goodness of Rimmon. Rimmon showed himself kind or good. Good pomegranate. The navel. The middle. Pleasing to Rimmon. Rimmon is good. Good is Rimmon.

Tachmonite (tak'-mun-ite) - You will make me wise. Wisdom. (Same as Hachmonite - Very wise). Sagacious. Wise. Most wise or sagacious. Thou will make me wise.

Tadmor (tad'-mor) - You will scatter myrrh. City of palms. The palm tree. Bitterness. Palm.

Tahan (ta'-han) - You will decline. You will encamp. Supplication of parents. Camp. Preciousness. Inclination. Earnest prayer. Station. Beseeching. Merciful. Encampment. Graciousness.

Tahanites (ta'-han-ites) - (Descendants of Tahan - You will decline. You will encamp. Supplication of parents. Camp. Preciousness. Inclination). Earnest prayer. Station. Beseeching. Merciful. Encampment. Graciousness.

Tahapanes (ta-hap'-a-neze) - You will fill hands with pity. The beginning of the age. Head of the land. Gift of the serpent. Temptation. Secret temptation. Head of the age.

Tahath (ta'-hath) - Depression. Humility. Substitute. Subordinate. Descent. Station. Fear. Going down.

Tahpanhes (tah'-pan-heze) - You will fill hands with pity. The beginning of the age. Head of the land. Gift of the serpent. Temptation. Standard. Flight. Head of the age. Thou will fill hands with pity. Secret temptation.

Tahpenes (tah'-pe-neze) - You will cover flight. (Same as Tahpanhes - The beginning of the age. Head of the age. Given of the serpent). Gift of the serpent. Temptation. Head of the age. Secret temptation. Wife of the king.

Tahrea (tah'-re-ah) - Separate the friend. Delaying cries i.e., a son slowly born. Cunning adroitness. Flight. Delay of rejoicing. Cunning. Craft. Anger. Wicked contention.

Tahtim-hodshi (tah'-tim-hod'-shi) - The lower ones of my new moon. Under the new moon. Netherland newly inhabited under the new moon. Land of the inhabited. Lowlands of Hodshi. Lowest moon.

Talitha-Cumi (tal'-ith-ah cu'-mi) - Maid arise. Damsel arise. Young woman arise.

Talmai (tal'-ma-hee) - Abounding in furrows i.e., as long as a furrow. Ridges. My furrows. Bold. Spirited. A furrow. Suspending the waters. Ridged. Heap of waters. Full of furrows. Furrowed. That suspends the waters.

Talmon (tal'-mon) - Injurious. Oppression. Oppressed (intense form). Oppressor. Violent. Outcast. Captive. Violent oppression.

Tamah (ta'-mah) - Joy. Laughter. You will be fat with inner joy. Clapping of the hands. Blotting or wiping out. Smiting. Combat.

Tamar (ta'-mar) - A palm tree. Palm. To be erect. The palm tree.

Tammuz (tam'-mu) - You will be shriveled up. Hidden. Giver of the vine. Sprout of life. Son of life. Concealed. Departure. Dissolution. Abstruse. Consumed. An idol god. A sort of incarnation of the sun. The fourth month of the Jewish sacred year (June-July).

Tanach (ta'-nak) - (Same as Taanach - Wandering through. Castle). Progress in traveling. Afflicting thee. Sandy.

Tanhumeth (tan'-hu-meth) - Consolation. His comfort. Solace. Repentance. Gift. Comfort.

Taphath (ta'-fath) - Distillation. Drop of myrrh. Stacte i.e., myrrh flowing spontaneously. A drop. Oil of myrrh. Drop. Little one. Ornament.

Tappuah (tap'-pu-ah) - You will cause to breathe. Apple. Fruitful in apples. High place. An apple tree. Swelling in the body. Swelling.

Tarah (ta'rah) - You may breathe. Delay. Station. A wretch. A banished man. A hair. One banished. Wretch.

Taralah (tar'-a-lah) - Release the curse. Reeling. His increase. Searching out of slander. A reeling. Searching out slander. Strength.

Tarea (ta'-re-ah) - Mark out a neighbor. Chamber of a neighbor (Same as Tahrea - Delaying cries i.e., a son slowly born). Delay of joy. Chamber of guile. Howling. Doing evil. Craft. Cunning.

Tarpelites (tar'-pel-ites) - They of the fallen or wonderous mountain. Ravishers. Hill of wonder. Succession of miracles.

Tarshish (tar'-shish) - She will cause poverty. She will shatter. Breaking subjection i.e., of enemies. Hard. Contemplation. Contusion. Battering. Subjection. Examination. Subdued. Yellow jasper. Jasper.

Tarsus (tar'-sus) - A flat basket. Joy. Pleasantness. Flat. Firmness. Hardness. Winged. Feathered.

Tartak (tar'-tak) - You shall be enchanted. The moon, the mother of gods. The sun in his regular return. Shut-up. Intense darkness. Chained. Bound. Prince of darkness.

Tartan (tar'-tan) - Release the dragon. Great increase. Military chief. The greatest extension. Commander in chief. A general (an official title). A title.

Tatnai (tat'-na-hee) - Gift. Overseer of gifts. Rewarding. A rewarder. The overseer of the gifts and tributes. That gives. A gift.

Tebah (te'-bah) - Confidence of parents. Slaughter. Slaughter of cattle. Thick. Strong. Confidence. Guarding of the body. Cook. Murder. Butchery. A cook.

Tebaliah (teb-a-li'-ah) - Baptized of the Lord i.e., purified. Whom Jehovah has immersed. Jehovah is protector. Jehovah has purified. The Lord dipped. Purified. Goodness of God. Baptism. Jehovah purifies.

Tebeth (te'-beth) - Goodness. Tenth Jewish month (Dec. - Jan.). Good.

Tehaphnehes (te-haf'-ne-heze) - You will fill hands with pity. (Same as Tahapanes - The beginning of the age. Head of the land). The gift of the serpent. Temptation.

Tehinnah (te-hin'-nah) - Grace. Prayer. Cry for mercy. Entreaty. Supplication. Earnest prayer. Merciful. Graciousness. A favor.

Tekel (te'-kel) - Weighed. Weight. Be weighed. Weighed and found wanting. Too light. Lacking in moral worth.

Tekoa (te-ko'-ah) - Sound of trumpet. Blowing a trumpet. Pitching of tents. Firm. Settlement. Fixing of a tent.

Sound of the trumpet. That is confirmed. Trumpet blast.

Tekoah (te-ko'-ah) - (Same as Tekoa - Sound of a trumpet. Blowing a trumpet. Pitching of tents. Firm. Settlement). Pitching of a tent. Trumpet clang. A trumpet. Trumpet blast. Fixing of a tent. Sound of the trumpet. That is confirmed.

Tekoite(s) (te-ko'-ite(s)) - (Inhabitants of Tekoah - Sound of a trumpet. Blowing a trumpet. Pitching of tents. Firm. Settlement). Pitching of a tent. Trumpet clang. A trumpet. Trumpet blast. Fixing of a tent. Sound of the trumpet. That is confirmed.

Tel-abib (tel-a'-bib) - Hill of ears of corn. Corn hill. A mound of green grain heap. A heap of new grain. A corn hill. A heap of grain. Hill of grain.

Telah (te'-lah) - Rejuvenator. Invigorator. Fracture. Vigor. Rupture. Breach. Making green. Moistening. Greenness.

Telaim (tel'-a-im) - Young lambs. Lambs i.e., spotted ones. Prey taken by force.

Telassar (te-las'-sar) - Weariness of the prince. Hang thou the prince. Hill of Assur. Oath of the princes. Assyrian hill. Taking away. Heaping up. Hill.

Telem (te'-lem) - Covering them. Casting them out. Oppression. A lamb. Shadow of them. Their due. Their shadow.

Tel-haresha (tel-ha-re'-shah) - Heap of artifice. Heap of the artificer. Hill of plowing. Forest hill. Plowed mound. Hill of the magus. Suspension of the plow. Mound of workmanship. Hill of workmanship. Mound of the forest. Mound of magic.

Tel-harsa (tel-har'-sah) - (Same as Tel-haresha - Heap of artifice. Heap of the artificer. Hill of plowing. Forest hill). Plowed mound. Hill of the magus. Suspension of the plow. Mound of workmanship. Hill of workmanship. Mound of the forest. Mound of magic.

Tel-melah (tel-me'-lah) - Hill of salt. Salt hill. Heap of salt.

Tema (te'-mah) - Southern. A desert. An untilled region. Sunburnt. Admiration. Great fear. Marveling south wind. Perfection. Consummation. South desert. South country. Desert.

Temah (te'-mah) - Laughter.

Teman (te'-man) - Southern quarter. The south. On the right hand. Perfect. Southward. Noonday. South desert. To breathe. Scent. Blow. The right or south.

Temani (te'-ma-ni) - (descendant of Teman - Southern quarter. The south. On the right hand. Perfect). The south. Moist. Ordained. To breathe. Scent. Blow. Southward. The right or south.

Temanite(s) (te'-man-ite(s)) - (Same as Teman - Southern quarter. The south. On the right hand. Perfect). Descendant of Teman. To breathe. Scent. Blow.

Temeni (tem'-e-ni) - You shall go to the right hand. My right hand. Fortunate. The south. Moist. Ordained. Southern.

Terah (te'-rah) - You may breathe. Delay i.e., slowly born. Stopping. Station. Smelling. Breathing. The senses. To breathe. Scent. Blow. Position. Turning. Duration.

Teraphim (ter'af-im) - Nourishers. Images. Idols. Literally enfeeblers or healers. Avoidances.

Teresh (te'-resh) - Possession. You will possess. Sever. Austere. Reverence. Driving away. Rude. Severe. Solid.

Tertius (tur'-she-us) - The third. Third.

Tertullus (tur-tul'-lus) - Triple hardened. Liar. Imposter. Third.

Tetrarch (te'-trarch) - Ruler of a fourth part of a country. Governor of a fourth part. Ruler of the fourth part of a realm.

Thaddaeus (thade-de' us) - Sucking plenty. Breast. Man of heart. One that praises. Praising. Confessing. Courageous. That praises or confesses. Aramaic word for the female breast. Large hearted.

Thahash (tha'-hash) - Badger. A seal. Keep silent. Reddish. A yew tree. Friction. That makes haste. That keeps silent. Dolphin. A badger.

Thamah (tha'-mah) - You will be fat. Laughing i.e., joy of parents. Laughter. Suppresses. Combat. Who blots out. That suppresses. That blots out.

Thamar (tha'-mar) - Palm tree. (Greek equivalent of Tamar - A palm tree. Palm). See Tamar.

Thara (tha'-rah) (Greek form of Terah - Delay i.e., slow born). Delayed. Late.

Tharshish (thar'-shish) - She will cause poverty or shattering. (Same as Tarshish - Breaking. Subjection of enemies. Hard. Contemplation). Contusion. Battering. A precious stone. Subdued.

Thebez (the'-bez) - Brightness. Mire. Clay. Whiteness. Brilliancy. He shone. Prominent. He gushed out. Muddy.

Eggs. Fine linen or silk. The head. City of the god, Amon. Splendor.

Thelasar (the-la'-sar) - (same as Telessar - Weariness of the prince. Hang thou the prince. Hill of Assur). The oath of the prince. That grants suspension. Hill.

Theophilus (the-of-'-il-us) - Loved by God. Lover of God. Friend of God. Loving God. Beloved of God. God given.

Thessalonians (thes-sa-lo'-ne-uns) - (Same as Thessalonica - Victory of falsity. Victory over the tossing of law. Victory over falsity). People of Thessalonica. Victory at sea.

Thessalonica (thes-sa-lo-ni'-cah) - Victory of falsity. Victory over the tossing of law. Victory over falsity. Victory of God. Victory against the Thessalonians. Victory at sea.

Theudas (thew'-das) - Gift of God. He shall be praised. Praise. False teacher. Acknowledgment. Flowing with water. God given.

Thimnathah (thim'-nath-ah) - Portion. (Same as Timnah - Portion assigned i.e., separated a portion. Gift). A portion there. You shall number there. A great portion. Portion assigned.

Thomas (tom'-us) - A twin. Depth without bottom. Twin.

Thummin (thum'-mim) - Perfection. Completion. Truth. Perfections. Judgment. Completeness.

Thyatira (thi-a-ti'-rah) - High tower. Castle. Feminine oppression. Odor of affliction. Sacrifice of love or labor. Perfume. Burning incense. Sacrifice of labor.

Tiberias (ti-be'-re-as) - A place named after Tiberius Caesar - Son of Tiber. from the river Tiber (as god river). Good vision. Observance. Breaking asunder. Prison. The navel.

Tiberius (ti-be'-re-us) - Son of Tiber. From the Tiber as god river. Good vision. Watching.

Tibhath (tib'-hath) - Security i.e., to dwell safely. Butchery. The slaughter place. Confidence. Slaughter. Extensive. Level. Place of slaughter.

Tibni (tib'-ni) - Building of the Lord. Made of straw. My straw. Straw. Intelligent. A structure. Pattern. Building of Jah. Hay.

Tidal (ti'-dal) - You shall be cast out of the Most High. You shall be cast out from heaven. Fear. Reverence i.e., of the object of fear. Dread. Easing the yoke. Veneration. Breaking the yoke. Knowledge of elevation. That breaks the yoke. Splendor. Renown. Great son.

Tiglath-pileser (tig'-lath-pi-le'-zur) - You will uncover the wonderful bond. You will carry away the wonderful bond. Mother of the gods (the son of the temple of Sorra). Hinders. Binds. My strength is the god, Ninib. Lord of the Tigris. Majesty of the great prince. Adoration be to the sun of Zodiac. That binds or takes away captivity. My trust is in the son of Asharra. Thou wilt uncover the wonderful bond.

Tikvah (tik'-vah) - Expectation. Strength. Hope. His assembling. A little line. A cord.

Tikvath (tik-vath) - You shall be gathered. (Same as Tikvah - Expectation. Strength. Hope). His assembling. A cord.

Tilgath-pilneser (til'-gath-pil-ne'-zur) - Winepress, heap of the wonderful bond. Winepress, heap of the distinguished captive. (Same as Tiglathpileser - Mother of the gods (the son of the temple of Sorra. Hinders. Binds. My strength is the god of Ninib. Lord of the Tigris). Majesty of the great prince. That takes away captivity.

Tilon (ti'-lon) - You shall murmur. You shall abide. Gift. Scorn. Suspension. Distinguished gift. Murmuring. Mockery.

Timaeus (ti-me'-us) - Highly prized. Polluted. Honored. Perfect. Admirable. Useless. Honorable.

Timna (tim-nah) - Restraint. Restrained. Unapproachable. Inaccessible. You will withhold. Restraining himself.

Timnah (tim'-nath) - Portion assigned i.e., separated. A portion. Gift. You will withhold. Restraining himself. Restraint. One withheld. Portion assigned. Forbidding. Allotted portion.

Timnath (tim'-nah) - (Same as Timnah - Portion assigned i.e., separated. A portion. Gift). Separation of one from another. Portion assigned. Image. Enumeration. Figure. Allotted portion.

Timnath-heres (tim'-nath-he'-rez) - Portion of the sun. Redundant portion. Image of the sun. Honorable. Worthy. Portion of Heres.

Timnath-serah (tim'-nath-se'-rah) - Portion redundant. Abundant portion i.e., that which is leftover and above. Portion of the remainder. Portion of abundance. Fruitful portion.

Honorable. Worthy. Remaining portion. Portion of the sun.

Timnite (tim'-nite) - Inhabitants of Timnah - Portion assigned i.e., separated. A portion. Gift.

Timon (ti'-mon) - Honorable. Deemed worthy Honoring. Precious. Valuable. Worthy.

Timotheus (tim-o'-the-us) - Honoring God. Zealot. To be honored of God. Worshipping God. Valued of God. Honor of God.

Timothy (tim'-o-thy) - Honoring God. English form of Timotheus - Honoring God. Zealot. To be honored of God. Valued of God. Worshiping God. Honored by God.

Tiphsah (tif'-sah) - Passage. She shall Passover. Passing over. Halting. Ford. Leap. Step. Passover. A fording place.

Tiras (ti'-ras) - He crushed the search. Desire of parents. Desire. Longing. A destroyer.

Tirathites (ti'-rath-ites) - Openings. From a place (gate). Men of the gate. Nourishers. Singing persons.

Tirhakah (tur-ha'-kah) - He searched out the pious. He searched out the waiter. Bought forth. Exalted. Inquirer. Beholder. Examiner. Dull observer.

Tirhanah (tur-ha'-nah) A camp spy. Inclination. Favor. Kindness. Inhabiting a residence i.e., a most secure dwelling place. Permanent dwelling. Condescension.

Tiria (tir'e-ah) - Fear. Foundation. Searching out. Beholding.

Tirshatha (tur'-sha-thah) - You shall possess there. The feared. Who overturns the foundation. Stern.

Severe. A governor. Dread sovereign. Feared. Your excellence.

Tirzah (tur'-zah) - Pleasantness. Delight. She is willing. Liberal. His delight. Well pleasing. Willing. Benevolent. Complaisant. Pleasing.

Tishbite (tish'-bite) – Captivity. (Inhabitant of Tishbeh - A captive. Adding. You shall lead captive. To take captive. Turning back. Recourse. That makes captive. The Gentile name for Elisha (Elijah)). The inhabitant.

Tishri (tish'-ri) - Seventh Jewish month (Sept - Oct). Beginning.

Titus (ti'-tus) - Nurse. Rearer. Protected. Honorable. From "I honor." Honored. Pleasing. Pleasant.

Tizite (ti'-zite) - You shall go forth. A scattering. Scattered. Going out. Extension. Patron. Thou shalt go forth.

Toah (to'-ah) - Prostration. Low. Depression. Humility. Sinking. Declension. Inclination. Humble. Weapon. Dart. Low or lowly. Inclined.

Tob (tob) - Good place. Good. Goodness.

Tob-adonijah (tob'-ad-o-ni'-jah) - Distinguished of my Lord. Jehovah. Good is my Lord. Jehovah my good God. The goodness of the Lord God. My good God. The goodness of the foundation of the Lord. God is Adonijah. The Lord Jehovah is Good. Pleading to Jehovah.

Tobiah (to-bi'-ah) - Distinguished of the Lord. Jehovah is good. The Lord is good. Goodness of Jah. Middle.

Tobijah (to-bi'-jah) - Goodness of Jehovah (Same as Tobiah - Distinguished of the Lord. Jehovah is good). The Lord is good. Pleasing to Jah. Middle. Jehovah is good.

Tochen (to'-ken) - Portion cut out. A measure. Measurement. Fixed quantity. Task. Middle. Measure.

Togarmah (to-gar'-mah) - Breaking bones. All bone. Strong. Rugged. A strong hold. You will break her. Excessive fear. Gnawing of the bones. Bony. Which is all bone. House of Torgum. Thou wilt break her.

Tohu (to'-hu) - Humility. Depression. Lowly. Inclined. That lives. (Same as Toah - Prostration. Law. They sank down). Declension. Abasement. Living. Declaring. That lives. That declares.

Toi (to'-i) - Error. Erring. Straying. Wanderer. Do thou mock. Laughter. Wandering. Who wanders. Terror.

Tola (to'-lah) - Little worm. Scarlet (from the color of a worm). Worm. Very red. Grub. Crimson worm. Certain worms have a scarlet color and are used in dyeing cloth crimson or scarlet.

Tolad (to'-lad) - Generation i.e., posterity. Birth. Let her bring forth. You may beget. His propagation. Generation. Nativity. Posterity. A generation.

Tolaites (to'-lah-ites) - (Descendants of Tola - Little worm. Scarlet (from the color of a worm). Worm. Very red. Grub. Crimson worm.

Topaz (to'-paz) - Affliction has fled away.

Tophel (to'-fel) - Unseasonable. Insipid. Lime. A murmuring. Ruin. Decay. Mortar. Foolishness. Quagmire. Folly. Without understanding.

Tophet (to'-fet) - A spitting (as object of contempt). Place of burning. Burning. A place abhorred. Place of graves. Detestable. Detestation. Execration. Drum. Betraying. Contempt. Spittle. Spitting out.

Topheth (to'-feth) - Spitting. (Same as Tophet - Place of burning. Burning. A place abhorred. Place of graves. Detestable). Execration. Curse. Leading aside. Smithing. Spittle. A drum. Spitting out.

Tou (to'-u) - Do you mock. Do you stray away. (Same as Toi - Error. Erring. Straying. Wanderer). Laughter. Declaring. Who wanders. Wandering.

Trachonitis (trak-o-ni'-tis) - Rugged. Rugged or stony tract. A heap of stones. Rocky region. Rough. Stony Place. Cruel. Stony. Hilly region.

Troas (tro'-as) - A Trojan. Bored through. Penetrated. I perforate.

Trogyllium (tro-jil'-le-um) - A cache i.e., a hole in the ground for preserving food. (A narrow channel used for shipping). A cavern. Fruit port.

Trophimus (trof'-im-us) - Master of the house. Nourishing. Well educated. Fit for nourishing. Nourished. Nutritive. Well brought up.

Tryphena (tri-fe'-sah) - Delicate. Dainty one. Luxurious. Tender. Soft. Delicious.

Tryphosa (tri-fo'-sah) - Luxuriating. (Same as Tryphena - Delicate. Dainty one). Tender. Soft. Thrice shining.

Tubal (tu'-bal) - Flowing forth i.e., increase and diffusion of a race. Worldly possessions. Production. Brought. You shall be brought.

Flowing forth. The earth. Confusion. Carried or led. The world. Offspring of Cain. Thou will be brought.

Tubal-cain (tu'-bal-cain) - Flowing forth of Cain i.e., increase of the race of Cain. Production. Forged work. You shall be brought of Cain. Possessor of the world. Flowing forth of Cain. Possessed of confusion. Worldly possessions. The smith. Thou wilt be brought of Cain.

Tychicus (tik'-ik-us) - Fortuitous. Fortunate. Happy Casual. Fate. By Chance. Fateful.

Tyrannus (ti-ran'nus) - Absolute rule. Sovereign. A despot. A tyrant. Prince ruling or reigning. A prince. One that reigns.

Tyre (tire) - To distress. Rock. A bundle tied fast together. A flint. A rock. Strength. A siege. Binding.

Tyrus (ti'-rus) - To distress (Same as Tyre - Rock. A bundle tied fast together. A flint). A rock. Strength. Binding. Breaking.

U

Ucal (u'-cal) - I shall be completed. I shall be established. I shall prevail. Power. Overcame. Consumed. He became chief. Mighty. Prevailing. Devoured. I am strong. To be consumed.

Uel (u'-el) - Will of God. Desired of God. The strength of God. Wish or will of God. Desiring god. Wish of God.

Ulai (ul'-lah) - My leaders (mightiest). Pure water. Muddy water. Peradventure (perhaps). Strength. Pool. Senseless. Strong water. Fool.

Ulam (u'-lam) - Their leaders. First of all i.e., a firstborn. Foremost. Porch. Vestibule. The court. Their strength. First of all. Their folly. Leader. Their leader or vestibule.

Ulla (ul'-lah) - He was taken up. Yoke. Elevation. Burden. A lifting up. Sacrifice. Killed on the altar. Burden or yoke. Leaf. Young child.

Ummah (um'-mah) - He was associated. Juxtaposition. Union i.e., community of inhabitants. Community. Gathering. Roof. Darkened. Covered. His people. Association. Kindred.

Unni (un'-ni) - Afflicted of the Lord. Answering is with Jehovah. Afflicted. Poor. Depressed. He was afflicted. An answer. Song. That answers. Answered.

Upharsin (u-far'-sin) - And dividers. Divided. To split up. Divide. Split up.

Uphaz (u'-faz) - Desire of fine gold. Island of gold. Glittering gold. Pure gold. A gold region. Gold of Phasis or Pison.

Ur (ur) - Light. Fire. Furnace. Luminous. Glorious. Flame.

Urbane (ur'-bane) - End of the way. Of the city. Of a city. Pleasant. Refined. Polite. Courteous.

Uri (u'-ri) - Light of the Lord. Light of Jehovah. Enlightened. Fiery. Burning. My furnace. My light.

Uriah (u-ri'-ah) - Jehovah is light. Light of the Lord. Light of Jehovah. The Lord my light. Light or fire of the Lord. Flame of Jehovah.

Urias (u-ri'-as) - Jehovah is light. My light is Jah. Flame of Jah. Greek form of Uriah.

Uriel (u'-re-el) - A light or flame of God. God is my light or fire. Fire of God. Flame of God. Light of God.

Urijah (u'-ri-ah) - Flame of Jehovah (Same as Uriah - Jehovah is light. Light of the Lord. Light of Jehovah. The Lord my light). Light or fire of the Lord.

Urim (u'-rim) - Light. Fire. Lights. Shining. Manifesting. Enlightening. Perfections. Doctrine of Truth.

Uthai (u'-tha-hee) - My helper (by teaching). Jehovah is help. Jehovah succors. Opportune of the Lord. i.e., a son given in the season of the Lord. Helpful. Seasonableness of God. Whom Jehovah succors. Mine iniquity.

Uz (uz) - Counselor. Counsel. Firmness. Fertile. Fruitful in trees. Consultation. Fastened. Fixed. Words. Wooded.

Uzai (u'-za-hee) - Velocity of the Lord. Robust. Hoped for. I shall have my sprinklings. Haste of God. Strong. He.

Uzal (u'-zal) - Going to and fro. Wanderer. I shall be flooded. Constant progress. A continual going forth. Wandering. Small.

Uzza (uz'-zah) - Strength. He was strengthened. A goat.

Uzzah (uz'-zah) - (Same as Uzza - strength. He was strengthened). A goat. Strength.

Uzzen-sherah (uz'-zen'she'-rah) - Ear of Sherah. Corner of Sherah. Provision of Sherah. Ear of the flesh. Tip of Sherah. Portion of Sherah.

Uzzi (uz'-zi) - The might of Jehovah. Power of the Lord. My strength. Of divine strength. My kid. Strength. Jehovah is strong.

Uzzia (uz-zi'-ah) - Power of the Lord. Strength of Jehovah. Might of Jehovah. Strength of God. Kid of God. Strength. Jehovah is strong.

Uzziah (uz-zi'-ah) - Strength of the Lord. Might of Jehovah. The Lord my strength. Strength of God. Kid of God. Strength. Light. Jehovah is strong or my strength is Jehovah. Strength of Jehovah.

Uzziel (uz-zi'-el) - Strength of God. Power of God. God is strong. God my strength. Might of God. God is my strength.

Uzzielites (uz-zi'-el-ites) - Descendants of Uzziel - Strength of God. Power of God. God is strong. God is my strength.

V

Vaheb (va'-heb) - Now, come on and do thou give. (ASV)

Vajezatha (va-jez'-a-thah) - White. Sincere. Pure. Strong as the wind. Sincere. Born of Ized. And he sprinkled there. Bright. Sprinkling the chamber. Olive trees. Hot or sunny.

Vaniah (va-ni'-ah) - And we were oppressed. God is praise. Weak. Distress. Weapons of the Lord. Oppression. Jah is praise. Nourishment. Praise or nourishment of Jehovah. Jehovah is praise.

Vashni (vash'-ni) - Wherefore sleep thou. Jehovah is praise. God is strong. Gift of God. Strong. Changeable. Gift. Changed. My year. Second. Jah is strong. Jah is praise. The second. A tooth.

Vashti (vash'-ti) - Wherefore waste thou away. Wherefore banquet thou. Beautiful. Beautiful woman. Fair. Lovely. Drinking. Doubling. Beauty. That drinks. Thread. Best.

Vedan (va'-dan) - And Dan.

Via Dolorosa (vi-a' dol-o-ro'-sa) - Way of sorrow.

Vophsi (vof'-si) - Wherefore vanish thou. Fragrant. Rich. Addition of the Lord. Expansion. Addition of God. Fragment diminished. Additional. Diminution.

W

Wonderful - A miracle. A marvelous thing. A wonderful counselor. A name given to Jesus in Isaiah 9:6.

X

Xerxes (xer'-xes) - Greek name of the Persian king, Ahasuerus. (See Ahasuerus)

Y

Yah - An abbreviation of Yahweh

Yan'shuph (yan'-shuph) - Twilight.

Yaudi (ya'-u-de) - Judah. A form of Judah used in II Kings 14:28. (See Judah)

YHWH (Yahweh) - The Hebrew name of the God of Israel considered to be too sacred to pronounce. In Exodus 3:14-16 the sacred name YHWH is given to Moses as a revelation of who God is. The word is a form of the verb "hayah" which is translated "to be," which is difficult to translate, though it may be rendered "I am who I am" or "I will be what I will be." English versions of the Old Testament tend to translate this word as Lord or Jehovah. The Hebrew name of God is pronounced "Yahweh."

Z

Zaanaim (za-an-a'-im) - Enormous. Migrations. Wanderings. Great migration. Removals. Changing. Departures. A person asleep. Journeys

Zaanan (za'-an-an) - Rich in flocks. Place of flocks. Their flocks. Going forth. Going out.

Zaanannim (za-an-an'-nim) - Same as Zaanaim - Enormous migrations. Wanderings. Departures. Journeys. Great migrations. Removals. One sleeping.

Zaavan (za'-av-an) - Great agitation (intense form). Conquest. Causing fear. Disturbed. Disquieted. Their removal. Their disquiet. Commotion. Great tremor. Tremblings. Unquiet. Quake. Terror.

Zabad (za'-bad) - Given i.e., given of God. Gift. Endower. He has given a gift. Present. He has given a dowry. Endowed. Dowry. Giver. He has endowed. Has endowed.

Zabbai (zab-bahee) - Clemency of the Lord. Pure. Innocent. Roving about. Humming. My flitings. My wanderings. The justice of God. Portion of God. Flowing.

Zabbud (zab'-bud) - Gift bestowed i.e., bestowed by God. Given. Bestowed. Well remembered. Endowed. A donation. A gift. A dowry. Mindful. Remembered.

Zabdi (zab'-di) - Jehovah gave. A dowry. The gift of Jehovah. Jehovah is endower or dowry. My dowry. The

gift of God. Giving. Jehovah is endower.

Zabdiel (zab'-de-ol) - Gift of God. The gift of God. My gift is God. God is endower. Portion of God.

Zabud (za'-bud) - Gift bestowed i.e., bestowed by God. Endower. Gift. Given. Given by gift. Dowry. Endowed. Bestowed.

Zabulon (zab'-u-lon) - A habitation. (Greek form of Zebulon - Wished for habitation). Dwelling. Habitation desired. Abiding.

Zaccai (zac'-cahee) - Pure of the Lord i.e., whom the Lord has cleansed. Pure. Innocent. My pure ones. He was pure. Just. Pure meat.

Zaccheus (zak-ke-us) - Pure. Justified. Clean. Just.

Zacchur (zac'-cur) - Mindful. Well remembered. Pure. Remembrance. Attentive. Careful.

Zaccur (zac'-cur) - (Same as Zacchur - Mindful. Well remembered. Pure.) Remembrance. Of the male kind. Attentive. Careful.

Zachariah (zak-a-ri'-ah) - Remembered of the Lord. Whom Jehovah remembers. Remember God. The Lord is remembered. Jah has remembered. Memory of the Lord. Jehovah has remembered.

Zacharias (zak'-a-ri'-as) - Jehovah is renowned. The Lord is remembered. Remembered of God. Mindful. Jehovah remembers or has remembered. Jehovah has remembered. Greek form of Zechariah. Remembered of Jehovah.

Zacher (za'-kur) - Remembrance. Memorial. Fame. Remembered. Whom Jehovah remembers.

Zadok (za'-dok) - Just. Righteous. Upright. Justified. Just or righteous.

Zaham (za'-ham) - Loathing. Fatness. He loathed. Pride. Filthiness. Crime. Impurity.

Zair (za'-ur) - Insignificant. Lesser. Little. Young. Small. Few. Ignoble. In tribulation. Afflicted.

Zalaph (za'-laf) - The shadow beautified. Fracture. Bruise. Wound. Purification. An opening. Fraction. A shadow. Ringing. Shaking. Shadow. Caper plant.

Zalmon (zal'-mon) - Resemblance. Image. Shady. Ascent. Very shadowy. Darkness. His image. His shade. Peaceable.

Zalmonah (zal-mo'-nah) - Representation. Imagery. (Same as Zalmon - Resemblance. Image. Shady. Ascent). Gift of a shadow or shade. Shady. The shade. The sound of the number. His image. Shade.

Zalmunna (zal-mun'-nah) - Shadow is withheld. A moving shadow. Withdrawn from protection. Shelter is denied. The covering or shade of an exile. Shadow. Image. Idol. Forbidden. Shade refused. Deprived of shade. Shade denied.

Zamzummims (zam-zum'-mims) - Intriguers. Tribes making a noise. Devisers. Wickedness. Most proud. Intriguing. Projects of crime. Enormous crimes. Murmurers. Mumblers. Plotters.

Zanoah (za-no'-ah) - To cast off. Stinking. Marsh. Bog. Broken district. Placed far distant. Desertion. Rejected. Forgetfulness.

Zaphnath-paaneah (zaf'-nath-pa-a-ne'-ah) - Saviour of the age. Saviour of the world. Giver of the nourishment of life. Prince of the life of the age. Revealer of a secret. The concealed treasure. Treasury of the glorious rest. Revealer of secrets. Discovering hidden things. One who discovers hidden things. Supporter of life. The Saviour.

Zaphon (za'-fon) - North. North wind i.e., a place exposed to the north wind. Northward. Hidden. Boreal. Beholder. Northeast wind.

Zara (za'-rah) - A rising (as of the sun). Brightness. Sprout. Clearness. Rising. Sunrising.

Zarah (za'-rah) - Rising of light; i.e., joy of parents. Shining. Brightness. Rising. Clearness. East. Sunrising.

Zareah (za'-re-ah) - Hornet. Place of hornets. She was smitten with leprosy. An assembly. Leprosy. A hornet - Wasp. Hornets town.

Zareathites (za'-re-ath-ites) - (Same as Zorathites - Inhabitants of Zorah. A nest of hornets i.e., a place of troublesome men. A place of hornets. She was smitten with leprosy). Dwellers in Zareah or Zorah.

Zared (za'-red) - Luxuriant growth of trees. Exuberant growth. Thick foliage. The stranger subdued. The bond subdued. The luxuriant branches of trees cut off. Strange. Descent. Luxuriance. Brook.

Zarephath (zar'-e-fath) - Place of refining. She has refined. Refined. Smelting house. Workshop of melting and refining metals. Pouring forth. Refinement. Perplexity of bread. Ambush of the mouth. Place of refinement. Dyeing place.

Zaretan (zar'-e-tan) - Their distress. Narrowness of dwelling place i.e., a small dwelling place. Cooling. Straitness of the dwelling. To pierce. Tribulation. Puncture. Perplexity.

Zareth-shahar (za'-reth-sha'-har) - Splendor of the morning i.e., a town situated facing the rising sun. Brightness of dawn. Brightness of the morning. Beauty of dawn. Splendor of dawn.

Zarhites (zar'-hites) - Descendants of Zerah - (Same as Zarah - Rising of light i.e., joy of parents. Dawn. Shining). Clear ones.

Zartanah (zar'-ta-nah) - (Same as Zoretan and Zarthan - Their distress. Narrowness of dwelling place i.e., a small dwelling place. Cooling). Straitness. Ambush. Perplexity.

Zarthan - (Same as Zaretan - Their distress. Narrowness of dwelling place i.e., a small dwelling place. Cooling). Straitness of the dwelling. To pierce. Cooling.

Zatthu (zath'-u) - Brightness of him. Ornament. Beauty. Lovely. Pleasant. An honor. Sprout. Olive tree.

Zattu (zat'-tu) - (Same as Zatthu - Brightness of him. Ornament. Beauty. Lovely. Pleasant). An ornament. An honor. Branch. Sprout. Lovely. Pleasant.

Zavan (za'-van) - (Same as Zaavan - Great agitation (intense form). Conquest. Causing fear. Disturbed. Disquieted. Their removal. Their disquiet). Commotion. Great tremor. Disquiet. Unquiet.

Zaza (za'-zah) - Brightness. Fullness. Abundance. Projection. Shining.

Prominent. Going back. Belonging to all.

Zealot (zeal'-ot)- Zealous one.

Zebadiah (zeb-ad-I'-ah) - Jehovah has endowed. Gift of the Lord. Given of the Lord. The Lord is my portion. God has given. Portion of the Lord. Gift of Jehovah. Jehovah is endowerer. The Lord has given.

Zebah (ze'-bah) - Sacrifice i.e., devoted to Molech. Victim. A sacrifice. Killing.

Zebaim (ze-ba'-im) - Hyenas. Gazelles. Roes. Antelopes. The gazelles.

Zebedee (zeb'e-dee) - Jehovah's gift. The gift of God. Dowry. Abundant portion. Abundant. Portion. Jehovah has given or bestowed. Gift of the Lord.

Zebina (ze-bi'-nah) - Bought. One who is bought. Purchasing. A precious possession. Flowing now. Selling. Buying. Acquired. Purchase. Bought or sold.

Zeboiim (ze-boy'-im) - Gathering of troops of soldiers i.e., a military city of the serpent breed. Fair. Deer. Goats. Gazelles. Hyenas. Valley of wild beasts.

Zeboim (ze-bo'-im) - (Same as Zeboiim - Gathering of troops of soldiers i.e., a military city): of the serpent breed. Fair. Deer. Goats. Gazelles. Hyenas. Valley of wild beasts.

Zebub (ze'-bub) - Prince of evil spirits.

Zebudah (ze-bu'dah) - Bestowing a gift. Given. Endowment. Given by a free gift. Endowed. Bestowed. Endowing. Gift.

Zebul (ze'-bul) - Habitation. Dwelling together. Abiding. Chamber. A habitation. Exalted.
Zebulonite (zeb'-u-lon-ite) - (Descendants of Zebulon - Wished for habitation. Dwelling). Member of the tribe of Zebulon.
Zebulun (zeb'-u-lun) - Wished for habitation. Dwelling. Dwelling wished for.
Zebulunites (zeb'-u-lun-ites) - (Same as Zebulonite - Descendants of Zebulun - Wished for habitation. Dwelling). Member of the tribe of Zebulun.
Zechariah (zek-a-ri'-ah) - Jehovah remembers. Jehovah is renowned. The Lord is remembered. Jah has remembered. Whom Jehovah remembers. Jehovah remembers or has remembered. The Lord remembers.
Zedad (ze'-dad) - Turned aside. A mountain. Side of a mountain. Steep place. Side. Coast. Mountainside. His side. His hunting.
Zedekiah (zed-e-ki'-ah) - Jehovah is might. Jehovah is righteous. Justice of the Lord. Justice of Jehovah. My righteous God. Righteousness of the Lord. The justice of the Lord. The Lord is my justice. Jehovah my righteousness. Righteousness of Jehovah.
Zeeb (ze'-eb) - To be yellow. A wolf.
Zelah (ze'-lak) - Side i.e., a place situated on the side of a mountain. Limping. One-sided. A rib. Slope. Halting.
Zelek (ze'-lek) - Fissure i.e., an opening. Rent. A shadow. Cleaving. Shadow of noise of one licking. The

shadow or noise of him that licks or laps. A cleft.
Zelophehad (ze'-lo'-fe-had) - First rupture i.e., firstborn. The firstborn. Fracture. Anxious for shade. Shadow of fear. First opening. Being burnt. Alike. The shade or tingling of fear.
Zelotes (ze-lo'-teze) - Zealous. Full of zeal. Jealous.
Zelzah (zel'-zah) - Shade in the heat of the sun. A distinct shadow. Double shadow. A clear or dazzling shadow. A shade. Noon tide. Clear shade.
Zemaraim (zem-a-ra'-im) - Two cuttings off. Two fleeces. Double woolens. Cold. Double fleece. Double mountain forest. Wool. Pith. Double peak.
Zemarite (ze'-a-rite) - (Same as Zemaraim - Two cuttings off. Two fleeces. Double woolens). A tribe from the sons of Canaan,
Zemira (ze-mi'-rah) - Song i.e., of joy. A melody. Causing singing. Vine. Palm. Music.
Zenan (ze'-nan) - (Same as Zaanan - Rich in flocks. Place of flocks. Their flock. Very fruitful). Cold. Coldness. Target. Weapon. Pointed.
Zenas (ze'-nas) - The gift of Zeus. Jupiter (as the father of gods). Gift of Jove. Living. Gift of Zeus.
Zephaniah (zef-a-ni'-ah) - Hid of the Lord i.e., protected by the Lord. Whom Jehovah hid. Concealed of God. Watcher of the Lord. Treasured of Jehovah. He hid. Jah Secreted i.e., protected. To protect. Cover over. Hidden. The Lord is my secret. Jehovah has hidden or hides.
Zephath (ze'-fath) - A watch tower. A cave beholds. That attends. That

covers. Beacon. That beholds. Which beholds that attends or covers.

Zephathah (zef'-a-thah) - (Same as Zephath - A watch tower. Place of watching). A cave beholds. That attends. That covers. Vale of the watchtower. Watchtower.

Zephi (ze'-fi) - Expectation i.e., hope of parents. Watch tower. Watch thou. An observer. Expectation. Watch.

Zepho (ze'-fo) - (Same as Zephi - Expectation i.e., hope of parents. Watch tower. A watcher. Watch. That sees. His watching). Perplexity.

Zephon (ze'-fon) - Earnest expectation. Intense longing. A looking out. Dark. Wintry. A watcher. Watchfulness. Hiding. Watchman. Looking out. Perplexity. Expectation. The act of watching or observing.

Zephonites (zef'-on-ites) - (Descendants of Zephon - Earnest expectation. Intense longing. A looking out). To look out.

Zer (zur) - Flint. Strait. Tribulation. Straitness. Rock or flint.

Zerah (ze'-rah) - Rising. Origin. Same as Zarah - Rising of light i.e., joy of parents. Shining. The beginning of. Sprout. Dawn.

Zerahiah (zer-a-hi'-ah) - Rising of the light of the Lord. Whom Jehovah caused to rise. The Lord is risen. Jehovah is appearing. Jehovah caused to spring forth. Jah caused to be born. Jehovah has risen. The Lord rising. Brightness of the Lord. Jehovah has come forth. Jehovah has appeared or risen up.

Zered (ze'-red) - Dense forest. (Same as Zared - Luxuriant growth of trees.

Exuberant growth). Power spreading. Luxuriance. Exuberant growth.

Zereda (zer'-e-dah) - The adversary rules. Cooling. Straitness. Ambush. Pierced. Change of dominion. Fortress.

Zeredathah (ze-red'a-thah) - Scene of the adversary's rule. Fortress. A straitening. To pierce. Puncture. Pierced. Cool.

Zererath (zer'e-rath) - Oppression. Straitness. A straitening. Pierced.

Zeresh (ze-resh) - Star of adoration. Gold. Star of gold. A stranger in want. Star of Venus. Misery. Strange. Dispersed. Inheritance.

Zereth (ze'-reth) - Splendor. Brightness. Straitness. A bond. Tribulation.

Zereth-Shahar (zer'-eth-sha'-har)- Splendor of dawn. Splendor of the dawn.

Zeri (ze'-ri) - Same as Jezer - Frame. Form i.e., of his parents. Anything made. Balm. Shape. Bringing together. Distillation. Built.

Zeror (ze'-ror) - Small bundle. Bundle. That straitens. Pocket. Pebble. Grain. A particle. That straitens or binds. That keeps tight. Tied. Bundle or pouch or particle of stone.

Zeruah (ze-ru'-ah) - Leprous. A hornet. Wasp. Smitten.

Zerubbabel (ze-rub'-ba-bel) - An offspring of Babel. Born at Babylon. Dispersed or begotten in Babylon. Scattered in Babylon. The dispersed in Babylon. Melted by Babylon. Dispersion of confusion i.e., dispelling human illusions. Sown in Babylon. A stranger at Babylon. Disperser of confusion. Born. Sown or scattered in

Babylon (Confusion). Seed of Babylon. Offspring of Babylon.

Zeruiah (ze'ru-i'ah) - Balsam from Jehovah. Cleft. Troubled by God. Pierce ye Jah. Pain. Wounded. Tribulation of the Lord. Balm.

Zetham (ze'-tham) - Olive. Place of olives. Shining. Chiefest olive tree. Olive tree.

Zethan (ze'-than) - Olive tree (intense form). Place of olives. Shining. Choice olive tree. Olive.

Zethar (ze'-thar) - Very great. Sacrifice. He that examines. This is the spy (searcher). Very high. Olive of vision. Stair. Star. He that examines or beholds. Conqueror.

Zeus (zeus) - Bright sky of the day. A father of help.

Zia (zi-ah) - Shaking i.e., fear. Terror. Terrified. Motion. Commotion. Agitation. Smelling. Sweat. Swelling. Movement. Fear.

Ziba (zi'-bah) - Plant. Planter. Plantation. Appointed. Host. Strength. Statue. A ship. Army. Fight. Post.

Zibeon (zib'-e-um) - Dyed. A dyer. Variegated. Wild robber. Seizing prey. A garment of many colors. Iniquity that dwells. Colored. Hyena.

Zibia (zib'-e-ah) - Female gazelle. Strength. A roe. A doe. Honorable chief. Gazelle.

Zibiah (zib'-e-ah) - (Same as Zibia - Female gazelle. Strength). Roe deer. The Lord dwells. A roe. A deer. Goat. Gazelle.

Zichri (zik'-ri) - Remembered of the Lord. Famous. Renowned. Memorable. Do thou remember. Remembrance of the Lord. That remembers. That is a man.

Ziddim (zid'-dum) - Sides. Lying in wait. Borders. Huntings. Destructions. Declivities. Treasons. Flanks.

Zidkijah (zid-ki'-jah) - (Same as Zedekiah - Justice of the Lord. Justice of Jehovah. My righteous God. Jehovah is might). Right of Jah. Righteousness of Jehovah. Jehovah my righteousness.

Zidon (zi'-don) - (Same as Sidon - Fishing. Plenty of fish. A place for hunting). Hunting. Fishing. Ship of judgment. Fishery. Venison.

Zidonians (zi-do'-ne-uns) - Inhabitants of Zidon. (Same as Zidon or Sidon - Fishing. Plenty of fish). Hunting. Fishing. Ship of judgment. Fishery. Venison.

Zif (zif) - Blossom. Bloom. Brightness. Beauty. Blossom month. This or that. Comeliness. In bloom. Flowing. Second month of Jewish sacred year.

Ziha (zi'-hah) - Drought. Dry. Thirsty. Sunniness. Causing dryness. Parching. Victory. Brightness. Whiteness. Draught.

Ziklag (zik'-lag) - Winding. Bending. A measure of oppression. Enveloped in grief. Pouring out of water. Flowing. Thirsty. Measure pressed down.

Zillah (zil'-lah) - A shadow. Shade. Shadow of darkness or protection. He wasted. Roasting. Roaring. Ringing. Shadow. The tingling of the ear.

Zilpah (zil'-pah) - A dropping. Drop. Flippant mouth. Action of dropping. Dripping. Gathering together. Contempt of the mouth. Distillation from the mouth. Myrrh dropping.

Zilthai (zil'-tha-hee) - Shadow of the Lord i.e. under the Lord's protection. Shady. Shaded. Shade. The shade of the Lord. Shadow i.e., protection. My shadow. My talk. God is a shadow.

Zimmah (zim'-mah) - Wicked device. Planning. Plan. Purpose. Counsel. Consideration. Lewdness. A chain. Thought. Wickedness. Damage. Mischief.

Zimram (zim'-ran) - Celebrated. Sung. A chanter. The singer. Celebrated in song. Famous. Great wild goat. A song. Musical. Singer. Vine. Musician.

Zimri (zim-ri) - Song of the Lord. Celebrated. Vine. My song. Famous. Celebrated in song. Song or praise of God. Musical. My field. My vine. My protection. God is my protection.

Zin (zin) - A low palm tree. Thorn. Mud. A small palm tree. Shrub. To prick. A crag. Buckler. Coldness. Swelling. Flat.

Zina (zin'-a) - Abundance. Borrowed. Nourishing. Ornament. Shining. Bright. Fruitful. Going back. Well fed.

Zion (zi'-un) - Very dry. Sunny. Parched place. Monument raised up. Guiding. Spiritual illumination. Sepulcher. Monument. Fortress. Citadel. Sunny mount.

Zior (zi'-or) - Smallness. Diminution. Very small. Ship of him who watches. Littleness. Insignificance.

Ziph (zif) - Refining place. Melting place. Borrowed. Mutual pledge. Flowing. A flowing. This mouth or mouthful. Battlement. Flux.

Ziphah (zi'-fah) - Borrowed. Lent. Refinery. Flowing. Flux. Mutual pledge. A flowing. Battlement.

Ziphims (zif'-ims) - (Inhabitants of Ziph - Refining place. Melting place. Borrowed. Smelters). Mutual pledge.

Flowing. A flowing. Battlement. Flux. This mouth or mouthful.

Ziphion (zif'-e-on) - (Same as Zephan - Earnest expectation. Intense longing. A looking out. To the flow of song). Eager expectation. Expectation much desired. Watch tower. Looking out. Dark. Wintry. Lookout. The act of observing. To watch.

Ziphites (zif'-ites) - (Same as Ziphims - Inhabitants of Ziph. Borrowed.) Smelters. Mutual pledge. A flowing. Battlement. This mouth or mouthful. Flux.

Ziphron (zif'-e-on) - Sweet smell. Fragrance. Sweet odor. Pleasant. Falsehood of a song. Rejoicing. A stench or odor.

Zippor (zip'-por) - A sparrow. Little bird. A bird. Descent. Hopping. Crown. Desert.

Zipporah (zip-po'-rah) - (Same as Zipper (feminine) - A sparrow. Little bird). A mourning. Trumpet. Beauty. Female bird.

Zithri (zith'-ri) - Protection of the Lord. Protection of Jehovah. Jehovah's protection. My hiding place. A cave. My secret. Protective. Over turned. Demolished. To hide. Jehovah conceals.

Ziv (ziv) - Bloom.

Ziz (ziz) - A flower. A blossom. Bloom. Lock of hair. Branch.

Ziza (zi'-zah) - Fertility. Full breast. Brightness. (Same as Zina - Abundance. Exuberance. Raving as a beast). Shining. The glory. Prominence.

Zizah (zi'zah) - (Same as Ziza/Zina - fertility. Full breast. Brightness.

Abundance). Shining. The glory. Prominence. Full breast.

Zoan (zo'-an) - A place of departure. A traveler. Removal. Motion. Moved.

Zoar (zo'-ar) - Smallness. Little. The younger. Bringing low. Small.

Zoba (zo'-bah) - Statue. Public place. A host. A plantation. A station. Standing. White. Bright. Dryness. Pressing down. An encampment. Army. Bronze. Copper.

Zobah (zo'-bah) - (Same as Zoba - Statue. Public place. A host. A plantation. A station. Standing). White. Bright. Dryness. Pressing down. Station. Army. Warning. Bronze. Copper.

Zobebah (zo-be'-bah) - Going slowly. Walking slowly. Slow moving. Sluggish. Covered. The slow coming. White Bright. Dryness. Fleshy. Slothful. The slow moving. An army. Affable. Slow movement.

Zohar (zo'-har) - Whiteness. White. Light. Shining. Distinction. Bright. Dryness. Nobility.

Zoheleth (zo'-he-leth) - Serpent. The serpent stone. Serpents of the dust. Creepers of the dust. That creeps. Smooth. Crawling. Drawing. Creeping one.

Zoheth (zo'-heth) - Strong. Corpulent. Releasing. Separation. Amazing. A separation. Removal of that which is torn.

Zophah (zo'-fah) - A cruse of water. A watch. Expanse. Expanding. A cruse. Vial. Honeycomb. Double extension. Bellied jug.

Zophai (zo'-fahee) - Sweet. Honey as dropping from the comb. Honeycomb. Watcher. My

honeycombs. My overflows. Honeycombed. Honey of the Lord.

Zophar (zo'-far) - Chirping. Insolence. Chatterer. Sparrow. Departing early. A climber. Rising early. Crown. Constant exultation. Twittering bird.

Zophim (zo'-fim) - Watchmen. Watchers. Field of dropping i.e., fertile. Place for a watchman. Of viewers. Seeing at a distance.

Zorah (zo'-rah) - A nest of hornets i.e., a place of troublesome men. A place of hornets. Leprosy. Scab. Hornets town. Congregation. Place of hornets. Wasp. Hornet.

Zorathites (zo'-rath-ites) - (Inhabitants of Zorah - A nest of hornets i.e., a place of troublesome men. A place of hornets). Leprosy. Scab. Hornets town. Congregation. Place of hornets. Wasp. Hornet.

Zoreah (zo'-re-ah) - (Same as Zorah - A nest of hornets i.e., a place of troublesome men. A place of hornets). Hornets town. Congregation. Leprosy. Wasp.

Zorites (zo'-rites) - (Same as Zorathites - Inhabitants of Zorah - A nest of hornets i.e., a place of troublesome men. A place of hornets). Descendants of Salma of Judah.

Zorobabel (zo-rob'-a-bel) - Born at Babel i.e., Babylon. Greek form of Zerubbabel - an offspring of Babel. Born at Babylon. Dispersed or begotten in Babylon. Scattered in Babylon. The dispersed in Babylon. Same as Zerubbabel. Dispersion of confusion i.e., dispelling of human illusions. Born. Sown or scattered in Babylon (confusion).

Zuar (zu'-ar) - Very small. Smallness. Little. He was belittled. Restraint. To make narrow.

Zuph (zuf) - Same as Zophai - Sweet honey as dropping from the comb. Honeycomb. That beholds. Honeycombed. Honey.

Zur (zur) - A rock. Rock. Stone. To besiege. That besieges. Great stone.

Zuriel (zu're-el) - Rock of God. God is the rock. My rock is God. Rock or strength of God. God is my rock. God a rock. Strength of God.

Zurishaddai (zu-re-shad'-da-i) - Rock of the Almighty. Whose Almighty is a rock. My rock is Almighty. The Almighty is my rock and strength. My rock is the Almighty. Omnipotent rock. My strength. My beauty.

Zuzims (zu'-zims) - Commotions i.e., terrors. The wanderers. Prominent. Strong. The posts of a door. Splendor. Beauty. Shining. Powerfulness. Roving creatures.

BIBLIOGRAPHY

1. The Exhaustive Dictionary of Bible Names – Stelman Smith & Judson Cornwall. Bridge-Logos. 1998.

2. Dictionary of Bible Proper Names – Cyrus A. Potts. Forgotten Book Originally published 1922.

3. Exhaustive Concordance – Strong.

4. Analytical Concordance to the Holy Bible – Robert Young.

5. Bible People & Places – Thomas Nelson Press. 1993.

6. All the Names in the Bible, A to Z – Thomas Nelson Press. 2014

7. Hitchcock's Bible Names Dictionary – Hitchcock. Pantianos Classics 1869.

8. Bible Names Pronunciations and Meanings – E. N. Hamilton. Kessinger Legacy Reprints. 1939.

9. A Guide to Pronouncing Biblical Names – T. S. Scott-Craig. Church Publishing. 1982.

10. People & Places in the Bible. John Farrer. Barbour & Company.

11. Who's Who in the Bible – Publications International. 1998.

12. Who Was Who in the Bible – MJF Books. 1999.

13. The Names of God in Holy Scripture – Jukes. 1888.

14. The Name of God – Conner. City Christian Publishing. 1975.

15. The God Manual – Samuel Greene. Glory Publishing. 2008.

16. Dictionary of Bible Themes – Manser. McGrath. Packer. Wiseman. Zondervan Publishing.

17. Bible Names and Their Meanings – CPA Book Publisher.

18. Names of God – Rose Publishing. 2003.

19. Baker Encyclopedia of Bible People – John Hunt. Baker Publishing. 2006.

ABOUT THE AUTHOR

For additional study and ordering information on Dr. Greene's "Principle of Names in Scripture" study manual, please visit us online at www.nwmin.org. Dr. Samuel Greene is president and founder of Narrow Way Ministries International, an outreach missionary arm of the body of Christ seeking to disciple and teach believers everywhere foundational truths and sound doctrine helping the body of Christ grow up into Jesus in all things. He was ordained into the ministry in 1976 and has pastored all over the United States as well as started churches and Bible Schools all over the world. Throughout his ministry, he has brought God's glory all over the world by leading worship with abandonment. He's written many worship choruses over the years that help usher people into the presence of God. Dr. Greene has also written books and study manuals to help solidify and found the body of Christ in basic sound doctrine as well as revelational truths about the coming Kingdom of God and the doctrine of the remnant. God spoke to him at the age of fifteen and said he was going to teach the doctrine to the remnant in the last days. Not knowing what this meant, he simply began to search the Scriptures as God brought into his life many men and women of God who taught him faithfully. Dr. Greene's guiding passion is to bring forth the message of the bride of Christ and preparing God's people for the last great move of God that's coming.

Foundational Series Study Manuals
Searching The Scriptures
Repentance From Dead Works
Faith Toward God
Doctrine of Baptisms
Laying on of Hands
Resurrection of the Dead
Eternal Judgment
Doctrine of Perfection

Revelational Series Study Manuals
Ashes of the Red Heifer
Call of the Bride
Crowns of the Believers
Glory of God
Mystery Babylon
Order of Melchisedec
Remnant Principle
Slaying Our Giants
Tabernacle of Moses

Dictionaries
The God Manual
Deeper Truth Dictionary
Greene's Dictionary of Bible Names

Sermon Archives
The Doctrine of First Things: Vol. 1
A Lamp That Burneth: Vol. 2
Precepts Of The Lord: Vol. 3
Way of Truth: Vol. 4

Devotional
The Little Book, A Spirit-Filled – Devotional

Present Truth Series Study Manuals
Dealings of God
Eternal Salvation
Fasting
Grace of Giving
Healing
Kingdom of Darkness
Kingdom of God
O Worship The Lord
Prophetic Utterance
Principle of Names
Scriptural Happiness
Teach Us To Pray
Walking Before Him
Women In Ministry

Commentary Books
To Comfort All That Mourn
A Fresh Look At Divorce
A Fresh Look At Hell
The Swelling Of Jordan
The Call To Aloneness
A Stone's Throw Further
Hast Thou Considered My Servant Job?
The Anointing Of God
The Israel Of God
Face To Face Communion
Handfuls of Purpose Vol. 1 & 2
Digging In The Valley
The Sound Of God
I Am Black But Comely
Words Fitly Spoken

www.ingramcontent.com/pod-product-compliance
Lightning Source LLC
Chambersburg PA
CBHW031432270326
41930CB00007B/670